FROM THE FILMS OF

Harry Potter

THE OFFICIAL BOOK OF
CROCHET AMIGURUMI

FROM THE FILMS OF

Harry Potter

THE OFFICIAL BOOK OF
CROCHET AMIGURUMI

Written by Juli Anne
with Jody Revenson

INSIGHT
EDITIONS

SAN RAFAEL · LOS ANGELES · LONDON

CONTENTS

PROJECT SKILL LEVELS

⚡ Beginner

⚡ ⚡ Intermediate

⚡ ⚡ ⚡ Advanced

INTRODUCTION

In an early lesson of Professor Minerva McGonagall's Transfiguration Class, she teaches her second-year students to transform a hornbill bird into a water goblet, as seen in *Harry Potter and the Chamber of Secrets*. By performing the physical action necessary for the transformation—tapping the bird lightly three times with her wand—and saying the words of the spell—*Vera Verto*—the result is a shining crystal goblet with a golden rim. By following these directions, her students can then transform their own animals into water goblets. (Of course, having a wand that isn't broken also helps, as Ron Weasley learns when he performs the spell and his rat, Scabbers, turns into a very furry version of the goblet, still wiggling his tail.) The magic of Transfiguration offers endless possibilities of new and exciting magical creations.

Crochet offers a similar kind of wizardry: By performing the stitches that make up crochet—chains and slip stitches, for example—and following the words—the instructions and the pattern—your work is transformed into colorful, beautiful, and fun creations.

Crocheting is a craft that involves creating fabric using a hook and some yarn or thread. However, amigurumi holds a special place in the world of crochet due to its unique characteristics. While amigurumi is a specialized form of crochet, it's not exclusively for those who are already experienced with the craft. In fact, most of the time you only need to know one or two types of stitches to complete an amigurumi project, making it very easy for new crocheters!

Unlike traditional crochet, which mainly involves flat or linear patterns, amigurumi projects are often crocheted in rounds to create three-dimensional shapes, which within this book can be anything from a Hippogriff to a Golden Snitch. The complexity of designing amigurumi is in the sculpting techniques, such as knowing where to increase or decrease stitches to create the desired curves and angles for your finished piece.

Crocheting amigurumi could even be considered as having similar elements to making potions: The yarn, crochet hooks, and stuffing materials are the ingredients, and the amigurumi patterns are the step-by-step potion recipes.

The crochet magic happens when you transform simple materials like yarn and stuffing into adorable characters, creatures, and objects right before your eyes.

Characters, creatures, and artifacts seen in the Harry Potter films are featured here for a (wizarding) world of creations, from the enigmatic Professor Snape to the jovial Professor Sprout. There is also the golden trio of Harry, Ron, and Hermione, and their friends and frenemy: Luna, Cho, and Draco. Every generation at Hogwarts is represented here, from the wise and caring Headmaster Albus Dumbledore to a merperson from the Black Lake.

Amigurumi lends itself especially well to the scales of the merpeople. It also defines the wings of Buckbeak the Hippogriff, whom Harry rides in *Harry Potter and the Prisoner of Azkaban*. Is there anything more adorable than Norbert, the baby Norwegian Ridgeback hatched in Hagrid's hut in *Harry Potter and the Sorcerer's Stone,* or the Pygmy Puff Ginny shows Luna in *Harry Potter and the Half-Blood Prince*? The cuddly crocheted versions included here definitely come close.

Artifacts in the wizarding world offer their own form of magic, from the chiding reprimands of a Howler sent to Ron Weasley in *Harry Potter and the Chamber of Secrets*, to the mysteries of the Golden Egg, clue to the second task of the Triwizard Tournament in *Harry Potter and the Goblet of Fire*. Wizards and Witches should take care not to let their Chocolate Frog escape (with its one good jump) or their Golden Snitch fly away (they'd get 150 points if they catch it).

The amigurumi patterns featured in *Harry Potter: The Official Book of Crochet Amigurumi* are well-suited for crocheters of different skill levels. Whether you're a seasoned crocheter seeking a fresh challenge or a novice eager to embark on a new creative journey, these projects offer a rewarding and enjoyable—and dare we say enchanting?—experience for all.

Chapter 1

CAPTIVATING CHARACTERS

HARRY POTTER

Designed by Juli Anne
Skill Level: ⚡⚡

When Harry Potter turns eleven years old, he learns something quite surprising: he's a wizard! Harry receives his acceptance letter from Hogwarts School of Witchcraft and Wizardry, where he will learn spells, charms, and potions, and meet other young witches and wizards who will become his friends for life.

In order to convey the idea of Hogwarts being a traditional English school, *Harry Potter and the Sorcerer's Stone* costume designer Judianna Makovsky felt that the students needed a unified look. Each uniform consisted of a white shirt and house tie, with gray flannel trousers for boys and gray flannel pleated skirts for girls. Traditional academic robes were given sleeves deemed more wizardy, and included pockets for their pointed hats and wands. Makovsky confesses she never could figure out how to put the wand in the pocket or take it out quickly. The robes were so comfortable Daniel Radcliffe (Harry) described them as feeling like pajamas, but admits he got a bit hot wearing them in the Great Hall, which often had fires lit in the fireplaces.

Step into the magical world of amigurumi with this 5.5-inch-tall Harry Potter amigurumi doll, complete with Harry's Hogwarts uniform. This miniature wizard's iconic round glasses are made using wire wrapped with black yarn. His lightning-bolt scar is carefully stitched onto his forehead using embroidery thread. His black robes are crocheted in one piece and are removable.

"I'm Harry. Harry Potter."

Harry Potter, *Harry Potter and the Sorcerer's Stone*

FINISHED MEASUREMENTS

Height: 5.5 in. / 14 cm
Width: 2.5 in. / 6.5 cm

YARN

DK weight (#3 light) yarn, shown in Hobbii *Friends Cotton 8/8* (100% cotton, 82 yd. / 75 m per 1.75 oz. / 50 g skein).
Color A: #04 Cream, 1 skein
Color B: #118 Silver, 1 skein
Color C: #124 Black, 1 skein
Color D: #112 Anthracite, 1 skein
Color E: #01 White, 1 skein
Color F: #41 Pomegranate, 1 skein
Color G: #24 Sunflower, 1 skein

Worsted weight (#4 medium) yarn, shown in Hobbii *Amigo XL* (100% acrylic, 109 yd. / 100 m per 1.8 oz. / 50 g skein).
Color H: A06, Chocolate, 1 skein

HOOK

• US D / 3.25mm crochet hook

NOTIONS

• Stitch markers
• Pair of 6.0mm safety eyes
• Polyester stuffing
• Embroidery thread, small amt. of pink or dark red, and black
• Jewelry wire, 20-gauge
• Tapestry needle
• Plastic or paper straw (optional)

GAUGE

24 sts and 24 rnds = 4 in. / 10 cm in sc
Gauge is not critical for this project. Ensure your stitches are tight so the stuffing won't show through.

SPECIAL ABBREVIATIONS

Back Loop Only (blo): Work through back loop only
Front Loop Only (flo): Work through front loop only

- Use the yarn-under-single-crochet technique to achieve tighter and more aligned stitches when crocheting in the round.
- Use the underside (WS) of the Hair piece as the wig.
- Pieces worked in the round are continuous rounds; do not join.
- Use the half-color changing. technique to achieve cleaner lines when changing colors from one row to another (optional).

BEHIND THE MAGIC

The glasses Daniel Radcliffe wore as Harry Potter rarely had lenses in them, in order to avoid reflections of the lights or cameras. After the final film, Radcliffe took his first and last pairs of glasses as a souvenir.

HEAD

With **A**, make a magic ring.
Rnd 1: 6 sc in ring—6 sc.
Rnd 2: Inc around—12 sc.
Rnd 3: [Sc in next sc, inc in next sc] around—18 sc.
Rnd 4: [Sc in next sc, inc in next sc, sc in next sc] around—24 sc.
Rnd 5: [Sc in next 3 sc, inc in next sc] around—30 sc.
Rnd 6: [Sc in next 2 sc, inc in next sc, sc in next 2 sc] around—36 sc.

Rnd 7: [Sc in next 5 sc, inc in next sc] around—42 sc.
Rnds 8–14: Sc around—42 sc.
Rnd 15: [Sc in next 5 sc, dec over next 2 sc] around—36 sc.
Rnd 16: [Sc in next 2 sc, dec over next 2 sc, Sc in next 2 sc] around—30 sc.
Rnd 17: [Sc in next 3 sc, dec over next 2 sc] around—24 sc.
Place eyes between Rnds 10 and 11, 7 stitches apart. Begin stuffing the head.
Rnd 18: [Sc in next sc, dec over next 2 sc, sc in the next sc] around—18 sc.

Rnd 19: [Sc in next sc, dec over next 2 sc] around—12 sc.
Rnd 20: Sc in blo around—12 sc.
Rnds 21–23: Sc around—12 sc.
Fasten off, leaving a tail. Stuff the Head until firm.

ARMS (MAKE 2)

With **A**, make a magic ring.
Rnd 1: 6 sc in ring—6 sc.
Rnd 2: Sc around—6 sc.
Change to **B**.
Rnds 3–5: Sc around—6 sc.
Fasten off, leaving a tail.

LEG 1

With **C**, make a magic ring.
Rnd 1: 6 sc in ring—6 sc.
Rnd 2: Inc around—12 sc.
Rnd 3: Sc in blo around—12 sc.
Rnd 4: Sc in next 4 sc, [dec over next 2 sc] 4 times—8 sc.
Change to **D**.
Rnds 5–9: Sc around—8 sc.
Fasten off, leaving a tail.

LEG 2 and BODY

With **C**, make a magic ring.
Rnd 1: 6 sc in ring—6 sc.
Rnd 2: Inc around—12 sc.
Rnd 3: Sc in blo around—12 sc.
Rnd 4: [Dec over next 2 sc] 4 times, sc in next 4 sc—8 sc.
Change to **D**.
Rnds 5–9: Sc around—8 sc.
Rnd 10: Ch 2, sc in the next 8 sc around Leg 1, sc into next 2 ch, sc in the next 8 sc around Leg 2, sc into the next 2 ch on the other side—20 sc.
Rnds 11–12: Sc around—20 sc.
Change to **B**.
Rnds 13–15: Sc around—20 sc.
Rnd 16: Sc in next 4 sc, sc in next 6 sc around one Arm, sc in next 10 sc, sc in next 6 sc around the second Arm, sc in next 6 sc—32 sc.
Stuff the Legs and Body as you continue to decrease in the next 2 rounds.
Rnd 17: [Dec over next 2 sc] around—16 sc.
Rnd 18: [Dec over next 2 sc] around—8 sc.
Change to **A**.
Rnd 19: Sc in blo around—8 sc.
Rnds 20–24: Sc around—8 sc.
Fasten off with a long tail to sew on the Head.

SHIRT COLLAR

Rnd 1: With the Legs facing toward you, using **E**, sc join to flo of Rnd 18 starting from the front of the doll, sc inc around; do not join—16 sts.
Fasten off and weave in the end.

ROBE

With **B**.
Row 1: Ch 18, sc in 2nd ch from hook, sc in the next 4 ch, inc in the next ch, sc in the next 5 ch, inc in the next ch, sc in the next 5 ch, turn—19 sc.

Row 2: Ch 1 (does not count as st), sc in the next sc, ch 4, sk next 5 sc (makes an armhole), sc in the next 7 sc, ch 4, sk next 5 sc, turn—9 sc, 8 ch.

Row 3: Ch 1, sc in the next sc, sc in the next 4 ch, sc in the next 7 sc, sc in the next 4 ch, sc in the next sc, turn—17 sc.

Rows 4–11: Ch 1, sc across, turn—17 sc.

Row 12: Ch 1, sc along the edge of the Robe 11 times, sc along the initial foundation 17 ch, sc down the other side of the edge of the Robe 11 times—39 sc.

Invisible fasten off and weave in the end.

SLEEVES

With **B**.

Rnd 1: Sc join to the opening of the armhole on row 2 of the robes, sc in the next 3 sc, sc in the sp between Rows 1 and 2, sc in the next 5 sc at the top of the armhole, sc in the sp between Rows 1 and 2—11 sc.

Rnds 2–3: Sc around—11 sc.

Invisible fasten off and weave in the end.

HAIR

With **H**, make a magic ring.

Rnd 1: 6 sc in ring—6 sc.

Rnd 2: Inc around—12 sc.

Rnd 3: [Sc in next sc, inc in next sc] around—18 sc.

Rnd 4: [Sc in next sc, inc in next sc, sc in next sc] around—24 sc.

Rnd 5: [Sc in next 3 sc, inc in next sc] around—30 sc.

Continue by working straight for strands.

Strs 1–4: Ch 9, sc in 2nd ch from hook and in each ch across, sl st into next sc in Rnd 5—8 sc.

Strs 5–6: Sl st into next sc in Rnd 5—1 sl st.

Strs 7–8: Ch 9, sc in 2nd ch from hook and in each ch across, sl st into next sc in Rnd 5—8 sc.

Str 9: Ch 9, hdc in 3rd ch from hook and in each ch across, sk next sc in Rnd 5, sl st into next sc—7 hdc.

Str 10: Ch 13, hdc in 3rd ch from hook and in each ch across, sk next sc in Rnd 5, sl st into next sc—11 hdc.

Strs 11–17: Ch 14, hdc in 3rd ch from hook and in each ch across, sk next sc in Rnd 5, sl st into next sc—12 hdc.

Str 18: Ch 13, hdc in 3rd ch from hook and in each ch across, sk next sc in Rnd 5, sl st into next sc—11 hdc.

Str 19: Ch 9, hdc in 3rd ch from hook and in each ch across, sk next sc in Rnd 5, sl st into next sc—7 hdc.

Fasten off with a long tail.

SCARF

Row 1: With **G**, Ch 4, [with **F**, ch 4; with **G**, ch 4] 6 times, ch 2, turn—54 ch.

Row 2: Hdc in 3rd ch from hook, hdc in next 3 ch, [with **F**, hdc in next 4 ch; with **G**, hdc in next 4 ch] 6 times—52 hdc.

Fasten off and weave in the end.

ASSEMBLY

Attach the Head to the Body

Cut a straw to approximately 2 inches, fold it in half twice, and insert it into the neck on the Body to make the neck sturdier. Thread the long tail from the neck through the tunnel on the bottom of the Head. Secure the Head to the Body by making stitches between the crown of the Head and the neck. The Head should be turnable. Using black embroidery thread, embroider a small mouth 3 rows below the eyes in the center, spanning 1 stitch.

Attach the Hair

Use the WS of the Hair as the side facing up. Secure the center of the magic ring of the Hair to the magic ring of the Head (i.e. the crown of the Head). Arrange the fringe (Strands 1 to 4, and 7 to 8) of the Hair loosely above the eyes and centered. Keeping the fringe loose, use the yarn tail to secure the Hair piece and each strand of the Hair onto the Head.

Uniform Details

With **F**, embroider a row to the bottom of the uniform sweater between Rows 13 and 14 of the Body and a V-neck collar for the sweater.

Glasses

Using jewelry wire, shape the eyeglasses. Then use black yarn to wrap around the glasses. Sew the glasses onto the face.

RON WEASLEY

Designed by Juli Anne
Skill Level: ⚡ ⚡

Ron Weasley meets Harry Potter on the Hogwarts Express, as they travel toward Hogwarts school in Scotland. Ron comes from a large family of ginger-haired wizards. While the two get to know each other on the train, Harry treats them to a smorgasbord of sweets off the sweets trolley, to Ron's delight.

Harry Potter and the Prisoner of Azkaban costume designer Jany Temime admits Ron was one of her favorite characters to dress, but she sometimes felt embarrassed by his outfits. "Every teenager wanted to look cool and good, and Ron never seemed to. He always looked ridiculous," she says, "but [Rupert Grint] pulled it off brilliantly. He wore everything with one hundred percent sincerity." Temime felt Grint understood his character better than anyone else. "He never felt ashamed to wear any of the costumes, which was very appreciated," she adds. "I always enjoyed dressing Ron because Rupert always made me laugh." Ron was definitely challenged by the sweaters his mum knitted over the years in the Weasley palette of oranges, greens, and, of course, maroon.

This charming Ron Weasley amigurumi doll is crafted with love and meticulous detail. The miniature wizard captures the spirit of Harry Potter's loyal and brave best friend. He's dressed in his hand-me-down uniform and robes, complete with a house scarf, and will undoubtedly weave his way into your heart and become a cherished companion for all your wizarding adventures.

"I'm Ron, by the way.
Ron Weasley."

Ron Weasley, *Harry Potter and the Sorcerer's Stone*

FINISHED MEASUREMENTS
Height: 5.5 in. / 14 cm
Width: 2.5 in. / 6.5 cm

YARN
DK weight (#3 light) yarn, shown in Hobbii *Friends Cotton 8/8* (100% cotton, 82 yd. / 75 m per 1.75 oz. / 50 g skein).
Color A: #04 Cream, 1 skein
Color B: #118 Silver, 1 skein
Color C: #124 Black, 1 skein
Color D: #122 Anthracite, 1 skein
Color E: #01 White, 1 skein
Color F: #41 Pomegranate, 1 skein
Color G: #24 Sunflower, 1 skein

Worsted weight (#4 medium) yarn, shown in Hobbii *Amigo XL* (100% acrylic, 109 yd. / 100 m per 1.8 oz. / 50 g skein).
Color H: A40, Rust, 1 skein

HOOK
• US D / 3.25mm crochet hook

NOTIONS
• Stitch markers
• Pair of 6mm safety eyes
• Polyester stuffing
• Tapestry needle
• Embroidery thread, small amount of black
• Plastic or paper straw (optional)

GAUGE
24 sts and 24 rnds = 4 in. / 10 cm in sc
Gauge is not critical for this project. Ensure your stitches are tight so the stuffing won't show through.

NOTES
- Use the yarn-under-single-crochet technique to achieve tighter and more aligned stitches when crocheting in the round.
- Use the underside (WS) of the Hair piece as the wig.
- Pieces worked in the round are continuous rounds; do not join.
- Use the half-color changing technique to achieve cleaner lines when changing colors from one row to another (optional).

BEHIND THE MAGIC

Costume designer Jany Temime describes Ron Weasley's personal style as a combination of "clumsiness" and "awkwardness," but says that made Ron "almost cool to be dressed that wrong."

HEAD

With **A**, make a magic ring.
Rnd 1: 6 sc in ring—6 sc.
Rnd 2: Inc around—12 sc.
Rnd 3: [Sc in next sc, inc in next sc] around—18 sc.
Rnd 4: [Sc in next sc, inc in next sc, sc in next sc] around—24 sc.
Rnd 5: [Sc in next 3 sc, inc in next sc] around—30 sc.
Rnd 6: [Sc in next 2 sc, inc in next sc, sc in next 2 sc] around—36 sc.
Rnd 7: [Sc in next 5 sc, inc in next sc] around—42 sc.
Rnds 8–14: Sc around—42 sc.
Rnd 15: [Sc in next 5 sc, dec over next 2 sc] around—36 sc.
Rnd 16: [Sc in next 2 sc, dec over next 2 sc, Sc in next 2 sc] around—30 sc.
Rnd 17: [Sc in next 3 sc, dec over next 2 sc] around—24 sc.
Place safety eyes between Rnds 10 and 11, 7 stitches apart.
Begin stuffing the Head.
Rnd 18: [Sc in next sc, dec over next 2 sc, sc in the next sc] around—18 sc.
Rnd 19: [Sc in next sc, dec over next 2 sc] around—12 sc.
Rnd 20: Sc in blo around—12 sc.
Rnds 21–23: Sc around—12 sc.
Fasten off. Stuff the Head until firm.

ARMS (MAKE 2)

With **A**, make a magic ring.
Rnd 1: 6 sc in ring—6 sc.
Rnd 2: Sc around—6 sc.
Change to **B**.
Rnds 3–5: Sc around—6 sc.
Fasten off.

LEG 1

With **C**, make a magic ring.
Rnd 1: 6 sc in ring—6 sc.
Rnd 2: Inc around—12 sc.
Rnd 3: Sc in blo around—12 sc.
Rnd 4: Sc in next 4 sc, [dec over next 2 sc] 4 times—8 sc.
Change to **D**.
Rnds 5–9: Sc around—8 sc.
Fasten off Leg 1.

LEG 2 and BODY

With **C**, make a magic ring.
Rnd 1: 6 sc in ring—6 sc.
Rnd 2: Inc around—12 sc.
Rnd 3: Sc in blo around—12 sc.
Rnd 4: [Dec over next 2 sc] 4 times, sc in next 4 sc—8 sc.
Change to **D**.
Rnds 5–9: Sc around—8 sc.
Rnd 10: Ch 2, sc in the next 8 sc around Leg 1, sc into next 2 ch, sc in the next 8 sc around Leg 2, sc into the next 2 ch on the other side—20 sc.
Rnds 11–12: Sc around—20 sc.
Change to **B**.
Rnds 13–15: Sc around—20 sc.
Rnd 16: Sc in next 4 sc, sc in next 6 sc around one Arm, sc in next 10 sc, sc in next 6 sc around second Arm, sc in next 6 sc—32 sc.
Stuff the Legs and Body as you continue to decrease in the next 2 rounds.
Rnd 17: [Dec over next 2 sc] around—16 sc.
Rnd 18: [Dec over next 2 sc] around—8 sc.
Change to **A**.
Rnd 19: Sc in blo around—8 sc.
Rnds 20–24: Sc around—8 sc.
Fasten off with a long tail to sew onto the Head.

SHIRT COLLAR

Rnd 1: With the doll's Legs facing toward you, using **E**, sc join to flo of Rnd 18 starting from the front of the doll, sc inc around; do not join—16 sts.

Fasten off and weave in the end.

ROBE

Row 1: With **C**, ch 18, sc in 2nd ch from hook, sc in the next 4 ch, inc in the next ch, sc in the next 5 ch, inc in the next ch, sc in the next 5 ch, turn—19 sc.

Row 2: Ch 1 (does not count as st), sc in the next sc, ch 4, sk next 5 sc (makes an armhole), sc in the next 7 sc, ch 4, sk next 5 sc, turn—9 sc, 8 ch.

Row 3: Ch 1, sc in the next sc, sc in the next 4 ch, sc in the next 7 sc, sc in the next 4 ch, sc in the next sc, turn—17 sc.

Rows 4—11: Ch 1, sc across, turn—17 sc.

Row 12: Ch 1, sc along the edge of the Robe 11 times, sc along the initial foundation 17 ch, sc down the other side of the edge of the Robe 11 times—39 sc.

Invisible fasten off and weave in the end.

SLEEVES

Rnd 1: With **C**, sc join to the opening of the armhole on Row 2 of the Robe, sc in the next 3 sc, sc in the sp between Rows 1 and 2, sc in the next 5 sc at the top of the armhole, sc in the sp between Rows 1 and 2—11 sc.

Rnds 2—3: Sc around—11 sc.

Invisible fasten off and weave in the end.

HAIR

With **H**, make a magic ring.

Rnd 1: 6 sc in ring—6 sc.

Rnd 2: Inc around—12 sc.

Rnd 3: [Sc in next sc, inc in next sc] around—18 sc.

Rnd 4: [Sc in next sc, inc in next sc, sc in next sc] around—24 sc.

Rnd 5: [Sc in next 3 sc, inc in next sc] around—30 sc.

Continue by working straight for strands.

Strs 1—3: Ch 9, sc in 2nd ch from hook and in each ch across, sl st into next sc in Rnd 5—8 sc.

Strs 4—5: Sl st into next sc in Rnd 5—1 sl st.

Strs 6—8: Ch 9, sc in 2nd ch from hook and in each ch across, sl st into next sc in Rnd 5—8 sc.

Str 9: Ch 9, hdc in 3rd ch from hook and in each ch across, sk next sc in Rnd 5, sl st into next sc—7 hdc.

Str 10: Ch 13, hdc in 3rd ch from hook and in each ch across, sk next sc in Rnd 5, sl st into next sc—11 hdc.

Strs 11–17: Ch 14, hdc in 3rd ch from hook and in each ch across, sk next sc in Rnd 5, sl st into next sc—12 hdc.

Str 18: Ch 13, hdc in 3rd ch from hook and in each ch across, sk next sc in Rnd 5, sl st into next sc—11 hdc.

Str 19: Ch 9, hdc in 3rd ch from hook and in each ch across, sk next sc in Rnd 5, sl st into next sc—7 hdc.

Fasten off with a long tail.

SCARF

Row 1: With **G**, ch 4, [with **F**, ch 4; with **G**, ch 4] 6 times, ch 2, turn—54 ch.

Row 2: Hdc in 3rd ch from hook, hdc in next 3 ch, [with **F**, hdc in next 4 ch; with **G**, hdc in next 4 ch] 6 times—52 hdc.

Fasten off and weave in the end.

ASSEMBLY

Attach Head to Body

Cut a straw to approximately 2 inches, fold it in half twice, and insert it into the neck on the Body to make the neck sturdier. Thread the long tail from the neck through the tunnel in the bottom of the Head. Secure the Head to the Body by making stitches between the crown of the Head and the neck. The Head should be turnable. Using black embroidery thread,

embroider a small mouth 3 rows below the eyes in the center, spanning 1 stitch.

Attach the Hair

Use the WS of the crocheted Hair piece as the side facing up. Secure the center of the magic circle of the Hair piece to the magic circle of the Head (i.e. the crown of the Head). Arrange the fringe (Strands 1-3 and 6-8) of the Hair loosely above the eyes and centered.

Keeping the fringe loose, use the yarn tail to secure the Hair piece and each strand of the Hair onto the Head.

Uniform Details

With **F**, embroider a row to the bottom of the uniform sweater between Rows 13 and 14 of the Body and a V-neck collar for the sweater.

HERMIONE GRANGER

Designed by Juli Anne
Skill Level: ⫻ ⫻

Hermione Granger was called "the brightest witch of her age" by Professor Lupin and "an insufferable know-it-all" by Professor Snape. She's also one of Harry Potter's most loyal friends, along with Ron Weasley.

For *Harry Potter and the Prisoner of Azkaban*, costume designer Jany Temime redesigned the Hogwarts robes to be in a darker color and manufactured in higher quality materials: 100 percent cotton shirts, wool robes, and silk ties. Robes were lined in the student's house colors for quick identification, and pointed hats were dropped in favor of a hood, "as all kids have a hoodie," she says.

As Hermione matured, Temime dressed her in clothes showing she was more concerned about her studies than anything else. "Hermione is a girl who felt her best asset was her brain," she explains, "and wasn't worried about making an effort with her clothes." That changed in *Harry Potter and the Goblet of Fire*, "when she became interested in Ron," laughs Temime, who chose a palette of pinks and grays for her simple, practical outfits.

Embark on an enchanting journey with this brilliant Hermione Granger amigurumi doll. This Hermione proudly wears her classic Hogwarts uniform with removable black robes and a long scarf in Gryffindor colors. She has long brown crocheted hair, each strand delicately stitched into place. Although this amigurumi doll stands only 5.5 inches tall, she embodies all the brilliance and bravery of the brightest witch of her age.

"I'm Hermione Granger. And you are . . . ?"

Hermione Granger,
Harry Potter and the Sorcerer's Stone

FINISHED MEASUREMENTS
Height: 5.5 in. / 14 cm
Width: 2.5 in. / 6.5 cm

YARN
DK weight (#3 light) yarn, shown in Hobbii *Friends Cotton 8/8* (100% cotton, 82 yd. / 1.75 oz. / 75 m per 50 g skein).
Color A: #04 Cream, 1 skein
Color B: #118 Silver, 1 skein
Color C: #124 Black, 1 skein
Color D: #122 Anthracite, 1 skein
Color E: #01 White, 1 skein
Color F: #41 Pomegranate, 1 skein
Color G: #24 Sunflower, 1 skein

Worsted weight (#4 medium) yarn, shown in Hobbii *Amigo XL* (100% acrylic, 109 yd. / 100 m per 1.8 oz. / 50 g skein).
Color H: #A39 Cognac, 1 skein

HOOK
• US D / 3.25mm crochet hook

NOTIONS
• Stitch markers
• Pair of 6.0mm safety eyes
• Polyester stuffing
• Tapestry needle
• Plastic or paper straw (optional)
• Embroidery thread, small amount of black

GAUGE
24 sts and 24 rnds = 4 in. / 10 cm in sc
Gauge is not critical for this project. Ensure your stitches are tight so the stuffing won't show through.

SPECIAL ABBREVIATIONS
Back Loop Only (blo): Work through back loop only
Front Loop Only (flo): Work through front loop only

BEHIND THE MAGIC

When the maturing Hogwarts students were able to wear more contemporary clothing in *Harry Potter and the Prisoner of Azkaban*, actor Emma Watson was relieved. "Thank goodness we didn't have to wear the uniforms all the time," she admits. "I was out of those itchy sweaters!"

HEAD

With **A**, make a magic ring.
Rnd 1: 6 sc in ring—6 sc.
Rnd 2: Inc around—12 sc.
Rnd 3: [Sc in next sc, inc in next sc] around—18 sc.
Rnd 4: [Sc in next sc, inc in next sc, sc in next sc] around—24 sc.
Rnd 5: [Sc in next 3 sc, inc in next sc] around—30 sc.
Rnd 6: [Sc in next 2 sc, inc in next sc, sc in next 2 sc] around—36 sc.
Rnd 7: [Sc in next 5 sc, inc in next sc] around—42 sc.
Rnds 8–14: Sc around—42 sc.
Rnd 15: [Sc in next 5 sc, dec over next 2 sc] around—36 sc.
Rnd 16: [Sc in next 2 sc, dec over next 2 sc, sc in next 2 sc] around—30 sc.
Rnd 17: [Sc in next 3 sc, dec over next 2 sc] around—24 sc.
Place eyes between Rnds 10 and 11, 7 stitches apart. Begin stuffing the Head.
Rnd 18: [Sc in next sc, dec over next 2 sc, sc in the next sc] around—18 sc.
Rnd 19: [Sc in next sc, dec over next 2 sc] around—12 sc.
Rnd 20: Sc in blo around—12 sc.
Rnds 21–23: Sc around—12 sc.
Fasten off. Stuff the Head until firm.

ARMS (MAKE 2)

With **A**, make a magic ring.
Rnd 1: 6 sc in ring—6 sc.
Rnd 2: Sc around—6 sc.
Change to **B**.
Rnds 3–5: Sc around—6 sc.
Fasten off.

LEG 1

With **C**, make a magic ring.
Rnd 1: 6 sc in ring—6 sc.
Rnd 2: Inc around—12 sc.
Rnd 3: Sc in blo around—12 sc.
Rnd 4: Sc in next 4 sc, [dec over next 2 sc] 4 times—8 sc.
Change to **B**.
Rnds 5–6: Sc around—8 sc.
Change to **A**.
Rnds 7–9: Sc around—8 sc.
Fasten off Leg 1.

LEG 2 and BODY

With **C**, make a magic ring.
Rnd 1: 6 sc in ring—6 sc.
Rnd 2: Inc around—12 sc.
Rnd 3: Sc in blo around—12 sc.
Rnd 4: [Dec over next 2 sc] 4 times, sc in next 4 sc—8 sc.
Change to **B**.
Rnds 5–6: Sc around—8 sc.
Change to **A**.
Rnds 7–9: Sc around—8 sc.
Change to **B**.
Rnd 10: Ch 2, sc in the next 8 sc around Leg 1, sc into next 2 ch, sc in the next 8 sc around Leg 2, sc into the next 2 ch on the other side—20 sc.
Rnds 11–12: Sc around—20 sc.
Change to **B**.
Rnd 13: Sc in blo around—20 sc.
Rnds 14–15: Sc around—20 sc.
Rnd 16: Sc in next 4 sc, sc in next 6 sc around Arm 1, sc in next 10 sc, sc in next 6 sc around Arm 2, sc in next 6 sc—32 sc.
Stuff the Legs and Body as you continue to decrease in the next 2 rounds.
Rnd 17: [Dec over next 2 sc] around—16 sc.
Rnd 18: [Dec over next 2 sc] around—8 sc.
Change to **A**.
Rnd 19: Sc in blo around—8 sc.

Rnds 20—24: Sc around—8 sc.
Fasten off with a long tail to sew
  onto the Head.

SHIRT COLLAR

Rnd 1: With the Legs facing
  toward you, using **E**, sc join to
  flo of Rnd 18 starting from the
  front of the doll, sc inc around;
  do not join—16 sts.
Fasten off and weave in the end.

UNIFORM SKIRT

With **D**.
Row 1: Ch 5, sc in 2nd ch from
  hook and in each ch across,
  turn—4 sc.
Rows 2—20: Ch 1, sc across—
  4 sc.
Fasten off with a long tail.

ROBE

With **C**.
Row 1: Ch 18, sc in 2nd ch from
  hook, sc in the next 4 ch, inc
  in the next ch, sc in the next
  5 ch, inc in the next ch, sc in
  the next 5 ch, turn—19 sc.
Row 2: Ch 1 (does not count as
  st), sc in the next sc, ch 4, sk
  next 5 sc (makes an armhole),
  sc in the next 7 sc, ch 4, sk
  next 5 sc, turn—9 sc, 8 ch.
Row 3: Ch 1, sc in the next sc, sc
  in the next 4 ch, sc in the next
  7 sc, sc in the next 4 ch, sc in
  the next sc, turn—17 sc.
Rows 4—11: Ch 1, sc across,
  turn—17 sc.
Row 12: Ch 1, sc along the edge
  of the Robe 11 times, sc
  along the initial foundation
  17 ch, sc down the other side
  of the edge of the Robe 11
  times—39 sc.
Invisible fasten off and weave in
  the end.

SLEEVES

With **C**.
Rnd 1: Sc join to the opening of
  the armhole on Row 2 of the
  Robe, sc in the next 3 sc, sc in
  the sp between Rows 1 and 2,
  sc in the next 5 sc at the top
  of the armhole, sc in the sp
  between Rows 1 and 2—11 sc.
Rnds 2—3: Sc around—11 sc.
Invisible fasten off and weave in
  the end.

HAIR

With **H**, make a magic ring.
Rnd 1: 6 sc in ring—6 sc.
Rnd 2: Inc around—12 sc.
Rnd 3: [Sc in next sc, inc in next
  sc] around—18 sc.
Rnd 4: [Sc in next sc, inc in next
  sc, sc in next sc] around—24 sc.
Rnd 5: [Sc in next 3 sc, inc in next
  sc] around—30 sc.
Continue by working straight for
  strands.

Str 1: Ch 16, sc in 2nd ch from hook and in each ch across, sl st into next sc in Rnd 5—15 sc.

Strs 2—5: Ch 9, sc in 2nd ch from hook and in each ch across, sl st into next sc in Rnd 5—8 sc.

Str 6: Ch 16, sc in 2nd ch from hook and in each ch across, sl st into next sc in Rnd 5—15 sc.

Strs 7—18: Ch 22, hdc in 3rd ch from hook and in each ch across, sk next sc in Rnd 5, sl st into next sc—20 hdc.

Fasten off with a long tail.

SCARF

Row 1: With **G**, Ch 4, [with **F**, ch 4; with **G**, ch 4] 6 times, ch 2, turn—54 ch.

Row 2: Hdc in 3rd ch from hook, hdc in next 3 ch, [with **F**, hdc in next 4 ch; with **G**, hdc in next 4 ch] 6 times—52 hdc.

Fasten off and weave in the end.

ASSEMBLY

Attach Head to Body

Cut straw to approximately 2 inches, fold it in half twice, and insert it into the neck on the Body to make the neck sturdier. Thread the long tail from the neck through the tunnel in the bottom of the Head. Secure the Head to the Body by making stitches between the crown of the Head and the neck. The Head should be turnable. Using black embroidery thread, embroider a small mouth 3 rows below the eyes in the center, spanning 1 stitch.

Attach the Hair

Use the WS of the crocheted Hair piece as the side facing up. Secure the center of the magic ring of the Hair piece to the magic ring of the Head (i.e. the crown of the Head). Arrange the fringe (Strands 2 to 5) of the Hair loosely above the eyes and centered. Keeping the fringe loose, use the yarn tail to secure the Hair piece and each strand of the Hair onto the Head. Strands 1 and 6 are slightly longer than the fringe and can be sewn on top of the longer strands on either side to give a finished look.

Uniform Details

With **F**, embroider a row to the bottom of the uniform sweater between Rows 13 and 14 of the Body and a V-neck collar for the sweater.

Attach the Skirt

Sew the foundation ch and the last row together to make a band. Sew to Body, matching one row to one stitch, just above the front loops of Row 12 on the Body.

DRACO MALFOY

Designed by Juli Anne
Skill Level: ⚡⚡

Draco Malfoy almost immediately becomes an archrival to Harry Potter after he insults Harry's new friend Ron and states that some wizards are better than others. His attitude isn't shocking, as he is the only child of a prosperous, pure-blood wizarding family who values status above all else.

For *Harry Potter and the Prisoner of Azkaban*, costume designer Jany Temime made noteworthy changes to the materials and design of the Hogwarts robes. Actor Tom Felton, who portrays Draco, was given one more change to his robes: the pockets were sewn shut! It turns out Felton had the habit of filling the pockets with food he could snack on in between filming scenes. After *Harry Potter and the Order of the Phoenix*, Draco no longer wears his robes, but instead wears a smart black suit to symbolize Draco's decision to follow his father with the goal of becoming a Death Eater. "We wanted to show that he is consciously separating himself from being a student," says Temime.

This confident and self-assured Draco Malfoy amigurumi doll dons his signature Hogwarts uniform, meticulously crocheted in the distinguished Slytherin house colors. His slicked-back blond crocheted hair perfectly captures Draco's handsome features and adds an air of sophistication.

"I'm Malfoy. Draco Malfoy. Think my name is funny, do you?"

Draco Malfoy, *Harry Potter and the Sorcerer's Stone*

FINISHED MEASUREMENTS
Height: 5.5 in. / 14 cm
Width: 2.5 in. / 6.5 cm

YARN
DK weight (#3 light) yarn, shown in Hobbii *Friends Cotton 8/8* (100% cotton, 82 yd. / 75 m per 1.75 oz. / 50 g skein).
Color A: #04 Cream, 1 skein
Color B: #118 Silver, 1 skein
Color C: #124 Black, 1 skein
Color D: #122 Anthracite, 1 skein
Color E: #01 White, 1 skein
Color F: #105 Emerald, 1 skein

Worsted weight (#4 medium) yarn, shown in Hobbii *Amigo XL* (100% acrylic, 109 yd. / 100 m per 1.8 oz. / 50 g skein).
Color G: #A35, Primrose, 1 skein

HOOK
• US D / 3.25mm crochet hook

NOTIONS
• Stitch markers
• Polyester stuffing
• Pair of 6mm safety eyes
• Tapestry needle
• Plastic or paper straw (optional)
• Embroidery thread, small amt of black

GAUGE
24 sts and 24 rnds = 4 in. / 10 cm in sc
Gauge is not critical for this project. Ensure your stitches are tight so the stuffing won't show through.

SPECIAL ABBREVIATIONS

Back Loop Only (blo): Work through back loop only

Front Loop Only (flo): Work through front loop only

NOTES

- Use the yarn-under-single-crochet technique to achieve tighter and more aligned stitches when crocheting in the round.
- Use the underside (WS) of the Hair piece as the wig.
- Pieces worked in the round are continuous rounds; do not join.
- Use the half-color changing. technique to achieve cleaner lines when changing colors from one row to another (optional).

BEHIND THE MAGIC

Actor Tom Felton received fan mail asking for more color in Draco's wardrobe, but as Felton responds, "There's no occasion where black doesn't fit in as far as Draco's concerned."

HEAD

With **A**, make a magic ring.
Rnd 1: 6 sc in ring—6 sc.
Rnd 2: Inc around—12 sc.
Rnd 3: [Sc in next sc, inc in next sc] around—18 sc.
Rnd 4: [Sc in next sc, inc in next sc, sc in next sc] around—24 sc.
Rnd 5: [Sc in next 3 sc, inc in next sc] around—30 sc.
Rnd 6: [Sc in next 2 sc, inc in next sc, Sc in next 2 sc] around—36 sc.
Rnd 7: [Sc in next 5 sc, inc in next sc] around—42 sc.
Rnds 8–14: Sc around—42 sc.
Rnd 15: [Sc in next 5 sc, dec over next 2 sc] around—36 sc.
Rnd 16: [Sc in next 2 sc, dec over next 2 sc, Sc in next 2 sc] around—30 sc.
Rnd 17: [Sc in next 3 sc, dec over next 2 sc] around—24 sc.
Insert safety eyes between Rnds 10 and 11 approximately 7 stitches apart. Begin stuffing the Head.
Rnd 18: [Sc in next sc, dec over next 2 sc, sc in the next sc] around—18 sc.
Rnd 19: [Sc in next sc, dec over next 2 sc] around—12 sc.
Rnd 20: Sc in blo around—12 sc.
Rnds 21–23: Sc around—12 sc.
Fasten off. Stuff the Head until firm.

ARMS (MAKE 2)

With **A**, make a magic ring.
Rnd 1: 6 sc in ring—6 sc.
Rnd 2: Sc around—6 sc.
Change to **B**.
Rnds 3–5: Sc around—6 sc.
Fasten off.

LEG 1

With **C**, make a magic ring.
Rnd 1: 6 sc in ring—6 sc.
Rnd 2: Inc around—12 sc.
Rnd 3: Sc in blo around—12 sc.
Rnd 4: Sc in next 4 sc, [dec over next 2 sc] 4 times—8 sc.
Change to **D**.
Rnds 5–9: Sc around—8 sc.
Fasten the first Leg.

LEG 2 and BODY

With **C**, make a magic ring.
Rnd 1: 6 sc in ring—6 sc.
Rnd 2: Inc around—12 sc.
Rnd 3: Sc in blo around—12 sc.
Rnd 4: [Dec over next 2 sc] 4 times, sc in next 4 sc—8 sc.
Change to **D**.
Rnds 5–9: Sc around—8 sc.
Rnd 10: Ch 2, sc in the next 8 sc around Leg 1, sc into next 2 ch, sc in the next 8 sc around Leg 2, sc into the next 2 ch on the other side—20 sc.
Rnds 11–12: Sc around—20 sc.
Change to **B**.
Rnds 13–15: Sc around—20 sc.
Rnd 16: Sc in next 4 sc, sc in next 6 sc around one Arm, sc in next 10 sc, sc in next 6 sc around second Arm, sc in next 6 sc—32 sc.
Stuff the Legs and Body as you continue to decrease in the next 2 rounds.
Rnd 17: [Dec over next 2 sc] around—16 sc.
Rnd 18: [Dec over next 2 sc] around—8 sc.
Change to **A**.
Rnd 19: Sc in blo around—8 sc.
Rnds 20–24: Sc around—8 sc.
Fasten off with a long tail to sew onto the Head.

SHIRT COLLAR

Rnd 1: With the doll's Legs facing toward you, using **E**, sc join to flo of Rnd 18 starting from the front of the doll, sc inc around; do not join—16 sts.
Fasten off and weave in the end.

ROBE

Row 1: With **C**, Ch 18, sc in 2nd ch from hook, sc in the next 4 ch, inc in the next ch, sc in the next 5 ch, inc in the next ch, sc in the next 5 ch, turn—19 sc.

Row 2: Ch 1 (does not count as st), sc in the next sc, ch 4, sk next 5 sc (makes an armhole), sc in the next 7 sc, ch 4, sk next 5 sc, turn—9 sc, 8 ch.

Row 3: Ch 1, sc in the next sc, sc in the next 4 ch, sc in the next 7 sc, sc in the next 4 ch, sc in the next sc, turn—17 sc.

Rows 4—11: Ch 1, sc across, turn—17 sc.

Row 12: Ch 1, sc along the edge of the Robe 11 times, sc along the initial foundation 17 ch, sc down the other side of the edge of the Robe 11 times—39 sc.
Invisible fasten off and weave in the end.

SLEEVES

Rnd 1: With **C**, sc join to the opening of the armhole on Row 2 of the Robe, sc in the next 3 sc, sc in the sp between Rows 1 and 2, sc in the next 5 sc at the top of the armhole, sc in the sp between Rows 1 and 2—11 sc.

Rnds 2—3: Sc around—11 sc.
Invisible fasten off and weave in the end.

HAIR

With **G**, make a magic ring.
Rnd 1: 6 sc in ring—6 sc.
Rnd 2: Inc around—12 sc.
Rnd 3: [Sc in next sc, inc in next sc] around—18 sc.
Rnd 4: [Sc in next sc, inc in next sc, sc in next sc] around—24 sc.
Rnd 5: [Sc in next 3 sc, inc in next sc] around—30 sc.
Continue by working straight for strands.

Str 1: Ch 11, hdc in 3rd ch from hook and in each ch across, sk next sc in Rnd 5, sl st into next sc—9 hdc.

Str 2: Ch 13, hdc in 3rd ch from hook and in each ch across, sk next sc in Rnd 5, sl st into next sc—11 hdc.

Strs 3—10: Ch 14, hdc in 3rd ch from hook and in each ch across, sk next sc in Rnd 5, sl st into next sc—12 hdc.

Str 11: Ch 13, hdc in 3rd ch from

hook and in each ch across, sk
next sc in Rnd 5, sl st into next
sc—11 hdc.

Str 12: Ch 11, hdc in 3rd ch from
hook and in each ch across, sk
next sc in Rnd 5, sl st into next
sc—9 hdc.

Cont. Rnd 6: Continue working in
the unworked sts of Rnd 5, ch
2, hdc inc in the next sc, hdc
in the next 4 sc, hdc inc in the
next sc, turn—8 hdc.

Str 13: Ch 12, hdc in 3rd ch from
hook and in each ch across, sk
next sc in Rnd 6, sl st into next
sc—10 hdc.

Strs 14–15: Ch 14, hdc in 3rd
ch from hook and in each ch
across, sk next sc in Rnd 6, sl
st into next sc—12 hdc.

Str 16: Ch 12, hdc in 3rd ch from
hook and in each ch across, sk
next sc in Rnd 6, sl st into next
sc—10 hdc.

Fasten off with a long tail.

SCARF

Row 1: With **F**, Ch 4, [with **B**, ch
4; with **F**, ch 4] 6 times, ch 2,
turn—54 ch.

Row 2: Hdc in 3rd ch from hook,
hdc in next 3 ch, [with **B**, hdc
in next 4 ch; with **F**, hdc in
next 4 ch] 6 times—52 hdc.

Fasten off and weave in the end.

ASSEMBLY

Attach Head to Body

Cut a straw to approximately
2 inches, fold it in half twice,
and insert it into the neck on
the Body to make the neck
sturdier. Thread the long tail
from the neck through the
tunnel on the bottom of the
Head. Secure the Head to the
Body by making stitches

between the crown of the
Head and the neck. The
Head should be turnable.
Using black embroidery
floss, embroider a small
mouth starting 2 rounds
below the eyes, off to the
side, diagonally, spanning
2 stitches.

Attach the Hair

Use the wrong side of the Hair as
the side facing up. Secure the
center of the magic ring of the
Hair to the magic ring of

the crown of the Head. Secure
Strands 1 to 12 to the sides
and back of the Head. Secure
Strands 13 to 16 to the top
of the Hair to create Draco's
slicked hair look.

Uniform Details

With **F**, embroider a row to the
bottom of the uniform sweater
between Rows 13 and 14 of
the Body and a V-neck collar
for the sweater.

LUNA LOVEGOOD

Designed by Juli Anne
Skill Level: ╱ ╱

When Hermione Granger introduces Luna Lovegood to her friends, she misspeaks and calls her "Loony Lovegood." But Luna is nonplussed. "A lot of people like her for being kooky," says actor Evanna Lynch (Luna), "but I like how wise she is, that nothing really affects her."

Costume designer Jany Temime wanted Luna Lovegood's clothes to exemplify a "wizardy" look, but also acknowledge her unique personality. "She is clearly a girl with her own tastes and her own hobbies," says Temime. "She has an approach to the world that nobody else has, and I wanted to reflect that in her clothing, because it mattered." Mismatched pieces with multiple layers featured fabrics with natural elements such as stars, flowers, or animals, giving them a folk-art feel. Lynch's familiarity with Luna proved valuable to the designer. "She was very specific about a few things that were from her character," Temime adds. "There was the Butterbeer-cap necklace, and shoes with strawberries on them. In fact, we put strawberries everywhere throughout her clothes because she liked strawberries."

This dreamy Luna Lovegood amigurumi doll is inspired by a loyal and compassionate friend who's unafraid to embrace her true self and follow her heart. She's dressed in her charming pink jacket with a stylish black skirt. Her long blonde hair is carefully crocheted and tied off to the side, showing her whimsical character. She sports a navy blue crossbody bag in which she carries the latest issue of *The Quibbler*. She's equipped with a pair of Spectrespecs, allowing her to see all the magical creatures and mysteries most others can't perceive, Nargles included.

"Everyone, this is Loony Love—Luna Lovegood."

Hermione Granger, *Harry Potter and the Order of the Phoenix*

FINISHED MEASUREMENTS
Height: 5.5 in. / 14 cm
Width: 2.5 in. / 6.5 cm

YARN
DK weight (#3 light) yarn, shown in Hobbii *Friends Cotton 8/8* (100% cotton, 82 yd. / 75 m per 1.75 oz. / 50 g skein).
Color A: #04 Cream, 1 skein
Color B: #54 Pink Berry Smoothie, 1 skein
Color C: #43 Bordeaux, 1 skein
Color D: #90 Capri Blue, 1 skein
Color E: #91 Aqua Blue, 1 skein
Color F: #124 Black, 1 skein
Color G: #45 Candyfloss, 1 skein
Color H: #51 Baby Pink, 1 skein
Color I: #86 Navy Blue, 1 skein

Worsted weight (#4 medium) yarn, shown in Hobbii *Amigo XL* (100% acrylic, 109 yd. / 100 m per 1.8 oz. / 50 g skein).
Color J: #A35 Primrose, 1 skein

HOOK
• US D / 3.25mm crochet hook

NOTIONS
• Stitch markers
• Pair of 6mm safety eyes
• Polyester stuffing
• Tapestry needle
• Plastic/paper straw (optional)
• Embroidery thread, small amt of black

GAUGE
24 sts and 24 rnds = 4 in. / 10 cm in sc
Gauge is not critical for this project. Ensure your stitches are tight so the stuffing won't show through.

SPECIAL ABBREVIATIONS

Back Loop Only (blo): Work through back loop only

Front Loop Only (flo): Work through front loop only

NOTES

- Use the yarn-under-single-crochet technique to achieve tighter and more aligned stitches when crocheting in the round.
- Use the underside (WS) of the Hair piece as the wig.
- Pieces worked in the round are continuous rounds; do not join.
- Use the half-color changing technique to achieve cleaner lines when changing colors from one row to another (optional).

BEHIND THE MAGIC

Actor Evanna Lynch was deeply knowledgeable about her character: When she was presented with a pair of red Dirigible Plum earrings, she immediately asked them to be redone in orange.

HEAD

With **A**, make a magic ring.

Rnd 1: 6 sc in ring; do not join—6 sc.

Rnd 2: Inc around—12 sc.

Rnd 3: [Sc in next sc, inc in next sc] around—18 sc.

Rnd 4: [Sc in next sc, inc in next sc, sc in next sc] around—24 sc.

Rnd 5: [Sc in next 3 sc, inc in next sc] around—30 sc.

Rnd 6: [Sc in next 2 sc, inc in next sc, Sc in next 2 sc] around—36 sc.

Rnd 7: [Sc in next 5 sc, inc in next sc] around—42 sc.

Rnds 8–14: Sc around—42 sc.

Rnd 15: [Sc in next 5 sc, dec over next 2 sc] around—36 sc.

Rnd 16: [Sc in next 2 sc, dec over next 2 sc, sc in next 2 sc] around—30 sc.

Rnd 17: [Sc in next 3 sc, dec over next 2 sc] around—24 sc.

Place safety eyes between Rnds 10 and 11, 7 stitches apart. Begin stuffing the head.

Rnd 18: [Sc in next sc, dec over next 2 sc, sc in the next sc] around—18 sc.

Rnd 19: [Sc in next sc, dec over next 2 sc] around—12 sc.
Rnd 20: Sc in blo around—12 sc.
Rnds 21–23: Sc around—12 sc.
Fasten off. Stuff the Head until firm.

ARMS (MAKE 2)

With **A**, make a magic ring.
Rnd 1: 6 sc in ring; do not join—6 sc.
Rnd 2: Sc around—6 sc.
Change to **B**.
Rnds 3–5: Sc around—6 sc.
Fasten off.

LEG 1

With **C**, make a magic ring.
Rnd 1: 6 sc in ring; do not join—6 sc.
Rnd 2: Inc around—12 sc.
Rnd 3: Sc in blo around—12 sc.
Rnd 4: Sc in next 4 sc, [dec over next 2 sc] 4 times—8 sc.
Change to **D**.
Rnd 5: Sc around—8 sc.
Change to **E**.
Rnd 6: Sl st in blo around—8 sl st.
Rnd 7: Sc in blo around—8 sc.
Rnds 8–10: Sc around—8 sc.
Fasten the first Leg.

LEG 2 and BODY

With **C**, make a magic ring.
Rnd 1: 6 sc in ring; do not join—6 sc.
Rnd 2: Inc around—12 sc.
Rnd 3: Sc in blo around—12 sc.
Rnd 4: [Dec over next 2 sc] 4 times, sc in next 4 sc—8 sc.
Change to **D**.
Rnd 5: Sc around—8 sc.
Change to **E**.
Rnd 6: Sl st in blo around—8 sl st.
Rnd 7: Sc in blo around—8 sc.
Rnds 8–10: Sc around—8 sc.

Rnd 11: Ch 2, sc in the next 8 sc around Leg 1, sc into next 2 ch, sc in the next 8 sc around Leg 2, sc into the next 2 ch on the other side—20 sc.
Rnd 12: Sc around—20 sc.
Change to **F**.
Rnd 13: Sc around—20 sc.
Change to **B**.
Rnd 14: Sl st blo around—20 sl st.
Rnd 15: Sc in blo around—20 sc.
Rnds 16–17: Sc around—20 sc.

Rnd 18: Sc in next 4 sc, sc in next 6 sc around Arm 1, sc in next 10 sc, sc in next 6 sc around Arm 2, sc in next 6 sc—32 sc.
Stuff the Legs and Body as you continue to decrease in the next 2 rounds.
Rnd 19: [Dec over next 2 sc] around—16 sc.
Rnd 20: [Dec over next 2 sc] around—8 sc.
Change to **A**.

Rnd 21: Sc in blo around—8 sc.
Rnds 22–26: Sc around—8 sc.
Fasten off with a long tail to sew onto the Head.

JACKET DETAILS

COLLAR

With **B**.
Rnd 1: With the Legs facing toward you, hdc join to flo of Rnd 20 starting from the front of the doll, hdc inc around; do not join—16 sts.
Fasten off and weave in the end.

HEM

With **B**.
Rnd 1: Sc join to flo of Rnd 14, sc around—20 sc.
Invisible fasten off and weave in the end.

SLEEVE CUFF (MAKE 2)

With **B**.
Row 1: Ch 7.
Fasten off with a tail to sew onto the Jacket.

FRONT

With **B**.
Row 1: Ch 5.
Fasten off with a tail to sew onto the Jacket.

SKIRT

With **F**.
Rnd 1: Sc join to flo of Rnd 13 on the Body, sc in each flo around—20 sc.
Rnds 2–4: Sc around—20 sc.
Invisible fasten off and weave in the end.

HAIR

With **J**, make a magic ring.
Rnd 1: 6 sc in ring; do not join—6 sc.

Rnd 2: Inc around—12 sc.
Rnd 3: [Sc in next sc, inc in next sc] around—18 sc.
Rnd 4: [Sc in next sc, inc in next sc, sc in next sc] around—24 sc.
Rnd 5: [Sc in next 3 sc, inc in next sc] around—30 sc.
Continue by working straight for strands.
Str 1: Ch 11, sc in 2nd ch from hook and in each ch across, sl st into next sc in Rnd 5—10 sc.
Strs 2–3: Ch 16, sc in 2nd ch from hook and in each ch across, sl st into next sc in Rnd 5—15 sc.
Str 4: Ch 11, sc in 2nd ch from hook and in each ch across, sl st into next sc in Rnd 5—10 sc.
Str 5: Ch 12, hdc in 3rd ch from hook and in each ch across, sk next sc in Rnd 5, sl st into next sc—10 hdc.
Str 6: Ch 14, hdc in 3rd ch from hook and in each ch across, sk next sc in Rnd 5, sl st into next sc—12 hdc.
Str 7: Ch 51, sc in 2nd ch from hook and in next 37 ch, hdc in next 12 ch, sk next sc in Rnd 5, sl st into next sc—38 sc + 12 hdc.
Str 8: Ch 14, hdc in 3rd ch from hook and in each ch across, sk next sc in Rnd 5, sl st into next sc—12 hdc.
Str 9: Ch 51, sc in 2nd ch from hook and in next 37 ch, hdc in next 12 ch, sk next sc in Rnd 5, sl st into next sc—38 sc + 12 hdc.
Strs 10–13: Ch 14, hdc in 3rd ch from hook and in each ch across, sk next sc in Rnd 5, sl st into next sc—12 hdc.
Str 14: Ch 41, sc in 2nd ch from hook and in next 27 ch, hdc in next 12 ch, sk next sc in Rnd 5, sl st into next sc—28 sc + 12 hdc.

Strs 15–16: Ch 14, hdc in 3rd ch from hook and in each ch across, sk next sc in Rnd 5, sl st into next sc—12 hdc.
Str 17: Ch 12, hdc in 3rd ch from hook and in each ch across, sk next sc in Rnd 5, sl st into next sc—10 hdc.
Fasten off with a long tail.

SPECTRESPECS

LENS (MAKE 2, one with D and one with G)

Rnd 1: 6 sc in ring; do not join—6 sc.
Rnd 2: Inc around—12 sc.
Invisible fasten off.

FRAME

With **H**.
Rnd 1: Sl st blo around one Lens; do not join—12 sl st.
Rnd 2: Sc blo in next 5 sl st, [Ch 4, sl st in 2nd ch from hook and in each ch across, sc blo in next sl st] 3 times, sc blo in the next 4 sl st, join, ch 2 (to create the bridge), repeat Rnds 1 and 2 on other Lens, sc in next 2 ch (bridge of the Spectrespecs).
Fasten off and weave in ends.

CROSSBODY BAG

Rnd 1: With **I**, ch 6, sc in 2nd ch from hook and in each ch across, turn and sc on the other side of the foundation ch in each ch across; do not join—10 sc.
Rnds 2–4: Sc around—10 sc.
Rnd 5: Sc in next 5 sc, sl st in next sc, ch 24, skip 4, sl st into the first st—24 ch to make the strap.

ASSEMBLY

Attach Head to Body

Cut a straw to approximately 2 inches, fold it in half twice, and insert it into the neck on the Body to make the neck sturdier. Thread the long tail from the neck through the tunnel on the bottom of the Head. Secure the head to the Body by making stitches between the crown of the Head and the neck. The Head should be turnable. Using black embroidery thread, embroider a small mouth 3 rows below the eyes in the center, spanning 1 stitch.

Attach the Hair

Use the WS of the crocheted Hair as the side facing up. Secure the center of the magic ring of the Hair piece to the magic ring of the Head (i.e. the crown of the Head). Arrange the fringe (Strands 1 to 4) of the Hair loosely above the eyes and centered. Keeping the fringe loose, use the yarn tail and secure the Hair piece and each strand of the Hair onto the Head.

Twist the first two long strands (7 and 9) together, secure it to the bottom of the Head along the hairline, and let the ponytail rest on the left shoulder. Then use the third long strand (14) to wrap around the twisted side ponytail for a finished look. Style the Hair so that the fringe frames the doll's face.

Jacket Details

Sew the cuffs onto the sleeves between Rnds 2 and 3 of the arms. Then sew the front of the Jacket to the Body where the opening of the Jacket would be.

Spectrespecs

If desired, you can sew the Spectrespecs directly onto the doll. To make them removable, sl st join at one side of the Spectrespecs and make a ch long enough (approx 30 to 35 ch) to go around the Head and sl st join on the other side of the Spectrespecs.

ALBUS DUMBLEDORE

Designed by Julia Chiang
Skill Level: ⚡ ⚡ ⚡

Albus Dumbledore is the headmaster of Hogwarts, and a fierce protector, adviser, and friend to Harry Potter. Dumbledore founded the Order of the Phoenix to fight Voldemort and his Death Eaters in both Wizarding Wars, and inspired Dumbledore's Army, formed by Hermione Granger and Harry Potter.

Harry Potter and the Sorcerer's Stone costume designer Judianna Makovsky was given the brief that Dumbledore, played by Richard Harris, was a clotheshorse, and so dressed him in thick robes of silk-screened velvets embroidered with Celtic symbols. With *Harry Potter and the Prisoner of Azkaban*, new costume designer Jany Temime saw Michael Gambon, who took over the role, as "an old hippie, though still chic." She dressed this version in layers of purple and lavender tie-dyed silks and a tasseled, flattened hat, and tied up his beard. When Dumbledore was injured in pursuit of a Horcrux, the color was washed out of his robes, and the hat was removed, giving Dumbledore a look of vulnerability.

Draped in purple robes accented with tasteful yellow edges and topped with his iconic tassel hat, this amigurumi Professor Dumbledore is ready to announce the winner of this year's House Cup. His long gray beard is crafted using a mix of different crochet stitches to add texture and charm, reflecting the character's aged wisdom and kind demeanor. Celebrate the magic of handmade crafting with this extraordinary amigurumi doll of the beloved Hogwarts headmaster.

> "It does not do to dwell on dreams and forget to live."

Albus Dumbledore, *Harry Potter and the Sorcerer's Stone*

FINISHED MEASUREMENTS
Height: 5.5 in. / 14 cm
Width: 3 in. / 8 cm

YARN
DK weight (#3 light) yarn, shown in Hobbii Yarns *Amigo*, (100% acrylic, 191 yd. / 175 m per 1.8 oz. / 50 g ball).
Color A: #A46 Light Peach, 1 ball
Color B: #A12 Black, 1 ball
Color C: #A09 Gray Melange, 1 ball
Color D: #A60 Violet, 1 ball
Color E: #A35 Primrose, 1 ball

HOOK
• US D-4 / 3.25mm crochet hook

NOTIONS
• Stitch markers
• Pair of 6.0mm safety eyes
• Polyester stuffing
• Tapestry needle
• 18-gauge wire for glasses (optional)

GAUGE
Gauge is not critical for this project. Ensure your stitches are tight so the stuffing won't show through.

SPECIAL ABBREVIATIONS
Bobble Stitch (bobble st): [Yarn over, insert hook into indicated st, yo, pull up lp, pull through two lps] 6 times, yo, pull through 6 lps on hook
Back Loop Only (blo): Work through back loop only
Front Loop Only (flo): Work through front loop only

NOTE
• Doll is worked primarily using single crochet stitches in the amigurumi style. The Robe, Hair piece, Beard, and Hat are worked separately and then attached to the doll.

LEGS (MAKE 2)

With **B**, make a magic ring.
Rnd 1: 6 sc in ring—6 sc.
Rnd 2: [2 sc, inc] 2 times—8 sc.
Rnds 3—5: Sc all around—8 sc.
Switch to **C**.
Rnds 6—11: Sc all around—8 sc.
Fasten off the first Leg (Leg 1).
    Make another (Leg 2), but do
    not fasten off.

BEHIND THE MAGIC

One of the robes Richard
Harris wore as Dumbledore
was appliquéd all over in
Celtic designs, which took
eight weeks to create.

CONNECTING THE LEGS

With the hook still connected to
    Leg 2, pick up a st on Leg 1,
    and work 8 scs all around Leg
    1. Then, pick up a st on Leg
    2 (the one immediately after
    the last st from Rnd 11), and
    then work the remaining 7 sts
    around Leg 2. The two Legs
    are now connected with a total
    of 16 sts. Continue to Body.

BODY

Rnds 1—8: Sc all around—16 sc.
Rnd 9: [6 sc, dec] 2 times—14 sc.
Rnd 10: Sc all around—14 sc.
Rnd 11: [5 sc, dec] 2 times, sl st to
    first st in rnd—12 sc.
Stuff firmly. Fasten off and weave
    in ends.

HEAD

With **A**, make a magic ring.
Rnd 1: 6 sc in ring—6 sc.
Rnd 2: Inc 6 times—12 sc.
Rnd 3: [Sc, inc] 6 times—18 sc.
Rnd 4: [2 sc, inc] 6 times—24 sc.
Rnd 5: [3 sc, inc] 6 times—30 sc.
Rnd 6: [4 sc, inc] 6 times—36 sc.
Rnd 7: [5 sc, inc] 6 times—42 sc.
Rnds 8—16: Sc all around—42 sc.
Insert the eyes between Rnds 13
    and 14, 8 sts apart. Using **A**,
    embroider a nose across 2 sts
    directly between the eyes.
Rnd 17: [5 sc, dec] 6 times—36 sc.
Rnd 18: [4 sc, dec] 6 times—30 sc.
Rnd 19: [3 sc, dec] 6 times—24 sc.
Rnd 20: [2 sc, dec] 6 times—18 sc.
Stuff firmly.
Rnd 21: [Sc, dec] 6 times—12 sc.
Rnd 22: Dec 6 times— 6 sc.
Fasten off, leaving a tail for
    sewing. Sew the Head to the
    Body. Weave in end.

ARMS (MAKE 2)

With **A**, make a magic ring.
Rnd 1: 6 sc in ring—6 sc.
Rnd 2: [2 sc, inc] 2 times—8 sc.
Rnd 3: Sc all around—8 sc.
Rnd 4: [2 sc, dec] 2 times—6 sc.
Rnds 5—9: Sc all around—6 sc.
Do not stuff. Fasten off leaving a
    short tail. Sew to one side of
    the Body at the seam between
    the Head and the Body. Repeat
    Rnds 1—9 to make another Arm
    and sew to the other side of
    the Body. Weave in ends.

BEARD

With **C**, ch 11.
Row 1 (RS): Sc in 2nd ch from
    hook and sc across, turn—
    10 sc.
Row 2: Ch, [bobble st, hdc]
    5 times, turn—5 hdcs,
    5 bobble sts.
Row 3: Ch, bobble st, sk, hdc,
    bobble st, hdc, bobble st, hdc,
    bobble st, sk, hdc, turn—8
    hdcs, 4 bobble sts.
Row 4: Ch, bobble st, sk, hdc,
    bobble st, hdc, bobble st, sk,
    hdc, turn—6 hdcs, 3 bobble sts.
Row 5: Ch, bobble st, sk, hdc,
    bobble st, sk, hdc, turn—4
    hdcs, 2 bobble sts.
Rows 6—7: Ch, [bobble st, hdc]
    2 times, turn—4 hdcs, 2
    bobble sts.
Row 8: Ch, sk, bobble st, sk,
    hdc—2 hdcs, 1 bobble st.
Fasten off, leaving a tail for
    sewing. Position the Beard
    so that Row 1 lies directly
    below the nose, at Rnd 15 of
    the Head. Sew it down. Then,
    using a piece of yarn **C**, tie a

small butterfly knot at row 6 of the Beard. Weave in ends.

HAIR

With **C**, make a magic ring.
Rnd 1: 6 sc in ring—6 sc.
Rnd 2: Inc 6 times—12 sc.
Rnd 3: [Sc, inc] 6 times—18 sts.
Rnd 4: [2 sc, inc] 6 times—24 sts.
We will now create 20 Hair strands (Str), leaving the last 4 sts in Rnd 4 unworked.

Str 1: Ch 21 off the side of Rnd 4. Sc in the 2nd ch from hook and sc across. Sl st into the next st in Rnd 4—20 sc.
Strs 2—20: Repeat Str 1, creating Hair strands all around Rnd 4, until there are 4 sts left, which will remain unworked.
Fasten off, leaving a tail for sewing. Lay the Hair flat and steam block so that each Hair strand is straight and does not curl. Place the blocked Hair on the Head with the **wrong side facing** up and with the unworked sts from Rnd 4 facing the front of the Head. Pin down the Hair to your liking and secure by sewing or with hot glue. Weave in end.

EYEGLASSES

Optional: *Using an 8 in. / 20 cm length of 18-gauge wire, wrap the wire around a ½ in. / 1 cm diameter object (e.g. pen) to form an eyeglass rim. Repeat to create a second rim. Bend the remaining wire backwards and insert into the front of the face to secure.*

ROBE

With **D**, ch 15.
Row 1 (RS): In the 2nd ch from

hook, [2 sc, 3 sc in one st]
2 times, 2 sc, [3 sc in one st,
2 sc] 2 times, ch and turn—
22 sc.

Row 2: 3 sc, ch 4, sk 4, 8 sc, ch 4,
sk 4, 3 sc, ch and turn—22 sc,
8 ch, 2 ch-4 sps.
Each of the ch-sps just created is
an armhole.

Row 3: 3 sc, 4 sc in ch-sp, 8 sc,
4 sc in ch-sp, 3 sc, ch and
turn—22 sc.

Rows 4—7: Sc across, ch and
turn—22 sc.

Row 8: 4 sc, inc, 12 sc, inc, 4 sc,
ch and turn—24 sc.

Row 9: 5 sc, inc, 12 sc, inc, 5 sc,
ch and turn—26 sc.

Row 10: 6 sc, inc, 12 sc, inc, 6 sc,
ch and turn—28 sc.

Row 11: Sc across, ch and turn—
28 sc.

Row 12: 7 sc, inc, 12 sc, inc, 7 sc,
ch and turn—30 sc.

Rows 15—16: Sc across, ch and
turn—32 sts.
Switch to **E**. Work a border in sc
all around the outside of the
robe, around 80 sc. Fasten off
and weave in end.

SLEEVES (MAKE 2)

With **D**, attach yarn to one of the
armholes created by the ch-4
sps in Row 2 of the Robe.

Rnd 1: [4 sc, inc] 2 times—12 sc.
Rnd 2: [2 sc, inc] 4 times—16 sc.
Rnd 3: [3 sc, inc] 4 times—20 sc.
Rnd 4: Sc all around—20 sc.
Switch to **E**.
Rnd 5: Sc all around—20 sc.
Fasten off and weave in end.
Repeat Rnds 1–5 for the
remaining Sleeve. Place Robe
on Body.

HAT

With **D**, make a magic ring.
Rnd 1: 6 sc in ring—6 sc.
Rnd 2: Inc 6 times—12 sc.
Rnd 3: [Sc, inc] 6 times—18 sc.
Rnd 4: Sc, inc, [2 sc, inc] 5 times,
sc—24 sc.
Rnd 5: [3 sc, inc] 6 times—30 sc.
Rnd 6: 2 sc, inc, [4 sc, inc] 5 times,
2 sc—36 sc.
Rnd 7: In blo, sc all around—36 sc.
Rnds 8—9: Sc all around—36 sc.
Switch to **E**.
Rnd 10: Sc all around—36 sc.
Fasten off, leaving a tail for
sewing. Using **E**, make a one-
inch long tassel. Block tassel
to remove wrinkles and sew
to the top of the Hat at the
center of rnd 1. Sew the Hat
to the top of the Head.

MINERVA McGONAGALL

Designed by Pham Hien Hahn
Skill level: ⟋ ⟋

Minerva McGonagall is head of Gryffindor house, Transfiguration professor, and a fiery fan of Quidditch. But she is, more than anything else according to actor Dame Maggie Smith, *Scottish*.

Harry Potter and the Sorcerer's Stone costume designer Judianna Makovsky appreciated the actor's input. "Dame Maggie's ideas were quite wonderful," recalls Makovsky. "She wanted something that was Scottish because she *is* a McGonagall. She wears a Scottish Tam, traditionally made with a band and feather, but it just happens to be a witch's hat. She also has her own tartan, which is, of course, green." Tartan plaids are seen throughout her wardrobe, even to the pajamas she wears in *Harry Potter and the Prisoner of Azkaban*. Costume designer Jany Temime changed the color of her robes to a darker green and incorporated more "wizardy" elements, such as high points to the shoulders and collars. Her dress robe worn to the Yule Ball in *Harry Potter and the Goblet of Fire* was given a unique texture on the lapels and back by utilizing a complicated pleating technique.

This amigurumi doll brings Professor McGonagall to life with remarkable accuracy. Standing at approximately 8 inches, Professor McGonagall is dressed in her distinctive green robes. Her black pointy witch hat, like her robes, can be easily removed, revealing her silver crocheted hair, neatly styled in a bun. This meticulously crocheted amigurumi doll perfectly captures the strong yet kind persona of the beloved Transfiguration professor.

"Welcome to Hogwarts!"
Minerva McGonagall, *Harry Potter and the Sorcerer's Stone*

FINISHED MEASUREMENTS
Height: 8 in. / 20.5 cm (without hat)
Width: 2.5 in. / 6.5 cm

YARN
Sport weight (#2 fine) yarn shown in YarnArt *Jeans* (55% cotton 45% polyacrylic, 174 yd. / 160 m per 1.76 oz. / 50 g ball).
Color A: #73 Pinkish Orange, 1 ball
Color B: #01 White, 1 ball
Color C: #49 Light Gray, 1 ball
Color D: #53 Black, 1 ball
Color E: #28 Smoked, 1 ball
Color F: #82 Green, 1 ball

HOOK
• US B-1 / 2.25mm crochet hook

NOTIONS
• Stitch markers
• Polyester fiberfill
• Pair of 5mm safety eyes in black
• Tapestry needle
• Embroidery thread or yarn, small amount of black

GAUGE
Gauge is not critical for this project. Ensure your stitches are tight so the stuffing won't show through.

SPECIAL ABBREVIATIONS
Half Double Crochet Increase (Hdc-inc): Two half double crochet in one stitch
Back Loop Only (blo): Work through back loop only
Front Loop Only (flo): Work through front loop only

HEAD

With **A**, make a magic ring.
Rnd 1: 7 sc in ring—7 sc.
Rnd 2: 7-inc—14 sc.
Rnd 3: (Sc, inc) * 7 times—21 sc.
Rnd 4: (2 sc, inc) * 7 times—28 sc.
Rnd 5: Sc, inc, (3 sc, inc) * 6 times, 2 sc—35 sc.
Rnd 6: (4 sc, inc) * 7 times—42 sc.
Rnd 7: 48 sc—48 sc.
Rnd 8: 2 sc, inc, (5 sc, inc) * 6 times, 3 sc—49 sc.
Rnds 9−16: 49 sc—49 sc.
Insert the eyes between Rnds 18 and 19, with 8-stitch space between them.
Rnd 17: (6 sc, inc) * 7 times—56 sc.
Rnds 18−21: 56 sc—56 sc.
Rnd 22: (5 sc, dec) * 8 times—48 sc.
Rnd 23: 48 sc—48 sc.
Rnd 24: (4 sc, dec) * 8 times—40 sc.
Rnd 25: (3 sc, dec) * 8 times—32 sc.
Rnd 26: (2 sc, dec) * 8 times—24 sc.
Start to stuff the Head firmly.
Rnd 27: (Sc, dec) * 8 times—16 sc.
Rnd 28: Blo (dec, 14 sc)—15 sc.

Rnds 29−35: Blo 15 sc—15 sc.
Rnd 36: 7-dec, sc—8 sc.
Cut the yarn, leaving a long tail. Thread a needle with your yarn tail and close the remaining gap. Pull your needle straight to the top of the Head. Use your crochet hook handle or a stick to push the neck you have formed inside the doll's Head. Weave in the end. **Do not sew the Head to the neck.**

ARMS (MAKE 2)

With **A**, make a magic ring.

Left Arm

Rnd 1: 6 sc in ring—6 sc.
Rnd 2: (Sc, inc) * 3 times—9 sc.
Rnd 3: 9 sc—9 sc.
Rnd 4: 2 sc, dec, 3 sc, dec—7 sc.
Rnds 5−18: 7 sc—7 sc.
Crochet 1 sc more. Cut the yarn.

BEHIND THE MAGIC

Minerva McGonagall's robes were frequently decorated with Celtic-inspired brooches and pins.

Right Arm

Work the Right Arm in the same way till Rnd 18. Crochet 4 sc more. Do not stuff the Arm. Invisible fasten off. Cut the yarn.

LEGS (MAKE 2)

With **B**, chain 5, start in the 2nd stitch from the hook.

Rnd 1: Inc, 2 sc, 5 sc in the last chain, 2 sc in the other side of the chain, inc in last stitch—13 sc.

Rnd 2: Inc, 3 sc, 5-inc, 3 sc, inc—20 sc.

Rnds 3−4: 20 sc—20 sc.

Rnd 5: 6 sc, 4-dec, 6 sc—16 sc.

Rnd 6: 5 sc, 3-dec, 5 sc—13 sc.

Rnd 7: 4 sc, dec, sc, dec, 4 sc—11 sc.

Rnd 8: 10 sc, inc—12 sc.

Rnds 9−14: 12 sc—12 sc.

Switch to **A**.

Rnd 15: Blo 12 sc—12 sc.

Rnds 16−21: 12 sc—12 sc.

Switch to **B**.

Rnd 22: 10 sc, end round here. Crochet the second Leg in the same way till Rnd 21. Crochet 5 sc more to reach to the crotch. Do not cut the yarn, chain 3, join in to the first Leg and keep going onto the Body with **B**.

BODY

With **B**.

Rnd 1: (on the first Leg) 6 sc, inc, 5 sc, (on chains) 3sc (on the second Leg) 5 sc, inc, 6 sc, (on chains) 3 sc—32 sc.

Rnds 2−6: 32 sc—32 sc.

Switch to **A**.

Rnd 7: (6 sc, dec) * 4 times—28 sc.

Rnd 8: 28 sc—28 sc.

Rnd 9: (5 sc, dec) * 4 times—24 sc.

Rnds 10−17: 24 sc—24 sc. Start to stuff the Body firmly. Join the Arms to the Body.

Rnd 18: (on the back of the Body) 7 sc, (on the Left Arm) 7 sc, (on the front of the Body) 12 sc, (on the Right Arm) 7 sc, (on the back of the Body) 5 sc—38 sc. End round. You have 12 sc on the back, 7 sc on each arm, 12 sc on the front of the Body. Total is 38 sc.

Rnd 19: 6 sc, dec, 5 sc, dec, 10 sc, dec, 5 sc, dec, 4 sc—34 sc.

Rnd 20: 5 sc, dec, 4 sc, dec, 9 sc, dec, 4sc, dec, 4sc—30 sc.

Rnd 21: (3 sc, dec) * 6 times—24 sc.

Rnd 22: (dec, 2 sc) * 6 times—18 sc.

Rnd 23: (4 sc, dec) * 3 times—15 sc.

Rnd 24: (3 sc, dec) * 3 times—12 sc.

Rnd 25: 10 sc, dec—11 sc.

Rnds 26−32: 11 sc—11 sc.

Rnd 33: 5-dec, sc—6 sc. Stuff the neck as tight as you can. Invisible fasten off. Close the remaining gap.

EARS (MAKE 2)

With **A**, leaving a long tail, make a magic ring.

4 sc in ring (4). Cut the yarn, leaving a long tail. Tighten the magic ring.

HAIR

With **C** make a magic ring.

Rnd 1: 6 sc in ring—6 sc.

Rnd 2: 6-inc—12 sc.

Rnd 3: Flo (sc, inc) * 6 times—18 sc.

Rnd 4: (2 sc, inc) * 6 times—24 sc.

Rnd 5: Sc, inc, (3 sc, inc) * 5 times, 2 sc—30 sc.

Rnd 6: (Ch 19, 18 sc on chain, sl st to the next st) * 4 times, Ch 16, (2 sc, 13-hdc) on chain, sl st to the next st, [Ch 15, (2 sc, 12-hdc) on chain, sl st to the next st] * 5 times, [Ch 15, (2 sc, 12-hdc) on chain, skip 1 st, sl st the next st] * 7 times, [Ch 15, (2 sc, 12-hdc) on chain, sl st to the next st] * 5 times, Ch 16, (2 sc, 13-hdc) on chain, sl st to the next st. You have 24 Hair strands in total. Insert your hook to the first flo stitch of blo rnd to crochet the second layer.

Rnd 7: [Ch 12, (2 sc, 9-hdc) on chain), sl st] * 5 times, [Ch 36, (2 sc, 33-hdc) on chain), sl st] * 6 times

BUN

With **C** make a magic ring.

Rnd 1: 6 sc in ring—6 sc.

Rnd 2: 6-inc—12 sc.

Rnds 3−4: 12 sc—12 sc.

Rnd 5: (2 sc, dec) * 3 times—9 sc. Cut the yarn. Invisible fasten off. Stuff the Bun gently and sew on the top of the Hair.

HAT

With **D**, make a magic ring.
Rnd 1: 4 sc in ring—4 sc.
Rnds 2—4: 4 sc—4 sc.
Rnd 5: 3 sc, inc—5 sc.
Rnds 6—8: 5 sc—5 sc.
Rnd 9: 4 sc, inc—6 sc.
Rnds 10—12: 6 sc—6 sc.
Rnd 13: (sc, inc) * 3 times—9 sc.
Rnds 14—16: 9 sc—9 sc.
Rnd 17: (2 sc, inc) * 3 times—12 sc.
Rnds 18—20: 12 sc—12 sc.
Rnd 21: (Sc, inc) * 6 times—18 sc.
Rnds 22—23: 18 sc—18 sc.
Rnd 24: (2 sc, inc) * 6 times—24 sc.
Rnd 25: 24 sc—24 sc.
Rnd 26: (3 sc, inc) * 6 times—30 sc.
Rnd 27: 30 sc—30 sc.
Rnd 28: (4 sc, inc) * 6 times—36 sc.
Rnd 29: 36 sc—36 sc.
Rnd 30: (5 sc, inc) * 6 times—42 sc.
Rnd 31: 42 sc—42 sc.
Rnd 32: (6 sc, inc) * 6 times—48 sc.
Rnd 33: 48 sc—48 sc.
Rnd 34: (7 sc, inc) * 6 times—54 sc.
Rnd 35: 54 sc—54 sc.
Rnd 36: (8 sc, inc) * 6 times—60 sc.
Rnd 37: 60 sc—60 sc.
Rnd 38: (9 sc, inc) * 6 times—66 sc.
Rnds 39—42: 66 sc—66 sc.
Rnd 43: Flo (10 sc, inc) * 6 times—72 sc.
Rnd 44: 72 hdc—72 sc.
Rnd 45: (11 hdc, hdc-inc) * 6 times, sl st—78 sc.
Cut the yarn. Invisible fasten off.

DRESS

With **E**, leaving a long tail. Chain 16, insert the hook to the first chain to make a circle. Start to crochet the Dress from the collar down.
Rnd 1: 16 sc on chain—16 sc.
Rnd 2: (3 sc, inc) * 4 times—20 sc.
Rnd 3: (4 sc, inc) * 4 times—24 sc.
Rnd 4: (5 sc, inc) * 4 times—28 sc.
Rnd 5: 4 sc, 4-inc, 10 sc, 4-inc, 6 sc—36 sc.
Rnd 6: 36 sc—36 sc.
Rnd 7: 4 sc, chain 5, skip 8 sts, 10 sc, chain 5, skip 8 sts, 6 sc—30 sc.
Rnd 8: 30 sc—30 sc.
Rnd 9: (4 sc, inc) * 6 times—36 sc.
Rnds 10—13: 36 sc—36 sc.
Rnd 14: (5 sc, inc) * 6 times—42 sc.
Rnds 15—19: 42 sc—42 sc.
Rnd 20: (6 sc, inc) * 6 times—48 sc.
Rnds 21—26: 48 sc—48 sc.
Rnd 27: (7 sc, inc) * 6 times—54 sc.
Rnds 28—35: 54 sc—54 sc.
Rnd 36: 54 sl st.
Cut the yarn. Invisible fasten off. Hide yarn tail. Use the long tail left at the start to crochet sl st around the collar.

SLEEVES

Insert your hook to the 6th stitch and the 23rd stitch of Rnd 6 on the Dress.
Rnds 1—15: 13 sc—13 sc.
Rnd 16: 13 sl st.
Cut the yarn. Invisible fasten off.

COAT

With **F**, leaving a long tail, chain 17, insert your hook to the 2nd chain from the hook.
Rnd 1: (3 sc, inc) * 4 times on chain—20 sc.
Rnd 2: Turn your hook, ch 1, (4 sc, inc) * 4 times—24 sc.
Rnd 3: Turn your hook, ch 1, inc, 3 sc, 4-inc, 3 sc, 2-inc, 3 sc, 4-inc, 3 sc, inc—36 sc.
Rnd 4: Turn your hook, ch 1, 5 sc, ch 9, skip 8 sts, 10 sc, ch 9, skip 8 sts, 5 sc—38 sc.
Rnd 5: Turn your hook, ch 1, inc, 36 sc, inc—40 sc.
Rnds 6—8: Turn your hook, ch 1, 40 sc—40 sc.
Rnd 9: Turn your hook, (4 sc, inc) * 8 times—48 sc.
Rnds 10—14: Turn your hook, ch 1, 48 sc—48 sc.
Rnd 15: Turn your hook, ch1, (5 sc, inc) * 8 times—56 sc.
Rnds 16—21: Turn your hook, ch 1, 56 sc—56 sc.
Rnd 22: Turn your hook, (6 sc, inc) * 8 times—64 sc.
Rnds 23—30: Turn your hook, ch 1, 64 sc—64 sc.
Rnd 31: Turn your hook, ch 1, (7 sc, inc) * 8 times—72 sc.
Rnd 32: Turn your hook, ch 1, 72 sc—72 sc.
Rnd 33: Turn your hook, ch 1, 71 sc, inc—73 sc.
Insert your hook to the chain you start each round with when you turn your hook, sc, to cover the edge till you reach to the collar, sl st along the collar, insert your hook to the chain you start each round with when you turn your hook, sc, to cover the edges. Cut the yarn. Invisible fasten off. Hide yarn tail. Use the long tail you left at beg to crochet sl st around the collar.

SLEEVES

Insert your hook to the first hdc on the Coat, ch 1.
Rnd 1: 17 sc—17 sc.
Rnd 2: 7 sc, inc, 9 sc—18 sc.

Rnd 3: 24 sc—24 sc.
Rnd 4: Blo 24 sc—24 sc.
Rnds 5–7: 24 sc—24 sc.
Rnd 8: 8 sc, 4-dec, 8 sc—20 sc.
Rnd 9: 7 sc, 3-dec, 7 sc—17 sc.
Rnds 10–12: 17 sc—17 sc.
Rnd 13: 17-sl st till the end of Rnd 12.
Cut the yarn. Invisible fasten off.
Insert your hook into flo stitches of the blo round, crochet 24-sl st along the blo round—24 sc.
Cut the yarn. Invisible fasten off.

ASSEMBLY

Put the Dress onto the Body before attaching the Head. To attach the Head to the Body, push the long neck from the Body into the tunnel at the bottom of the Head created by pushing the neck from the Head into the doll's Head.

Using black embroidery thread, embroider a small mouth starting from under the nose and two rows below the eyes, off to the side, diagonally, spanning two stitches. Using the yarn tail from the Ears, sew the Ears on the Head spanning Rnds 18 to 20, 6 sts apart from the eye.

Using the wrong side of the Hair as the side facing up, attach the Hair to the top of the Head with the shorter strands at the front. Part the Hair with 4 strands of Hair to the right side and 2 strands of Hair to the left. Secure the Bun to the top of the Head with a couple of stitches.

Finish dressing the doll with her Boots, Coat, and Hat.

Rnd 3: (5 sc, inc) * 3 times—21 sc.
Rnds 4–5: 21 sc—21 sc.
Rnd 6: (6 sc, inc) * 3 times—24 sc.
Rnds 7–9: 24 sc—24 sc.
Rnd 10: (7 sc, inc) * 3 times—28 sc.
Rnds 11–12: 28 sc—28 sc.
Cut the yarn. Invisible fasten off.

BOOTS (MAKE 2)

With **D**.
Chain 7, start in the 2nd stitch from the hook.
Rnd 1: Inc, 4 sc in next 4 chains, 5 sc in last chain, 4 sc in other side of the chain, inc in last stitch—17 sc.
Rnd 2: Inc, 5 sc, 5-inc, 5 sc, inc—24 sc.

SEVERUS SNAPE

Designed by Chloe Yuen
Skill Level: ✓✓

Severus Snape is the Potions professor at Hogwarts and a very enigmatic wizard. In all the interactions he has with Harry Potter during his years at school, it's hard to tell if Snape is a hindrance or a help to Harry.

When actor Alan Rickman came in to consult with costume designer Judianna Makovsky for *Harry Potter and the Sorcerer's Stone*, he had two requests. He wanted tight sleeves and lots of buttons. "[Snape] lives within very tight confines, physically as well as emotionally," said Rickman. "The costume helped me to understand somebody who lives absolutely alone." In fact, the costume for Severus Snape stayed exactly the same for all eight Harry Potter films. Rickman stated that thinking this outfit was the only one hanging in Snape's wardrobe helped him with the character. "He doesn't have much of a social life," said Rickman, "and clearly, he's only got one set of clothes."

This mysterious Professor Snape amigurumi doll encapsulates the very core of his enigmatic demeanor and complex presence. His dark, flowing crocheted locks frame his countenance, and his gaze penetrates like no other. His distinguished black robes, meticulously crocheted, drape elegantly and are easily removable. This amigurumi flawlessly captures Snape's iconic appearance.

"Oh, that's Professor Snape, head of Slytherin house."

"What's he teach?"

"Potions. But everyone knows it's the Dark Arts he fancies."

Percy Weasley and Harry Potter,
Harry Potter and the Sorcerer's Stone

FINISHED MEASUREMENTS
Height: 4.3 in. / 11.5 cm
Width: 3.14 in. / 8 cm

YARN
Fingering weight (#1 super fine) yarn, shown in Scheepjes *Catona* (100% cotton, 68 yd. / 62 m per 0.9 oz. / 25 g ball).
Color A: #255 Shell, 1 ball
Color B: #106 Snow White, 1 ball
Color C: #124 Ultramarine, 1 ball
Color D: #110 Jet Black, 1 ball

HOOK
• US C-2 / 2.5mm crochet hook

NOTIONS
• Stitch markers
• Polyester stuffing
• A pair of black 7mm safety eyes
• Dressmaking pins
• Tapestry needle
• DMC 6-Strand embroidery floss Color #310

GAUGE
28 sts and 28 rnds = 4 in. / 10 cm in sc
Gauge is not critical for this project. Ensure your stitches are tight so the stuffing won't show through.

SPECIAL ABBREVIATIONS
Back Loop Only (blo): Work through back loop only
Front Loop Only (flo): Work through front loop only
Invisible Slip Stitch (invisible sl st): [insert hook into front loop of indicated stitch, insert hook into front loop of next stitch (3 loops on hook). Yarn over, pull through 2 loops. Yarn over, pull through remaining 2 loops on hook]

BEHIND THE MAGIC

Severus Snape's robes were actually created in a dark, dark blue, which appeared black on film. The material became shiny when ironed.

HEAD

With **A**, make a magic ring.
Rnd 1: 6 sc in ring—6 sc.
Rnd 2: 2 sc in each sc—12 sc.
Rnd 3: [Sc in next sc, 2 sc in next sc] 6 times—18 sc.
Rnd 4: [Sc in next sc, 2 sc in next sc, sc in next sc] 6 times—24 sc.
Rnd 5: [Sc in next 3 sc, 2 sc in next sc] 6 times—30 sc.
Rnd 6: [Sc in next 2 sc, 2 sc in next sc, sc in next 2 sc] 6 times—36 sc.
Rnd 7: [Sc in next 5 sc, 2 sc in next sc] 6 times—42 sc.
Rnd 8: [Sc in next 3 sc, 2 sc in next sc, sc in next 3 sc] 6 times—48 sc.
Rnds 9–17: Sc around—48 sc.
Rnd 18: [Sc in next 3 sc, sc dec in next 2 sc, sc in next 3 sc] 6 times—42 sc.
Rnd 19: [Sc in next 5 sc, sc dec in next 2 sc] 6 times—36 sc.
Rnd 20: [Sc in next 2 sc, sc dec in next 2 sc, sc in next 2 sc] 6 times—30 sc.
Rnd 21: [Sc in next 3 sc, sc dec in next 2 sc] 6 times—24 sc.
Insert the eyes between Rnds 14 and 15, 5 stitches apart. Start stuffing the Head.
Rnd 22: [Sc in next sc, sc dec in next 2 sc, sc in next sc] 6 times—18 sc.
Rnd 23: [Sc in next sc, sc dec in next 2 sc] 6 times—12 sc.
Rnd 24: Sc dec in next 2 sc around—6 sc.
Fasten off and leave a long tail to close the hole. Weave through front loops and pull tightly to close the hole. Weave in loose ends.

EARS (MAKE 2)

With **A**, make a magic ring.
Rnd 1: 5 sc in ring—5 sc.
Pull the ring tight and fasten off. Leave a long tail for sewing. The Ear should be a semicircle.

ARMS (MAKE 2)

With **A**, make a magic ring.
Rnd 1: 6 sc in ring—6 sc.
Rnds 2–3: Sc around—6 sc.
Change to **B**.
Rnd 4: Sc around—6 sc.
Change to **C**.
Rnds 5–9: Sc around—6 sc.
Do not stuff the Arms.
Rnd 10: Fold the opening of the Arm down and sc through both loops to close the Arms—3 sc.
Fasten off.

LEGS (MAKE 2)

With **D**, make a magic ring.
Rnd 1: 6 sc in ring—6 sc.
Rnd 2: [Sc in next sc, 2 sc in next sc] 3 times—9 sc.
Rnd 3: Sc around—9 sc.
Change to **C**.
Rnds 4–6: Sc around—9 sc.
Stuff the Leg firmly. Fasten off and repeat Rnds 1 to 6 for the second Leg, but do not fasten off. Join the two Legs and continue to make the Body.

BODY

Continuing from the second Leg.
Rnd 7: Ch 3, join to the first Leg, sc around first Leg, sc in each ch, sc around in second Leg, sc in each ch—24 sc.
Rnd 8: [Sc in next 3 sc, 2 sc in next sc] 6 times—30 sc.
Rnds 9–12: Sc around—30 sc.

Rnd 13: Blo, sc around—30 sc.

Rnds 14–16: Sc around—30 sc.

Rnd 17: [Sc in next 3 sc, sc dec in next 2 sc] 6 times—24 sc.

Rnds 18–19: Sc around—24 sc.

Make sure the hook is at the center of the Body, you may need to add or remove sts. This will be the new start of the round. You will be joining the Arms in the next round.

Rnd 20: Sc in next 4 sc, place the first Arm against the Body and work sc in next 3 sc,

through both Body and Arm loops. Continue to work sc in next 10 sc in the Body, place the second Arm against the Body and work sc in next 3 sc, through both Body and Arm loops. Continue to work sc in next 4 sc, sl st to close the round—24 sc.

MAKE THE SHIRT COLLAR

Rnd 21: Flo of Rnd 20, ch 1, start crocheting in the second st from hook, sc in next 11 sc,

sl st in next 2 sc, sc in next 11 sc, sl st into the first st of round—24 sc.

Fasten off and weave in loose ends.

MAKE THE NECK

With **A**, join the yarn to the back loop of Rnd 20.

Rnd 21: Blo of Rnd 20, sc around—24 sc.

Sl st to close. Fasten off and leave a long tail for sewing. Stuff the Body firmly.

You will now crochet the shirt edge, with the Legs facing away from you, and using **C**, start at the front center front loop of Rnd 12 of the Body and sc around, do not join the round. Fasten off and weave in loose ends—30 sc.

With short piece of **C** embroider the shirt line down the center of the Body, starting at the middle of the collar to Rnd 12 of shirt edge. Fasten off and weave in loose ends.

CLOAK

With **D**, ch 26, starting in the second ch from hook work in rows.

Row 1: Sc in each ch, ch 1 and turn project—25 sc.

Row 2: Sc in next 4 sc, ch 4, skip next 3 sc, sc in next 11 sc, ch 4, skip next 3 sc, sc in next 4 sc, ch 1 and turn project—27 sc.

Row 3: Sc in next 4 sc, sc in each ch, sc in next 11 sc, sc in each ch, sc in next 4 sc, ch1 and turn project—27 sc.

Row 4: Sc across row, ch 1 and turn project—27 sc.

Row 5: 2 sc in next sc, sc in the next 25 sc, 2 sc in next sc, ch 1 and turn project—29 sc.

Row 6: Sc around, ch 1 and turn project—29 sc.

Row 7: 2 Sc in next sc, sc in next 8 sc, 2 sc in next sc, sc in next 9 sc, 2 sc in next sc, sc in next 8 sc, 2 sc in next sc, ch 1 and turn project—33 sc.

Rows 8—15: Sc along row, ch 1 and turn project—33 sc.

To clean up the edge of the Cloak, continue to work sc around the next 3 edges of the Cloak, work 3 sc in the corners. Do an invisible sl st at the end and weave in loose ends.

LEFT SLEEVE

With **D**, insert hook into the armhole opening of Cloak and join a piece of yarn.

Rnd 1: Sc in next 9 sc—9 sc.

Rnd 2: [Sc in next 2 sc, 2 sc in next sc] 3 times—12 sc.

Rnds 3—5: Sc around—12 sc.

For the Left Sleeve, make sure the last st is located at the top of the Sleeve, you may need to crochet extra or remove sts. Begin working in rows. Ch 1 and turn project.

Row 6: Sc in next 8 sc, leave the rest of the sc unworked, ch 1 and turn project—8 sc.

Row 7: Sc dec in next 2 sc, sc in 4 sc, sc dec in next 2 sc, ch 1 and turn project—6 sc.

Row 8: Sc along row, ch 1 and turn project—6 sc.

Row 9: Sc dec in next 2 sc, sc in next 2 sc, sc dec in next 2 sc, ch 1 and turn project—4 sc.

Row 10: Sc along row, ch 1 and turn project—4 sc.

Row 11: Sc dec in next 2 sc along row—2 sc.

To clean up the opening of the Sleeve, sc around the Sleeve edge, do an invisible sl st at the end. Fasten off and weave in loose ends.

RIGHT SLEEVE

With **D**, insert hook into the armhole opening of cloak and join a piece of yarn.

Rnd 1: Sc in next 9 sc—9 sc.

Rnd 2: [Sc in next 2 sc, 2 sc in next sc] 3 times—12 sc.

Rnds 3—5: Sc around—12 sc.

For the Right Sleeve, make sure the last st is located at the bottom of the Sleeve, you may need to crochet extra or remove sts. Begin working in rows. Ch 1 and turn project.

Row 6: Sc in next 8 sc, leave the rest of the sc unworked, ch 1 and turn project—8 sc.

Row 7: Sc dec in next 2 sc, sc in 4 sc, sc dec in next 2 sc, ch 1 and turn project—6 sc.

Row 8: Sc along row, ch 1 and turn—6 sc.

Row 9: Sc dec in next 2 sc, sc in next 2 sc, sc dec in next 2 sc, ch 1 and turn project—4 sc.

Row 10: Sc along row, ch 1 and turn project—4 sc.

Row 11: Sc dec in next 2 sc along row—2 sc.

To clean up the opening of the Sleeve, sc around the Sleeve edge, do an invisible sl st at the end. Fasten off and weave in loose ends.

HAIR

With **D**, make a magic ring.

Rnd 1: 6 sc in magic ring—6 sc.

Rnd 2: 2 sc in each sc—12 sc.

Rnd 3: [Sc in next sc, 2 sc in next sc] 6 times—18 sc.

Rnd 4: [Sc in next sc, 2 sc in next sc, sc in next sc] 6 times—24 sc.

Rnd 5: [Sc in next 3 sc, 2 sc in next sc] 6 times—30 sc.

Continue to make the Hair strands.

Strs 1—13: Ch 16, start crocheting in the third ch from hook, hdc along the ch, skip 1 sc, sl st in the next sc of Hair—14 hdc.

Str 14: Ch 15, start crocheting in the second ch from hook, sc along the ch, sl st in the next sc of Hair—14 sc.

Strs 15—16: Ch 13, start crocheting in the second ch from hook, sc along the ch, sl st in the next sc of Hair—12 sc.

Str 17: Ch 15, start crocheting in the second ch from hook, sc along the ch, sl st in the next sc of Hair—14 sc.

Fasten off and leave a long tail for sewing.

ASSEMBLY

Sew the Head to the Body.

Sew the Ears to either side of the Head, between Rnds 13 and 15, 5 sts from the eyes. With **A** embroider the nose in between the eyes, between Rnds 15 and 16, 3 sts wide. With embroidery floss in color #310, embroider the eyebrows one round above the eyes, and embroider a small mouth two rounds below the nose in the center, spanning 1 stitch.

Place the Hair to the top of the Head, with the underside facing up. First, sew Hair Strands 1 to 13 behind the ears and around the back of the Head. Then sew Strands 14 and 17 behind the Ears, over the Hair strands that have been sewn down. Sew Strands 15 and 16 in front of the Ears.

Place the Cloak onto the doll.

FINISHING

Weave in all ends.

POMONA SPROUT

Designed by Joy Pham Sontakke
Skill Level: 𝄃 𝄃

Professor Pomona Sprout, the Herbology professor at Hogwarts and head of Hufflepuff house, works with plants of all kinds. Some of them, however, have decidedly difficult natures, such as the squirming, squealing Mandrakes she teaches her second-year students to repot, or the Venomous Tentacula, a prickly plant that tries to seize its prey with its thorny vines.

As a precaution for her work, Sprout wears thick, sturdy robes that are, not surprisingly, rendered in earth-tone colors. There are two large pockets in the front, presumably to hold her tools for gardening. Complementing her robes is a cape-like collar fastened by two metal leaves and embroidered with ferns, leaves, and flowers that almost appear to be growing on it. She also wears a pair of dragon-hide gloves used enough to need to be bound with twine. Her witch's hat is also earth-toned and made in a burlap-type fabric, topped with a "sprout" of two leaves at the tip. For her lesson on Mandrakes, she also wears a pair of large pink earmuffs against the plant's deadly cries.

This delightful Professor Sprout amigurumi doll is ready to tend to her magical plants. She's dressed in a green jumpsuit, complete with an earthy brown cloak. Her crocheted gray curly hair adds to her wise and kindhearted personality, making her the ideal head of Hufflepuff house. She has a removable brown pointy witch hat similar to the one she wears while teaching her Herbology class. And that's not all! This Professor Sprout comes with a miniature Mandrake companion, perfect for teaching her second-year students about repotting the screaming plants.

"As our Mandrakes are only seedlings, their cries won't kill yet. However, they will knock you out for several hours. That is why I have provided each of you with a pair of earmuffs."

Pomona Sprout, *Harry Potter and the Chamber of Secrets*

FINISHED MEASUREMENTS

Height: 6.7 in. / 17 cm (excluding the hat)
Width: 4 in. / 10 cm

YARN

Sport weight (#2 fine) yarn, shown in Yarn Art *Jeans,* (55% cotton, 45% acrylic, 174 yd. / 160 m per 1.75 oz. / 50 g ball).
Color A: #05 Light Beige, 1 ball
Color B: #46 Gray, 1 ball
Color C: #69 Green, 1 ball
Color D: #29 Apple, small amount
Color E: #71 Cacao, 1 ball
Color F: #40 Brown, 1 ball

HOOK

• US 00 / 1.75mm crochet hook

NOTIONS

• Stitch markers
• Polyester stuffing
• Pair of 12mm black safety eyes
• Tapestry needle
• Sewing needle
• Embroidery thread, small amount of black and pink
• 30 cm of craft wire, for the earmuffs

GAUGE

Gauge is not critical for this project. Ensure your stitches are tight so the stuffing won't show through.

SPECIAL ABBREVIATIONS

Back Post Single Crochet (bpsc):
Insert your hook into the next st by first going through the WS of both loops of st; going around the post of the st; and second insert your hook going through the RS of both loops of the same st. Yo and pull up a loop through both insertion points of the hook. Yo pull through both loops on hook.

Front Post Single Crochet (fpsc):
Insert hook around the front of the post (from front to back to front), yo and draw up a loop, yo and draw through both loops to complete the st.

Picot Stitch (p): [3ch, sl st in the first st of the chain]

Back Loop Only (blo): Work through back loop only

Front Loop Only (flo): Work through front loop only

Reverse Single Crochet (r-sc)

Decrease (sc2tog)

Decrease (sc3tog)

NOTE

• I used cross single crochet stitches, but you can crochet normally. All the decreases are invisible. Stuff as you go except for when indicated.

BEHIND THE MAGIC

The important "auditory protection" Professor Sprout insists her students wear—fluffy earmuffs—were originally designed in psychedelic colors and animal prints, but changed to the uniformly brown, flecked material.

INNER NECK

With **A**, make a magic ring.
Rnd 1: 6 sc in ring—6 sc.
Rnds 2−10: Sc around—6 sc.
Stuff firmly. Fasten off and close the opening.

ARMS (MAKE 2)

With **F**, make a magic ring.
Rnd 1: 6 sc in ring—6 sc.
Rnd 2: [Sc in the next st, 2 sc in the next st] 3 times—9 sc.
Rnd 3: Sc around—9 sc.
Rnd 4: Sc in first st, ch 3, [2 hdc, sl st] in the first st of chain, sc in last 8 sc—9 sc.
Rnd 5: [Sc in next st, sc2tog over next 2 sc] 3 times—6 sc.
Rnd 6: Sc around—6 sc.
Switch to **C**, and keep **F** yarn attached, leaving the tail outside to crochet the cuff later.
Rnd 7: Sc in blo around—6 sc.
Rnd 8: Sc in first 3 sc, 2 sc in next sc, sc in last 2 sc—7 sc.
Rnd 9: Sc in first 6 sc, 2 sc in last sc—8 sc.
Rnd 10: Sc around—8 sc.
Rnd 11: Sc in first 4 sc, 2 sc in next sc, sc in last 3 sc—9 sc.
Rnds 12−18: Sc around—9 sc.
Fasten off. Cut **C** and hide the tail. Continue working with **F**.
Rnd 7: Flo ch 1, [hdc in next sc, 2 hdc in next sc] 3 times, sl st to join the round—9 hdc.
Fasten off. Hide the yarn tail.

SHOES (MAKE 2)

With **C**.
Rnd 1: Ch 7, 2 sc in 2nd ch from hook, sc in next 4 ch, 3 sc in the next ch, sc in next 5

ch on the other side of the chain, sl st to 1st sc to make a round—14 sc.
Rnd 2: Ch 1, fpsc around—14 fpsc.
Rnd 3: Sc around in each fpsc—14 sc.
Rnd 4: Sc2tog in first sc, sc in 3 next sc, sc2tog in next 3 sc, sc in last 3 sc—10 sc.

LEGS (MAKE 2)

LEG 1

Switch to **A**, keep **C** yarn attached, leaving the tail outside to crochet later.
Rnd 5: Blo sc2tog in first sc, sc in last 8 sc—9 sc.
Rnds 6−10: Sc around—9 sc.
Switch **C**.
Rnd 5: Sc in flo around, sl st to join the round—10 sc.
Fasten off. Cut **C** and hide the yarn tail. Stuff the Shoe.
Continue the Leg with **A**.
Rnd 11: Sc in first 4 sc, 2 sc in next sc, sc in last 4 sc —10 sc.
Rnd 12: 2 sc in first st, sc in each st around—11 sc.
Rnd 13: Sc in first 5 sc, 2 sc in next sc, sc in last 5 sc —12 sc.
Rnd 14: 2 sc in first st, sc in each st around—13 sc.
Rnd 15: Sc in first 6 sc, 2 sc in next sc, sc in last 6 sc —14 sc.
Rnd 16: 2 sc in first st, sc in each st around—15 sc.
Rnds 17−20: Sc around—15 sc.
Stuff the Leg.

LEG 2

Same as Leg 1.
Rnd 21: 10sc—10 sc.
Do not cut the yarn of Leg 2. We will join the two Legs in the next round.

BODY

Continuing with **A**.

Rnd 22: Ch 1, sc around [Leg 1], sc on one side of ch, sc around [Leg 2], sc on the other side of ch—32 sc.

Note: Before joining, place the Legs in the correct direction. Mark the new first st.

Rnd 23: [Sc in next 7 sc, 2 sc in next sc] 4 times—36 sc.

Rnds 24—26: Sc around—36 sc.

Rnd 27: [Sc in next 7 sc, sc2tog over next 2 sc] 4 times—32 sc.

Rnd 28: Sc around—32 sc.

Rnd 29: [Sc in next 6 sc, sc2tog over next 2 sc] 4 times—28 sc.

Rnd 30: [Sc in next 5 sc, sc2tog over next 2 sc] 4 times—24 sc.

Rnd 31: Sc around—24 sc.

Rnd 32: Sc in first 6 sc, 2 sc in next 5 sc, sc in next 2 sc, 2 sc in next 5 sc, sc in last 6 sc—34 sc.

Rnds 33—36: Sc around—34 sc.

Join the Arms to the Body in the next round.

Rnd 37: 2sctog, sc in next 5 sc (Body), sc in next 3 sc, sc3tog over next 3 sc, sc in next 3 sc (Arm), sc2tog in next 22 sc (Body), sc in next 3 sc, sc3tog over next 3 sc, sc in next 3 sc (Arm), sc in last 5 sc (Body)—36 sc.

Rnd 38: [Sc in next 4 sc, sc2tog over next 2 sc] 6 times—30 sc.

Rnd 39: [Sc in next 3 sc, sc2tog over next 2 sc] 6 times—24 sc.

Rnd 40: [Sc in next 2 sc, sc2tog over next 2 sc] 6 times—18 sc.

Stuff the Body and Arms firmly. Place the inner neck here and continue crocheting.

Rnd 41: [Sc in next sc, sc2tog over next 2 sc] 6 times—12 sc.

Rnd 42: [Sc in next 2 sc, sc2tog over next 2 sc] 3 times—9 sc.

HEAD

With **A**.

Rnd 1: 2 sc in each st around—18 sc.

Rnd 2: [Sc in next 2 sc, 2 sc in next sc] 6 times—24 sc.

Rnd 3: [Sc in next 3 sc, 2 sc in next sc] 6 times—30 sc.

Rnd 4: [Sc in next 4 sc, 2 sc in next sc] 6 times—36 sc.

Rnd 5: [Sc in next 5 sc, 2 sc in next sc] 6 times—42 sc.

Rnd 6: [Sc in next 6 sc, 2 sc in next sc] 6 times—48 sc.

Rnds 7—9: Sc around—48 sc.

Rnd 10: Sc in first 16 sc, [ch 2, sl st in upper loop of second previous round, turn, 4 sc in 1st ch] (to create first Ear), sc in next 22 sc, [ch 2, sl st in upper loop of second previous round, turn, 4 sc in 1st ch] (to create second Ear), sc in last 10 sc—48 sc.

Rnds 11—15: Sc around—48 sc.

Rnd 16: [Sc in next 6 sc, sc2tog] 6 times—42 sc.

Rnd 17: [Sc in next 5 sc, sc2tog] 6 times—36 sc.

Insert the eyes between Rnds 9 and 10, 6 sts from each ear. Embroider the face as in the photo.

Rnd 18: [Sc in next 4 sc, sc2tog] 6 times—30 sc.

Rnd 19: [Sc in next 3 sc, sc2tog] 6 times—24 sc.

Change to **B**

Rnd 20: Blo [sc in next 2 sc, sc2tog] 6 times—18 sc.

Rnd 21: Sc around—18 sc.

Stuff the Head.

Rnd 22: [Sc in next sc, sc2tog] 6 times—12 sc.

Rnd 23: Sc2tog around—6 sc.

Stuff the Head firmly.

Fasten off. Use a yarn needle to close the opening.

HAIR

Insert **B** into flo on Rnd 20 of the Head and align with the right Ear.

Strs 1—12: Sl st in the next st,

Strs 13—18: sk 1, sl st in the 2nd next st of Rnd 20 at the end of each strand.

Str 1: Ch 8, sc on the surface into Rnd 12 of the Head, ch 9, 2 hdc in 2nd ch from hook, 2 hdc in next 6 ch, hdc in last 10 ch—24 hdc.

Strs 2—12: Turn, ch 8, sc in the 9th hdc from crown on previous strand into the Head, ch 9, 2 hdc in 2nd ch from hook, 2 hdc in next 6 ch, hdc in next hdc, hdc in flo hdc of the previous strand—24 hdc.

Str 13: Turn, ch 15, 2 hdc in 2nd ch from hook, 2 hdc in next 7 ch, hdc in last 6 ch— 22 hdc.

Strs 14—17: Turn, ch 10, 2 hdc in 2nd ch from hook, 2 hdc in next 4 ch, hdc in last 4 ch— 14 hdc.

Str 18: as Strand 13.

Fasten off. Hide the yarn tail.

JUMPSUIT

With **C**, make a magic ring.

Working in rows, turn and ch at the end of each row.

Row 1: 3 sc in ring, sl st to 1st sc to create the button, ch 26, sl st in 6th ch from hook to create the buttonhole loop— 20 ch.

Row 2: [Hdc in next ch, 2 hdc in next ch] 10 times—30 hdc.

Row 3: Flo [hdc in next 2 hdc, 2 hdc in next hdc] 10 times— 40 hdc.

Row 4: Blo [hdc in next 3 hdc, 2 hdc in next hdc] 10 times— 50 hdc.

Row 5: Flo hdc in first 6 hdc, skip 10, [hdc in next 3 hdc, 2 hdc in next hdc] 5 times, skip 10, hdc in last 6 hdc—37 hdc.

Row 6: Hdc in next 18 hdc, 2 hdc in next hdc, hdc in last 18 hdc—38 hdc.

Rows 7—8: Hdc around—38 hdc.

Sl st to join the round. Working in rounds, sl st to join a round and ch at the end of each round.

Rnds 9—11: Hdc around—38 hdc.

Sl st through two opposite sts to create two Legs of the Jumpsuit.

LEG 1

Rnd 12: Hdc around—19 hdc.

Rnd 13: Hdc in first 8 hdc, hdc2tog over next 2 hdc, 9 hdc in last hdc—18 hdc.

Rnds 14—16: Hdc around— 18 hdc.

Fasten off. Hide the yarn tail.

LEG 2

As Leg 1.

POCKET

With **F**.

Work in rows, turn and ch at the end of each row.

Row 1: Ch 6, 2 hdc in 3rd ch from hook, hdc in next 2 hdc, 2 hdc in last hdc—6 hdc.

Row 2: 2 hdc in first hdc, hdc in next 4 hdc, 2 hdc in last hdc—8 hdc.

Row 3: 2 hdc in first hdc, hdc in next 7 hdc—9 hdc.

Row 4: 2 hdc in first hdc, hdc in next 8 hdc—10 hdc.

Edging: work 25 sc around the pocket.

Sew to the Jumpsuit.

EARMUFFS

With **E**, make a magic ring.

BACK PAD (MAKE 2)

Rnd 1: 6 sc in ring —6 sc.

Rnd 2: 2 sc in each st around—12 sc.

Rnd 3: [Sc in next sc, 2 sc in next sc] 6 times—18 sc.

Fasten off. Cut the yarn tail.

FRONT PAD (MAKE 2)

Rnds 1—3: as Back Pad.

Rnds 4—5: Sc around—18 sc.

Fasten off and cut the yarn in one piece.

Form the Earmuff frame with the 30 cm wire.

MUFF 1

Rnd 6: Place Front and Back Pads together (RS facing out), put the frame between two Pads, sc through 2 sts of two Pads, around—18 sc.

Stuff after 12 sts. Fasten off. Do not cut the yarn.

HEADBAND

Use the yarn tail of Muff 1 to cover the frame by wrapping yarn around the frame.

MUFF 2

Rnd 6: Same as Muff 1, using the yarn tail from the headband.

Fasten off. Hide the yarn tail. Put the Earmuffs on Professor Sprout.

WITCH HAT

With **F**, make a magic ring.

Work in rounds. Sl st to join the round and ch at the end of each round.

Rnd 1: 6 hdc in ring—6 hdc.

Rnds 2–3: Hdc around—6 hdc.

Rnd 4: 2 hdc in each st around—12 hdc.

Rnd 5: Hdc in flo around, sl st to join the round, 2 ch, sl st to blo 1st st, hdc in blo around—12 hdc in each layer.

Rnd 6: [Hdc in next hdc, 2 hdc in next hdc] 6 times—18 hdc.

Rnd 7: Hdc in flo around, sl st to join the round, 2 ch, sl st to blo 1st st, hdc in blo around—18 hdc in each layer.

Rnd 8: [Hdc in next 2 hdc, 2 hdc in next hdc] 6 times—24 hdc.

Rnd 9: Hdc in flo around, sl st to join the round, 2 ch, sl st to blo 1st st, hdc in blo around—24 hdc in each layer.

Rnd 10: [Hdc in next 3 hdc, 2 hdc in next hdc] 6 times—32 hdc.

Rnd 11: Flo 32 hdc, sl st to join the round, 2 ch, sl st to blo first st, blo 32 hdc—32 hdc.

Rnd 12: [Hdc in next 4 hdc, 2 hdc in next hdc] 6 times—36 hdc.

Rnd 13: Hdc in flo around, sl st to join the round, 2 ch, sl st to blo 1st st, hdc in blo around—36 hdc in each layer.

Rnd 14: [Hdc in next 5 hdc, 2 hdc in next hdc] 6 times—42 hdc.

Rnd 15: Hdc in flo around, sl st to join the round, 2 ch, sl st to blo 1st st, hdc in blo around—42 hdc in each layer.

Rnd 16: [Hdc in next 6 hdc, 2 hdc in next hdc] 6 times—48 hdc.

Rnd 17: Hdc in flo around, sl st to join the round, 2 ch, sl st to blo 1st st, hdc in blo around—48 hdc in each layer.

Rnd 18: Flo [2 hdc in next hdc, hdc in next hdc] 24 times—72 hdc.

Rnd 19: [2 hdc in next st, hdc in next 2 hdc] 24 times—96 hdc.

Rnd 20: [2 hdc in next st, hdc in next 3 hdc] 24 times—120 hdc.

Rnd 21: R-sc around, sl st to join the round—120 r-sc.

Fasten off. Hide the yarn tail.

LEAVES FOR HAT (MAKE 1 IN EACH COLOR)

With **C** or **D**, make a magic ring.

Rnd 1: 6 sc in ring—6 sc.

Rnd 2: Sc around—6 sc.

Rnd 3: [Sc in next sc, 2 sc in next sc] 3 times—9 sc.

Rnd 4: Sc around—9 sc.

Rnd 5: [Sc in next 2 sc, 2 sc in next sc] 3 times—12 sc.

Rnds 6–7: Sc around—12 sc.

Rnd 8: [Sc in next 2 sc, sc2tog over next 2 sc] 3 times—9 sc.

Rnd 9: Sc around—9 sc.

Rnd 10: [Sc in next sc, sc2tog over next 2 sc] 3 times—6 sc.

Fasten off. Close the opening. Use the yarn tail to attach to the Hat.

Put the Witch Hat on Professor Sprout.

WITCH COAT

With **E**.

Work in rows, turn, ch at the end of each row.

Row 1: Ch 22, [hdc in next st, 2 hdc in next st] 10 times, starting at 3rd ch from hook—30 hdc.

Row 2: [Hdc in next 2 hdc, 2 hdc in next hdc] 10 times—40 hdc.

Row 3: [Hdc in next hdc, ch] 5 times, hdc in next 30 hdc, [ch, hdc in next hdc] 5 times—50 hdc.

Rows 4–5: Hdc around—50 hdc.

Row 6: Hdc in first 2 hdc, [2 hdc in next hdc, hdc in next hdc] 3 times, skip 10, hdc in next 6 hdc, 2 hdc in next 2 hdc, hdc in next 6 hdc, skip 10, [2 hdc in next hdc, hdc in next hdc] 3 times, hdc in last 2 hdc—38 hdc.

Row 7: Hdc in first hdc, [hdc in next 5 hdc, 2 hdc in next hdc] 6 times, hdc in last hdc—44 hdc.

Row 8: Hdc in first hdc, [hdc in next 6 hdc, 2 hdc in next hdc] 6 times, hdc in last hdc—50 hdc.

Rows 9–16: Hdc around—50 hdc.

EDGING

Sc around the outside edges of the coat—23 sc.

SLEEVES

Insert yarn under Arm, ch. Crochet in rounds, sl st to join, ch at the end of each round.

Rnd 1: Hdc in 10 skipped sts of Row 6 of the Coat, 2 hdc in 2 sts in the underarm space—14 hdc.

Rnd 2: Hdc in 12 hdc, [3 hdc in next 2 hdc] twice—18 hdc.

Rnd 3: Hdc in 12 hdc, [2 hdc in next 2 hdc], hdc in last 4 hdc.—20 hdc.
Fasten off. Hide the yarn tail.

STRING TIE

With **C**.
Ch 7, [sl st, sc, 2 hdc, sc, sl st] in 2nd ch from hook to create a leaf, ch 3, sc in 22 sc in Row 1 of the Coat, ch 10, [sl st, sc, 2 hdc, sc, sl st] in 2nd ch from hook to create a Leaf, ch 3, sl st to Row 1 to create a hole.

COLLAR

Insert **F** on the String Tie.
Row 1: [Hdc in next st, 2 hdc in next st] 11 times—33 hdc.
Row 2: [Hdc in next 2 st, 2 hdc in next st] 11 times—44 hdc.
Row 3: [Hdc in next st, 3 hdc in next st] 11 times—55 hdc.
Row 4: [Ch 3, sk1, sl st in next st] 27 times.
Fasten off. Hide the yarn tail.
Put the Witch Coat on Professor Sprout.

BABY MANDRAKE

LEGS (MAKE 2)

With **A**, make a magic ring.
Rnd 1: 4sc in ring—4 sc.
Rnd 2: [2 sc in next sc, sc in next sc] twice—6 sc.
Rnd 3: Sc around—6 sc.
Do not cut the yarn on Leg 2.
Cut 6 in. / 15 cm of **F**, fold it in half, and make a knot. Use a yarn needle to insert the knot into each Leg, with the yarn tails outside.

BODY AND HEAD

Join two Legs together.
Rnd 4: Sc in each st (Leg 1), Sc in each st (Leg 2)—12 sc.

Rnd 5: [Sc in next 3 sc, 2 sc in next sc] 3 times—15 sc.
Rnds 6–7: Sc around—15 sc.
Rnd 8: Sc in first 5 sc, [ch 3, 2 hdc in 2nd ch from hook to create Arm 1], sc in next 6 sc, [ch 3, 2 hdc in 2nd ch from hook to create Arm 2], sc in last 4 sc—15 sc.
Rnd 9: Sc around—15 sc.
Rnd 10: [Sc in next 3 sc, sc2tog over next 2 sc] 3 times—12 sc.
Rnd 11: Sc around—12 sc.
Rnd 12: Sc2tog around—6 sc.
Fasten off. Close the opening. Embroider the face.

RUBEUS HAGRID

Designed by Valérie Prieur-Côté
Skill Level: ⭘ ⭘

Rubeus Hagrid is a half-giant, and a supporter and friend to Harry Potter. "It was Hagrid who told Harry he was a wizard," said actor Robbie Coltrane, "and he feels a very, very strong protective love for the wee fellow." As Keeper of Keys and Grounds, he is also a friend to all creatures, some of questionable reputation. "Hagrid is, as we know, obsessed with having pretty much lethal creatures as pets," laughs Daniel Radcliffe (Harry Potter).

When *Harry Potter and the Sorcerer's Stone* costume designer Judianna Makovsky researched Hagrid's outfits, she read that he had a moleskin coat. "Did the author mean a cotton moleskin fabric, or little moles?" asked Makovsky. "And she meant little moles. Clearly, we wouldn't use real fur," she confirms, "so we used imitation fur cut into mole-shaped pelts. If you look very closely, each has little ear shapes, and flanks and tails." *Harry Potter and the Prisoner of Azkaban* costume designer Jany Temime felt Hagrid should look more like a farmer as he took care of the grounds and animals. "I gave him an old waistcoat, an old shirt, thick trousers, and boots he could muck around in."

A heartfelt tribute to one of the most beloved characters of the wizarding world, this amigurumi Hagrid stands approximately 11 inches tall. Designed with precision, Hagrid's coat and undercoat are created as separate pieces. Each strand of his hair and beard is thoughtfully attached, capturing the wild charm of Hagrid's unruly locks. Crafted with care, this amigurumi adaptation gives off the warmth and generosity that defines the half-giant, Keeper of Keys and Grounds at Hogwarts School of Witchcraft and Wizardry.

> "I'm Rubeus Hagrid, Keeper of Keys and Grounds at Hogwarts."
>
> Rubeus Hagrid,
> *Harry Potter and the Sorcerer's Stone*

FINISHED MEASUREMENTS
Height: 11 in. / 28 cm
Width: 8.6 in. / 22 cm

YARN
Worsted weight (#4 medium) shown in WeCrochet *Brava Worsted* (100% acrylic, 218 yd / 199 m per 3.5 oz. / 100 g skein).
Color A: #28424 Cream, 1 skein
Color B: #28456 Wine, 1 skein
Color C: #29489 Espresso, 1 skein
Color D: #29490 Gingerbread, 1 skein
Color E: #28410 Almond, 1 skein
Color F: #28449 Sienna, 1 skein
Color G: #28413 Black, very small amount
Color H: #28420 Cobblestone Heather, very small amount

HOOKS
• US D-3 / 3.25 mm crochet hook
• US G-6 / 4 mm crochet hook
• US H-8 / 5 mm crochet hook

NOTIONS
• Stitch markers
• Polyester stuffing
• Pair of 12mm black safety eyes
• Tapestry needle

GAUGE
Gauge is not critical for this project. Ensure that your stitches are tight so the stuffing won't show through.

SPECIAL ABBREVIATIONS
Back Loop Only (blo): Work through back loop only
Invisible Decrease (inv dec): Insert hook into front loop of first st, insert hook into front loop of second st, yo, draw through 2 loops on the hook, yo, draw through 2 loops.

Bobble: Yarn over, insert hook in stitch and pull up a loop, yarn over and draw yarn through 2 loops on the hook. Repeat 3 more times. On the last time draw yarn through all of the remaining loops to finish the bobble.

Foundation Half-Double Crochet (fhdc):

Step 1: Make slip knot and ch 2. Yarn over, insert hook into second chain from the hook, yarn over. Draw yarn through 1 loop on the hook. Yarn over, draw yarn through remaining loops on the hook. You have completed 1 fhdc.

Step 2: Yarn over, insert hook under the 2 loops of the chain at the bottom of the previous fhdc. Yarn over and draw yarn through stitch, there are now 3 loops on the hook. Yarn over and draw yarn through 1 loop. Yarn over and draw yarn through remaining loops. You have now created your second fhdc. Repeat Step 2 for all of the remaining fhdc demanded in the pattern.

NOTES
• Pieces are worked in continuous rounds unless otherwise stated.

ARMS (MAKE 2)
With smallest hook and **A**, make a magic ring.

Rnd 1: 6 sc in magic ring— 6 sc.

Rnd 2: 2 sc in each st around— 12 sc.

Rnds 3—4: Sc in each sc around—12 sc.

Rnd 5: Sc in next 5, Bobble, sc in next 6—12 sc.

Rnds 6—7: Sc in each sc around—12 sc.

Change to **B**.

Rnd 8: Sc in each sc around—12 sc.

Rnd 9: Blo sc in each sc around—12 sc.

Rnds 10—20: Sc in each sc around—12 sc.

Stuff the hand and only lightly stuff for the rest of the Arm.

Rnd 21: Fold Arm opening in half and sc both sides together to close the Arm—6 sc.

Fasten off.

LEGS (MAKE 2)
With smallest hook and **B**.

Rnd 1: Ch 6, sc in second chain from the hook, sc in next 3 chains, 3 sc in last chain, go on the other side, sc in next 3 chains, 2 sc in first chain—12 sc.

Rnd 2: 2sc, sc in next 3, 2sc in next 3, sc in next 3, 2sc in next 2—18 sc.

Rnd 3: Sc, 2sc, sc in next 4, 2sc, [sc in next, 2sc] x 2, sc in next 3, [sc in next, 2sc] x 2—24 sc.

Rnd 4: Blo sc in each sc around—24 sc.

Rnd 5: Sc in next 8, [inv dec] x 3, sc in next 10—21 sc.

Rnd 6: Sc in next 7, [inv dec] x 3, sc in next 8—18 sc.

Rnd 7: Sc in next 6, [inv dec] x 2, sc in next 8—16 sc.

Rnds 8—9: Sc in each sc around—16 sc.

Change to **C**.

Rnd 10: Blo sc in each sc around—16 sc.

Rnds 11—17: Sc in each sc around—16 sc.

Stuff Legs firmly and fasten off Leg 1, do not fasten off Leg 2 but continue to Body and Head.

BODY AND HEAD
Starting from Leg 2.

Rnd 1: Starting from Leg 2, ch 2 and join to Leg 1 by making 1 sc, make sure that both Legs are facing the same way. Sc around each sc of Leg 1, 1 sc through both ch, sc in each sc around Leg 2, 1 sc into each chain from the other side—36 sc.

Rnds 2—6: Sc in each sc around—36 sc.

Change to **B**.

Rnd 7: Blo sc in each sc around—36 sc.

BEHIND THE MAGIC

Hagrid gave an unusual challenge to the films' costume designers: each costume needed to be constructed in two sizes, one for six-foot-one-inch Robbie Coltrane, and one worn by his double, six-foot-ten-inch Martin Bayfield, who "grew" to seven feet seven inches tall in the costume.

Rnds 8–17: Sc in each sc around—36 sc.

Rnd 18: [Sc in next 4, inv dec] around—30 sc.

Rnd 19: Sc in each sc around—30 sc.

Rnd 20: [Sc in next 3, inv dec] around—24 sc.

Rnd 21: Sc in each sc around—24 sc.

Stuff firmly as you go.

To join the Arms, position the Arms on each side of the Body, using stitch markers to attach them to make sure you like their placement. You can tweak the next round as long as there are 6 sc between each Arm. At the end of Rnd 21 you might not be perfectly aligned with the desired placement of the Arms. For Rnd 22, simply make sure that the Arms are on the sides 6 sc between each.

Rnd 22: 6 sc, for the next 6 stitches sc together Body with 6 sc of the Arm, make sure the thumb is facing out. 6 sc, join second Arm. (24)

Rnd 23: Sc in each sc around—24 sc.

Rnd 24: [Sc in next 2, inv dec]—18 sc.

Rnd 25: [Sc in next, inv dec]—12 sc.

Change to **A**.

Rnd 26: Blo, sc in each sc around—12 sc.

Rnd 27: [Sc in next, 2sc] around—18 sc.

Rnd 28: [Sc in next 2, 2sc] around—24 sc.

Rnd 29: [Sc in next 3, 2sc] around—30 sc.

Rnd 30: [Sc in next 4, 2sc] around—36 sc.

Rnd 31: [Sc in next 5, 2sc] around—42 sc.

Rnd 32: [Sc in next 6, 2sc] around—48 sc.

Rnds 33–43: Sc in each sc around—48 sc.

Continue stuffing as you go.

Insert the eyes between Rnds 37 and 38, with 7 to 8 sc between and aligned with middle of the Legs. If desired, insert a small piece of dowel, a pipe cleaner, or wires going from the Body through the neck and into the Head to keep it from wobbling.

Rnd 44: [Sc in next 6, inv dec] around—42 sc.

Rnd 45: Sc in next 2, inv dec, [sc in next 5, inv dec]x5, sc in next 3—36 sc.

Rnd 46: [Sc in next 4, inv dec] around—30 sc.

Rnd 47: Sc, inv dec, [sc in next 3, inv dec] x 5, sc in next 2—24 sc.

Rnd 48: [Sc in next 2, inv dec] around—18 sc.

Rnd 49: [Sc, inv dec] around—12 sc.

Rnd 50: [Inv dec] around—6 sc.

Cut yarn leaving a tail to sew to close.

Make the Face Details

With a long piece of **A** and a needle, go in from the top of the Head and come out in the second round under the eyes, two stitches on the right of the left eye. Pass the yarn a few times over the three stitches between the eyes to make a nose.

With **F** make 2 eyebrows.

VEST

With largest hook and **D**.

Front Panel

Rnd 1: Fhdc 30—30 hdc.

Rnds 2–8: Hdc in each hdc around—30 hdc.

Rnds 9–11: Hdc in next 5, ch 2, turn (you just made one of the Front Panels)—5 hdc.

Cut yarn leaving a tail.

Second Front Panel

Join yarn on the other side of the piece to make the Second Front Panel.

Rnds 1–3: Hdc in next 5, ch 2, turn—5 hdc.

Cut yarn leaving a tail.

Back Panel

Join yarn 5 hdc after a Front Panel.

Rnd 1: Hdc in next 10, ch 2, turn—10 hdc.

Rnd 2: 2hdc, hdc in next 8, 2hdc, ch2, turn—12 hdc.

Rnd 3: 2hdc, hdc in next 10, 2hdc—14 hdc.

Ch1, join Back Panel with Front Panel by sc together the next 5 stitches from both panels.

Do the same on the other side with the other Front Panel, use yarn tail to join them together.

You can flip it inside out to get smoother seams.

Starting at the bottom left corner, join new piece of yarn, ch1 and sc loosely around Vest to finish the outside edges.

VEST BELT LOOP (MAKE 4)

Rnd 1: Leaving a 4-inch tail, ch 6 and leave another 4-inch tail.

Place the first two Belt Loops 3 to 4 stitches in from the outside edge and the other two on the back of the Vest. Attach ends of each loop to Vest with the tails.

Weave in all the ends.

Put the Vest on Hagrid.

BELT AND BUCKLE

With largest hook and **G**.
Row 1: Fhdc 40—40 hdc.
Weave ends in.
With **H**.
Rnd 1: Ch 12, join with first ch to make a circle. Ch 4 join to other side of the circle to make a circle divided in 2 with a line.
Leave a 3- to 4-inch tail. Sew the bar of the Buckle on one of the ends of the Belt.
Put the Belt through the Belt Loops of the Vest and thread other end of Belt through the Buckle.

COAT

With largest hook and **E**.

Front Panel

Row 1: Fhdc 30—30 hdc.
Rows 2–12: Hdc in each hdc across—30 hdc.
Rows 13–16: Hdc in next 5, ch 2, turn—5 hdc.
Cut yarn leaving a tail.

Second Front Panel

Join yarn on the other side of the piece to make the Second Panel.
Rnds 1–3: Hdc in next 5, ch 2, turn—5 hdc.
Rnd 4: Hdc in next 5—5 hdc.
Cut yarn and leave long tail.

Back Panel

Join yarn 5 hdc after a Front Panel by chaining 2 and then hdc in same stitch.
Rnd 1: Ch 2, 2hdc, hdc in next 8, 2hdc, ch 2, turn—12 hdc.
Rnd 2: 2hdc, hdc in next 10, 2hdc, ch 2, turn—14 hdc.
Rnd 3: 2hdc, hdc in next 12, 2hdc—16 hdc.
Rnd 4: Hdc in each hdc across—16 hdc.
Rnd 5: Ch 1, join with one of the Front Panels by sl st next 5 stitches of both panels together.
Do the same on the other side with the other Front Panel, use yarn tail to join them together.
You can flip it inside out to get smoother seams.

COAT SLEEVES (MAKE 2)

Join new yarn in the stitch in the middle of the underarm of the Coat.
Rnd 1: Make 20 hdc around the armhole join to first hdc with a sl st, ch 1, turn—20 hdc.
Rnd 2: Hdc, [inv dec, hdc in next 2) x 4, inv dec, hdc, join to first hdc with a sl st, ch 1, turn—15 hdc.
Rnds 3–6: Hdc around, join to first hdc with a sl st, ch 1 and turn—15 hdc.
Cut yarn leaving a long tail. Fold the last row over the previous one and use tail to sew it in place. This will make a cuff. Weave ends in.

COAT POCKETS (MAKE 2)

Row 1: Fhdc 5—5 hdc.
Rows 2–4: Hdc in each hdc across—5 hdc.
Leave a long tail of approximately 11 inches for sewing.

Sew the Pockets on the Coat on Rows 4 to 8 about 3 to 4 stitches from the side.

Don't forget: don't sew the top closed, only sew the two sides and bottom.

Put the Coat on Hagrid.

HAIR

Note: The layers are made from Hair strands all linked to each other. Once a strand is done, you will start the next one right away with the loop on your hook.

With middle hook and **F**.

LAYER 1

Rows 1—13: Ch 26, sc in second ch from the hook, sc in all the remaining ch—25 sc.

Fasten off, leave a long tail to attach to the Head later.

LAYER 2

Rows 1—7: Ch 28, sc in second ch from the hook, sc in all the remaining ch—27 sc.

Fasten off, leave a long tail to attach to the Head.

Place Layer 1 around the Head (approximately around Rnd 35 of the Head, but can be a little lower or higher). Sew in place.

Place Layer 2 front to back, on top of the Head with the curly ends toward the back of the Head. The middle strands are centered with the nose. Use tail to secure some Hair strands around.

BEARD

Note: The Beard is made from Hair strands all linked to each other. Once a strand is done, you will start the next one right away with the loop on your hook.

With middle hook and **F**.

Rows 1—12: Ch 18, sc in second ch from the hook, sc in all the remaining ch—17 sc.

Fasten off, leave a long tail to attach to the Head later.

Use the tail or another piece of **F** to attach some of the strands together by weaving them together. To fix the Beard on the Head, place one edge on the side of the Head where the first strand from the Hair is, align with the eyes. Then shape the Beard in a small crescent under the nose and back up to the other side. Use the yarn tail to sew the Beard onto the Head.

MOUSTACHE (MAKE 2)

With middle hook and **F**.

Row 1: Ch 11, sc in second chain from the hook, sc in next 9—10 sc.

Cut yarn and leave tail to fix on the Head.

Place a piece of the Moustache on either side of the nose angled slightly downward diagonally, and stitch in place.

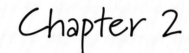

Chapter 2

MAGICAL CREATURES & ANIMAL COMPANIONS

SCABBERS

Designed by Irene Strange
Skill Level: ◣ ◣

Ron Weasley, the youngest male Weasley, often ends up with hand-me-downs—of his brothers' robes, books, cauldrons, and even his wand. For the small animal Hogwarts first-year students are allowed to bring, Ron has Scabbers, who originally belonged to his brother Percy.

Ron introduces Scabbers to his new friend, Harry, while on the Hogwarts Express. He tries to perform a magic spell on the rat suggested to him by his brother Fred, to turn "this stupid, fat rat yellow." Scabbers is enjoying himself in an empty box of Bertie Bott's Every Flavour Beans when Ron casts the spell, which only creates a yellow light and forces Scabbers out of the box.

For many of the scenes in the first three films, Scabbers was played by an animatronic rat, but a real rat, named Dex, also essayed the role. For this sequence, Dex was gently placed inside the candy box, which had a wire attached to it. When the time came, an animal trainer pulled on the wire, and the box popped off Dex, making it appear as if Scabbers backed out of the box and landed on Ron's lap.

Discover the charm of amigurumi Scabbers, Ron Weasley's loyal yet peculiar pet rat. His scruffy fur and the mischievous twinkle in his eyes bring this amigurumi rat to life. From his little whiskers to his missing toe, every stitch helps bring this iconic rat to life.

"This is Scabbers, by the way. Pathetic, isn't he?"

"Just a little bit."

Ron Weasley and Harry Potter,
Harry Potter and the Sorcerer's Stone

FINISHED MEASUREMENTS
Height: 7 in. / 17.7 cm
Width: 4 in. / 10 cm

YARN
Note: The project uses the two following yarns held and worked together to create a furry texture.

Sport weight (#2 light) yarn, shown in Scheepjes Stone Washed (78% cotton / 22% acrylic, 142 yd. / 130 m per 1.8 oz. / 50 g skein).
Color A: #802 Smokey Quartz, 1 skein

Lace weight (#0 lace) shown in Rico Design Essentials Super Kid Mohair Loves Silk (70% mohair / 30% silk, 218 yd. / 200 m per 0.9 oz. / 25 g skein).
Color B: #058 Grey Brown, 1 skein

DK weight (#3 light) yarn, shown in Rico Creative Ricorumi DK (100% cotton, 62 yd. / 57.5 m per 0.9 oz / 25 g ball).
Color C: #058 Silver Grey, 1 ball
Color D: #072 Lavender, 1 ball
Color E: #002 Cream, very small amount

HOOKS
• US G-6 / 4.0mm crochet hook
• US E- 4 / 3.5mm crochet hook

NOTIONS
• Pair of 12mm black safety eyes
• Polyester stuffing
• Wire or pipe cleaner
• Tapestry needle
• Wire brush (pet hair brush)

GAUGE
Gauge is not critical for this project. Ensure your stitches are tight so the stuffing won't show through.

BEHIND THE MAGIC

In *Harry Potter and the Prisoner of Azkaban*, Scabbers turns out to be the Animagus Peter Pettigrew, who betrayed Harry's parents to Voldemort. Pettigrew has been hiding as the Weasleys' family pet, Scabbers. When Scabbers is transformed back to Pettigrew, the texture and color of actor Timothy Spall's wig matched the color of Scabbers's fur.

HEAD

With larger hook, and **A** and **B** held together, make a magic ring.

Rnd 1: 6 sc in ring—6 sc.

Rnd 2: 2 sc in each st around—12 sc.

Rnd 3: [2 sc in next st, sc in next 3 st] 3 times—15 sc.

Rnd 4: [2 sc in next st, sc in next 4 st] 3 times—18 sc.

Rnd 5: [2 sc in next st, sc in next 5 st] 3 times—21 sc.

Rnd 6: [2 sc in next st, sc in next 6 st] 3 times—24 sc.

Rnd 7: [2 sc in next st, sc in next 7 st] 3 times—27 sc.

Rnd 8: [2 sc in next st, sc in next 8 st] 3 times—30 sc.

Rnds 9—16: Sc around—30 sc.

Add safety eyes between Rnds 12 and 13, about 12 stitches apart.

Rnd 17: [Sc2tog, sc in next 4 st] 5 times—25 sc.

Rnd 18: [Sc2tog, sc in next 3 st] 5 times—20 sc.

Rnd 19: [Sc2tog, sc in next 2 st] 5 times—15 sc.

Add stuffing.

Rnd 20: [Sc2tog, sc in next st] 5 times—10 sc.

Rnd 21: Sc2tog 5 times—5 sc.

Fasten off, pick up all the front loops with a tapestry needle and pull tight to close.

EARS (MAKE 2)

With smaller hook and **E,** make magic ring.

Rnd 1: 6 sc in ring—6 sc.

Rnd 2: 2 sc in each st around—12 sc.

Rnd 3: [2 sc in next st, sc in next st] 6 times—18 sc.

Rnds 4—7: Sc around—18 sc.

Rnd 8: [Sc2tog, sc in next 2 st].

Fasten off, leave a long tail for sewing.

INNER EARS (MAKE 2)

With smaller hook and **D,** make magic ring.

Rnd 1: 6 sc in ring—6 sc.

Rnd 2: 2 sc in next 5 st, skip last st—11 sc.

Fasten off, leave a tail for sewing.

TEETH

With smaller hook and **E,** ch 4, start 2nd ch from hook.

Row 1: Working in back hump of the chain, sc in next 3 ch, turn—3 sc.

Rows 2—3: Ch 1, sc in each st, turn—3 sc.

Fasten off, leave a tail for sewing.

TAIL

With smaller hook and **D,** make magic ring.

Rnd 1: 5 sc in ring—5 sc.

Rnds 2—5: Sc around—5 sc.

Rnd 6: 2 Sc in next st, sc in next 4

st—6 sc.

Rnds 7—10: Sc around—6 sc.

Rnd 11: 2 Sc in next st, sc in next 5 st—7 sc.

Rnds 12—15: Sc around—7 sc.

Rnd 16: 2 Sc in next st, sc in next 6 st—8 sc.

Rnds 17—20: Sc around—8 sc.

Rnd 21: 2 sc in next st, sc in next 7 st—9 sc.

Rnds 22—25: Sc around—9 sc.

Rnd 26: 2 sc in next st, sc in next 8 st—10 sc.

Rnds 27—30: Sc around—10 sc.

Rnd 31: 2 sc in next st, sc in next 9 st—11 sc.

Rnds 32—35: Sc around—11 sc.

Rnd 36: 2 sc in next st, sc in next 10 sc—12 sc.

Rnds 37—44: Sc around—12 sc.

Fasten off, leave a tail for sewing. Add a wire or a pipe cleaner to make the Tail bendable.

BODY

With larger hook, and **A** and **B** held together, make a magic ring.

Rnd 1: 6 sc in ring—6 sc.

Rnd 2: 2 sc in each st around—1 2 sc.

Rnd 3: [2 sc in next st, sc in next st] 6 times—18 sc.

Rnd 4: [2 sc in next st, sc in next 2 st] 6 times—24 sc.

Rnd 5: [2 sc in next st, sc in next 3 st] 6 times—30 sc.

Rnd 6: [2 sc in next st, sc in next 4 st] 3 times, sc in next 15 st—33 sc.

Rnd 7: [2 sc in next st, sc in next 5 st] 3 times, sc in next 15 st—36 sc.

Rnd 8: [2 sc in next st, sc in next 6 st] 3 times, sc in next 15 st—39 sc.

Rnd 9: [2 sc in next st, sc in next 7 st] 3 times, sc in next 15 st—42 sc.

Rnd 10: [2 sc in next

8 st] 3 times, sc in next 15 st—45 sc.

Rnd 11: [2 sc in next st, sc in next 9 st] 3 times, sc in next 15 st—48 sc.

Rnds 12—20: Sc around—48 sc.

Rnd 21: [Sc2tog, sc in next 9 st] 3 times, sc in next 15 st—45 sc.

Rnd 22: [Sc2tog, sc in next 8 st] 3 times, sc in next 15 st—42 sc.

Rnd 23: [Sc2tog, sc in next 7 st] 3 times, sc in next 15 st—39 sc.

Rnd 24: [Sc2tog, sc in next 6 st] 3 times, sc in next 15 st—36 sc.

Rnd 25: [Sc2tog, sc in next 5 st] 3 times, sc in next 15 st—33 sc.

Rnd 26: [Sc2tog, sc in next 4 st] 3 times, sc in next 15 st—30 sc.

Rnd 27: [Sc2tog, sc in next 3 st] 3 times, sc in next 15 st—27 sc.

Rnd 28: [Sc2tog, sc in next 2 st] 3 times, skip the remaining st—24 sc.

Fasten off, leave a tail for sewing.

BACK LEGS (MAKE 2)

With larger hook, and **A** and **B** held together, make a magic ring.

Rnd 1: 6 sc in ring—6 sc.

Rnd 2: 2 sc in each st around—12 sc.

Rnd 3: [2 sc in next st, sc in next st] 6 times—18 sc.

Rnd 4: [2 sc in next st, sc in next 2 st] 6 times—24 sc.

Rnd 5: [2 sc in next st, sc in next 3 st] 6 times—30 sc.

Rnd 6: [2 sc in next st, sc in next 4 st] 6 times—36 sc.

Rnd 7: Sc around—36 sc.

Left Leg

Rnd 8: [Sc2tog, sc in next 4 st] 3 times, ch 4, skip next 4 st, sc in next st, skip the remaining st of the main round and proceed to make the paw—

the paw is made over the 4 chains and 4 skipped stitches, ignoring the rest of the Leg.

Right Leg

Rnd 8: [Sc2tog, sc in next 4 st] 3 times, sl st in back loop only in next 13 st, ch 4, skip next 4 st, sc in next st, next make the paw.

Both Legs

Rnd 9: Turn and work along the chain, sc in next 4 ch, turn the piece and work along the skipped 4 st, sc in next 4 st—8 sc.

Rnds 10—14: Sc around—8 sc.

Rnd 15: [Sc2tog, sc in next 2 st] 2 times—6 sc.

Fasten off, pick up all the front loops with a tapestry needle and pull tight to close.

FRONT LEGS (MAKE 2)

With larger hook, and **A** and **B** held together, make a magic ring.

Rnd 1: 6 sc in ring—6 sc.

Rnd 2: Sc around—6 sc.

Rnd 3: Sc in next 3 st, sl st in next 3 st.
Rnds 4–6: Sc around—6 sc.
Fasten off, leave a tail for sewing.

TOES (MAKE 2)

With smaller hook and **C**.

Toes for Right Leg

Row 1: (Ch 5, start 2nd ch from hook, sl st in next 4 ch) repeat 3 times—3 Toes.

Toes for Left Leg

Row 1: (Ch 5, start 2nd ch from hook, sl st in next 4 ch) repeat 2 times—2 Toes.
Fasten off, leave a tail for sewing.

ASSEMBLY

Sew Inner Ear to the Outer Ear, then sew the Ears to the Head, behind the eyes, positioning them over Rnd 16, about 8 stitches apart. With **D** embroider a nose over Rnds 2–3. Sew the Teeth under the nose.

Add stuffing to the Body and sew it to the Head, adjust the angle of the Head until you like the pose.

Pin the Back Legs to the Body, checking that the Legs help the rat sit up. Carefully sew in place all around the round section of the Leg and the open section of the Leg, adding a bit of stuffing as you go. When sewing the Right Leg make sure to sew it through the free front loops, so the slip stitch section is hidden.

Next sew the Toes to the tips of the Back Legs—position the 3-toe section over the middle of the Leg, and the 2-toe section closer to the inside. When sewing catch the space in between the Toes with the yarn tail, keeping the stitches short. Then embroider a few small stitches in **D** at the base of the missing Toe—this will highlight its absence.

Sew the Tail to the base of the Body.

Sew the Front Legs to the Body, with the fold pointing down.

Embroider a few short stitches in **C** over the tip of each Front Leg to suggest toes.

Separate a small piece of **C** into single strands, tie a knot on the end of each and add to either side of the nose to make the whiskers.

Using a wire brush vigorously brush the top of the Head and the back of the Body to bring out the mohair fluff and make your Scabbers scruffier.

CROOKSHANKS

Designed by Irene Strange
Skill Level: ⚡ ⚡

While Ron brings Scabbers the rat, and Harry acquires Hedwig the owl for the first year at Hogwarts, Hermione does not bring an animal with her until her third year, in *Harry Potter and the Prisoner of Azkaban*. It's a large, fluffy, ginger-colored cat she names Crookshanks. Crookshanks and Scabbers become adversaries, with the cat the first one Ron suspects when Scabbers goes missing.

Several red Persian cats portrayed Crookshanks in the films, partly hired for their grumpy looks. To make them appear even grumpier, an animal-safe brown "eye shadow" was applied around their eyes and mouths. Their already fuzzy fur was added to with blobs of additional fur culled from the brushing of their undercoat. The excess fur was balled up and then clipped to their coat for a matted, wild effect. A cat named Crackerjack had the most on-screen time as Crookshanks, and learned a variety of behaviors including walking away with the Extendable Ear the Weasley kids, Harry, and Hermione use to eavesdrop on the grown-ups in *Harry Potter and the Order of the Phoenix*.

This amigurumi incarnation of Hermione's clever feline companion, Crookshanks, is crocheted with a keen eye. Crookshanks's vibrant, bushy orange fur is created using a slicker brush. Every part of this amigurumi Crookshanks is thoughtfully created with attention to detail, including his unique face and his bright yellow eyes.

> "A cat? Is that what they told you? Looks more like a pig with hair if you ask me."
>
> Ron Weasley, *Harry Potter and the Prisoner of Azkaban*

FINISHED MEASUREMENTS
Height: 6 in. / 15 cm
Length: 8 in. / 20 cm

YARN
Note: This project is worked with some of the yarns held together to create a furry texture.

Sport weight (#2 light) yarn, shown in Scheepjes Stone Washed (78% cotton / 22% acrylic, 142 yd. / 130 m per 1.8 oz. / 50 g ball).
Color A: #832 Enstatite, 2 balls

DK weight (#3 light) yarn, shown in Rowan Kidsilk Haze (70% mohair / 30% silk, 229 yd. / 210 m per 0.9 oz. / 25 g ball).
Color B: #732 Caramel, 1 ball

DK weight (#3 light) yarn, shown in Rico Design Ricorumi DK (100% cotton, 62.8 yd. / 58 m per 0.9 oz, 25 g ball).
Color C: #024 Smokey Orange, 1 ball
Color D: #070 Dk Apricot, 1 ball
Color E: #002 Cream, very small amount

Small amount of similar weight cotton yarn in brown

HOOKS
• US G / 4.0mm crochet hook
• US E / 3.5mm crochet hook

NOTIONS
• Pair of 22mm yellow or orange round or cat-eye-shaped safety eyes
• Polyester stuffing
• Wire or pipe cleaner with chenille stem
• Tapestry needle
• Wire brush (pet hair brush)

BEHIND THE MAGIC

When the Weasleys, Harry, and Hermione celebrate Christmas dinner with Sirius Black, Crookshanks watches on a stool. Sardine juice was rubbed on Crackerjack's mouth to encourage her to lick her lips.

HEAD

Working with **A** and **B** held together and larger hook, make a magic ring.

Rnd 1: 7 sc in ring—7 sc.
Rnd 2: 2 sc in each st around—14 sc.
Rnd 3: [Sc in next st, 2 sc in next st] 7 times—21 sc.
Rnd 4: [Sc in next 2 st, 2 sc in next st] 7 times—28 sc.
Rnd 5: [Sc in next 3 st, 2 sc in next st] 7 times—35 sc.
Rnd 6: [Sc in next 4 st, 2 sc in next st] 7 times—42 sc.
Rnd 7: [Sc in next 5 st, 2 sc in next st] 7 times—49 sc.
Rnd 8: Sc in next 48 st, 2 sc in next st—50 sc.
Rnds 9–17: Sc around—50 sc.
Rnd 18: [Sc2tog, sc in next 8 st] 5 times—45 sc.
Rnd 19: [Sc2tog, sc in next 7 st] 5 times—40 sc.
Fasten off, leave a tail for sewing.
Add the eyes between Rnds 8 and 9, approximately 7 sts apart.
Brush out the mohair yarn with a wire brush until the surface is very fluffy.

EARS (MAKE 2)

With **A** and smaller hook, make a magic ring.

Rnd 1: 6 sc in ring—6 sc.
Rnd 2: [Sc in next st, 3 sc in next st] 3 times—12 sc.
Rnd 3: [Sc in next 2 st, 3 sc in next st, sc in next st] 3 times—18 sc.
Rnd 4: Sl st in next 3 st, ch 1, sc in next 5 st, 3 sc in next st, sc in next 6 st, skip the remaining st—12 sc, not counting slip stitches or chains.
Fasten off, leave a tail for sewing.

INNER EARS (MAKE 2)

With **D** and smaller hook, make a magic ring.

Rnd 1: 6 sc in ring—6 sc.
Rnd 2: [Sc in next st, 3 sc in next st] 3 times—12 sc.
Rnd 3: [Sc in next 2 st, 3 sc in next st, sc in next st] 3 times—18 sc.
Fasten off, leave a tail for sewing.

BODY

Working with **A** and **B** held together and larger hook, make a magic ring.

Rnd 1: 7 sc in ring—7 sc.
Rnd 2: 2 sc in each st around—14 sc.
Rnd 3: [Sc in next st, 2 sc in next st] 7 times—21 sc.
Rnd 4: [Sc in next 2 st, 2 sc in next st] 7 times—28 sc.
Rnd 5: [Sc in next 3 st, 2 sc in next st] 7 times—35 sc.
Rnd 6: [Sc in next 4 st, 2 sc in next st] 7 times—42 sc.
Rnd 7: Sc around—42 sc.
Rnd 8: [Sc in next 13 st, 2 sc in next st] 3 times—45 sc.
Rnd 9: [Sc in next 14 st, 2 sc in next st] 3 times—48 sc.
Rnd 10: [Sc in next 15 st, 2 sc in next st] 3 times—51 sc.
Rnd 11: [Sc in next 16 st, 2 sc in next st] 3 times—54 sc.
Rnd 12: [Sc in next 17 st, 2 sc in next st] 3 times—57 sc.
Rnds 13–24: Sc around—57 sc.
Rnd 25: Sc in next 12 st, [sc2tog, sc in next 9 st] 3 times, sc in next 12 st—54 sc.
Rnd 26: Sc in next 12 st, [sc2tog, sc in next 8 st] 3 times, sc in next 12 st—51 sc.
Rnd 27: Sc in next 12 st, [sc2tog, sc in next 7 st] 3 times, sc in next 12 st—48 sc.
Rnds 28–32: Sc around—48 sc.

Rnd 33: [Sc2tog, sc in next 6 st] 6 times—42 sc.

Rnd 34: [Sc2tog, sc in next 5 st] 6 times—36 sc.

Rnd 35: [Sc2tog, sc in next 4 st] 6 times—30 sc.

Rnd 36: [Sc2tog, sc in next 3 st] 6 times—24 sc.

Rnd 37: [Sc2tog, sc in next 2 st] 6 times—18 sc.

Add lots of stuffing.

Rnd 38: [Sc2tog, sc in next 1 st] 6 times—12 sc.

Rnd 39: Sc2tog 6 times—6 sc.

Fasten off, pick up all the front loops with a tapestry needle and pull tight to close.

PAWS (MAKE 4)

Working with **A** and **B** held together and larger hook, make a magic ring.

Rnd 1: 6 sc in ring—6 sc.

Rnd 2: [Sc in next st, 3 sc in next st, sc in next st] 2 times—10 sc.

Rnd 3: [Sc in next 2 st, 2 sc in next st, sc in next 2 st] 2 times—12 sc.

Rnds 4—5: Sc around—12 sc.

Rnd 6: Sc in next 9 st, add a little bit of stuffing and fold the open edge closed, working through both layers sc in next 6 st.

Fasten off, leave a tail for sewing.

TAIL

With one strand of **A** held together with **2 strands** (*this will make the tail darker in color*) of **B** and larger hook, make a magic ring.

Rnd 1: 6 sc in ring—6 sc.

Rnd 2: 2 sc in each st around—12 sc.

Rnd 3: [2 sc in next st, sc in next 3 st] 3 times—15 sc.

Rnd 4: [2 sc in next st, sc in next 4 st] 3 times—18 sc.

Rnd 5: [2 sc in next st, sc in next 5 st] 3 times—21 sc.

Rnds 6—8: Sc around—21 sc.

Rnd 9: [Sc2tog, sc in next 5 st] 3 times—18 sc.

Rnds 10—14: Sc around—18 sc.

Rnd 15: [Sc2tog, sc in next 4 st] 3 times—15 sc.

Rnds 16—20: Sc around—15 sc.

Rnd 21: Sc2tog, sc in next 13 st—14 sc.

Rnd 22: Sc around—14 sc.

Rnd 23: Sc2tog, sc in next 12 st—13 sc.

Rnd 24: Sc around—13 sc.

Rnd 25: Sc2tog, sc in next 11 st—12 sc.

Rnd 26: Sc around—12 sc.

Rnd 27: Sc2tog, sc in next 10 st—11 sc.

Rnd 28: Sc around—11 sc.

Rnd 29: Sc2tog, sc in next 10 st—10 sc.

Rnd 30: Sc around—10 sc.

Fasten off, leave a tail for sewing. Add stuffing and a pipe cleaner.

MOUTH

With **D** and smaller hook, make a magic ring.

Rnd 1: 6 sc in a ring—6 sc.

Rnd 2: [Sc in next st, 3 sc in next st] 3 times—12 sc.

Rnd 3: [Sc in next 2 st, 3 sc in next st, sc in next st] 3 times—18 sc.

Rnd 4: Sc in next 4 st, ch 1, sl st in next 5 st, 3 sc in next st, sl st in next 6 st, ch1, sl st in next 2 st—23 sts.

Fasten off, leave a tail for sewing.

TUMMY

With **D** and smaller hook, make a magic ring.

Rnd 1: 6 sc in ring—6 sc.

Rnd 2: [Sc in next st, 3 sc in next st] 3 times—12 sc.

Rnd 3: [Sc in next 2 st, 3 sc in next st, sc in next st] 3 times—18 sc.

Rnd 4: [Sc in next 3 st, 3 sc in next st, sc in next 2 st] 3 times—24 sc.

Rnd 5: [Sc in next 4 st, 3 sc in next st, sc in next 3 st] 3 times—30 sc.

Rnd 6: [Sc in next 4 st, 2 sc in next 3 st, sc in next 3 st] 3 times—39 sc.

Rnd 7: Sc in next 6 st, ch 1, sc in next 10 st, 3 sc in next st, sc in next 4 st, 3 sc in next st, sc in next 10 st, ch 1, sc in next 7 st—45 sts.

Fasten off, leave a tail for sewing.

ASSEMBLY

Add stuffing to the Head and position it over the shorter section of the Body after the decreases in Rnds 25 to 27. Choose which way the Cat is looking by adjusting the angle of the eyes. After the Head is attached embroider the nose with **C**, placing it between the eyes. Next sew the Mouth to the Head a little below the nose.

Sew the Inner Ears to Outer Ears and then sew them to the top of the Head—choose your preferred position.

Add some wire and stuffing into the Tail and sew it to the back of the Body.

Brush out the Body and the Tail to bring out the fur.

Sew the Tummy to the front of the Body, then pin two of the Paws where the Tummy overlaps the Body, so that they help the toy stay upright.

Sew the other Paws to the bottom of the Body, about halfway.

Split up a small length of **E** into single strands and stitch them to the face, on either side of the nose, to make the whiskers.

Use brown yarn to embroider the mouth, following the top triangle shape of the sewn Mouth piece.

Then add some brown yarn lines to the Paws to suggest toes.

Brush out any fluff trapped under the seams to finish.

TREVOR

Designed by Irene Strange
Skill Level: ✄ ✄

Trevor, the toad brought to Hogwarts by student Neville Longbottom, disappears and reappears in unexpected places: on the Hogwarts Express, in the waiting area before the Sorting Ceremony, and on the arm of a chair in the Gryffindor common room. Fortunately, Neville is able to recover him, sometimes with help from Harry, Ron, and Hermione.

Four toads portrayed Trevor in the first three Harry Potter films. The toads were housed in a large terrarium covered with moss and specially heated for them when they weren't called to shoot a scene. In addition to his appearances (and disappearances) in *Harry Potter and the Sorcerer's Stone*, Trevor is seen in Professor McGonagall's Transfiguration class in *Harry Potter and the Chamber of Secrets*. And while he appears in a publicity photo for the third film, he disappeared for good after that. Matthew Lewis (Neville) remembers director David Yates asking him if he wanted Trevor back with him in *Harry Potter and the Goblet of Fire*. To which Lewis replied, "Honestly, David, no, I don't." And he was never seen again.

Neville Longbottom's devoted toad, Trevor, is a fitting companion to accompany you on your magical journey in crocheting (unless he gets lost!). Trevor's charming and gentle features come to life in every stitch. Using soft and plush chenille yarn, this crochet toad is velvety smooth, making it irresistible to snuggle.

> "Has anyone seen a toad? A boy named Neville's lost one."
>
> Hermione Granger,
> *Harry Potter and the Sorcerer's Stone*

FINISHED MEASUREMENTS
Height: 5 in. / 12 cm
Width: 6 in. / 15.25 cm

YARN
DK weight (#3 light) yarn, shown in Sirdar *Happy Chenille* (100% polyester, 41 yd. / 38 m per 15 g ball).
Color A: #028 Teddy, 2 balls

DK weight (#3 light) yarn, shown in Rico *Design Ricorumi DK* (100% cotton, 62 yd. / 57.5 m per 25 g ball).
Color B: #078 Khaki, 1 ball
Color C: #057 Chocolate, 1 ball

HOOK
• US E-3.5mm crochet hook

NOTIONS
• Pair of 18 or 20mm orange cat-eye safety eyes
• Polyester stuffing
• Straight pins
• Tapestry needle
• Wire (optional)

GAUGE
Gauge is not critical for this project. Ensure your stitches are tight so the stuffing won't show through.

NOTE
• Trevor's body is made in fluffy chenille, starting from the front. The eyes are shaped as you work with increases and decreases. The other elements are made in cotton yarn and are sewn onto the body. The top of the body is decorated with embroidery to finish.

BODY

With **A**, make a magic ring.
Rnd 1: 6 sc in ring—6 sc.
Rnd 2: 2 sc in each st around—12 sc.
Rnd 3: [Sc in next st, 2 sc in next st] 6 times—18 sc.
Rnd 4: [Sc in next 2 st, 2 sc in next st] 6 times—24 sc.
Rnd 5: [Sc in next 3 st, 2 sc in next st] 6 times—30 sc.
Rnd 6: [Sc in next 4 st, 2 sc in next st] 6 times—36 sc.
Rnd 7: [Sc in next 5 st, 2 sc in next st] 6 times—42 sc.
Rnd 8: [Sc in next 6 st, 2 sc in next st] 6 times—48 sc.
Rnd 9: [Sc in next 7 st, 2 sc in next st] 6 times—54 sc.

Rnd 10: [Sc in next 8 st, 2 sc in next st] 6 times—60 sc.
Next 9 rounds shape the eyes.
Rnd 11: Sc in next 18 st, 3 sc in next st, sc in next 8 st, 3 sc in next st, sc in next 32 st—64 sc.
Rnd 12: Sc in next 18 st, 2 sc in next 3 st, sc in next 8 st, 2 sc in next 3 st, sc in next 32 st—70 sc.
Rnd 13: Sc in next 18 st, [2 sc in next st, sc in next st] 3 times, sc2tog, sc in next 4 st, sc2tog, [2 sc in next st, sc in next st] 3 times, sc in next 32 st—74 sc.
Rnd 14: Sc in next 16 st, [sc2tog, sc in next 8 st, sc2tog, sc in next 4 st] 2 times, sc in next 26 st—70 sc.
Rnds 15–16: Sc around—70 sc.
Rnd 17: Sc in next 16 st, [sc2tog, sc in next 6 st, sc2tog, sc in next 4 st] 2 times, sc in next 26 st—66 sc.
Rnd 18: Sc in next 17 st, sc2tog 3 times, sc in next 6 st, sc2tog 3 times, sc in next 31 st—60 sc.
Rnd 19: Sc around— 60 sc.
Add safety eyes between Rnds 12 and 13, in the middle of the increase section for the eye shaping.
Rnd 20: [Sc2tog, sc in next 18 st] 3 times—57 sc.
Rnd 21: [Sc2tog, sc in next 17 st] 3 times—54 sc.
Rnd 22: [Sc2tog, sc in next 16 st] 3 times—51 sc.
Rnd 23: Sc around—51 sc.
Rnd 24: [Sc2tog, sc in next 15 st] 3 times—48 sc.
Rnd 25: Sc around—48 sc.
Rnd 26: [Sc2tog, sc in next 10 st] 4 times—44 sc.
Rnd 27: Sc around—44 sc.
Rnd 28: [Sc2tog, sc in next 9 st] 4 times—40 sc.
Rnd 29: Sc around—40 sc.
Add stuffing to the front of the Body, take care to stuff tightly around the eyes to exaggerate the shaping.
Rnd 30: [Sc2tog, sc in next 8 st] 4 times—36 sc.
Rnd 31: [Sc2tog, sc in next 7 st] 4 times—32 sc.
Rnd 32: [Sc2tog, sc in next 6 st] 4 times—28 sc.
Rnd 33: [Sc2tog, sc in next 5 st] 4 times—24 sc.
Rnd 34: Sc around—24 sc.
Top up stuffing for the rest of the Body.
Rnd 35: [Sc2tog, sc in next 2 st] 6 times—18 sc.
Rnd 36: [Sc2tog, sc in next st] 6 times—12 sc.
Rnd 37: Sc2tog around—6 sc.
Fasten off and sew up the end.

TUMMY

With **B**, make a magic ring.
Rnd 1: 7 sc in ring—7 sc.
Rnd 2: 2 sc in each st around—14 sc.
Rnd 3: [Sc in next st, 2 sc in next st] 7 times—21 sc.
Rnd 4: [Sc in next 2 st, 2 sc in next st] 7 times—28 sc.
Rnd 5: [Sc in next 3 st, 2 sc in next st] 7 times—35 sc.
Rnd 6: [Sc in next 4 st, 2 sc in next st] 7 times—42 sc.
Rnd 7: [Sc in next 5 st, 2 sc in next st] 7 times—49 sc.
Rnd 8: Sc around—49 sc.
Rnd 9: [Sc in next 6 st, 2 sc in next st] 7 times—56 sc.
Rnd 10: Sc around—56 sc.
Rnd 11: [Sc in next 7 st, 2 sc in next st] 7 times—63 sc.
Rnd 12: Sc around—63 sc.
Rnd 13: [Sc in next 8 st, 2 sc in next st] 7 times—70 sc.
Rnd 14: Sc around—70 sc.
Fasten off, leave a long tail for sewing.

BEHIND THE MAGIC

The toad most frequently used was already named "Harry" before filming began. However, Harry did not enjoy being held, and would try to jump out of Matthew Lewis's hands into his face or onto other actors.

BACK LEGS (MAKE 2)

With **C**, make a magic ring.

Rnd 1: 6 sc in ring—6 sc.

Rnd 2: [2 sc in next st, sc in next st] 3 times—9 sc.

Rnd 3: Sc around—9 sc.

Rnd 4: [2 sc in next st, sc in next 2 st] 3 times—12 sc.

Rnds 5−9: Sc around—12 sc.

Rnd 10: [Sc2tog, sc in next 2 st] 3 times—9 sc.

Rnds 11−12: Sc around—9 sc.

Add some stuffing to the first half of the Leg. Next rounds shape the knee fold.

Rnd 13: Sc in next 4 st, 3 sc in next st, sc in next 4 st—11 sc.

Rnds 14−15: Sc in next 4 st, hdc in next 3 st, sc in next 4 st—11 st (8sc + 3hdc).

Rnd 16: Sc in next 3 st, sc2tog, sc in next st, sc2tog, sc in next 3 st—9 sc.

Rnds 17−19: Sc around—9 sc.

Rnd 20: 2 sc in next st, sc in next 8 st—10 sc.

Rnd 21: Sc in next st, 2 sc in next st, sc in next 8 st—11 sc.

Rnd 22: Sc in next 2 st, 2 sc in next st, sc in next 8 st—12 sc.

Rnds 23−25: Sc around—12 sc.

Rnd 26: Sc in next 8 st, [ch 6, start 2nd ch from hook, sl st in next 3 ch, sc in next 2 ch, sc in next st along the main round] 3 times, sc in next st—12 sc + 3 toes.

Add some stuffing to the second half of the Leg, leaving the knee fold unstuffed.

Rnd 27: Sc2tog 4 times, skip the remaining st—4 sc.

Fasten off, pull the toes forward and close the gap with the yarn tail along the base of the toes. Secure the Leg into a folded pose with a tail of yarn.

FRONT LEGS (MAKE 2)

With **C**, make a magic ring.

Rnd 1: 6 sc in ring—6 sc.

Rnd 2: Sc around—6 sc.

Rnd 3: [2 sc in next st, sc in next 2 st] 2 times—8 sc.

Rnds 4−6: Sc around—8 sc.

Rnd 7: 2 sc in next st, sc in next 7 st—9 sc.

Rnd 8: 3 sc in next st, sc in next 8 st—11 sc.

Rnd 9: Sc in next st, 3 sc in next st, sc in next 9 st—13 sc.

Rnd 10: Sc in next 5 st, sl st in next 8 st—13 st (5 sc + 8 sl st).

Rnd 11: Sc in next st, sc3tog, sc in next 9 st—11 sc.

Rnd 12: Sc3tog, sc in next 8 st—9 sc.

Rnds 13−17: Sc around—9 sc.

Rnd 18: [2 sc in next st, sc in next 2 st] 3 times—12 sc.

Rnd 19: Sc in next 8 st, [ch 6, start 2nd ch from hook, sl st in next 3 ch, sc in next 2 ch, sc in next st along the main round] 3 times, sc in next st—12 sc + 3 toes.

Add some stuffing to the second half of the Leg, leaving the top and the knee fold unstuffed. Alternatively add in some wire.

Rnd 20: Sc2tog 4 times, skip the remaining st—4 sc.

Fasten off, pull the toes forward and close the gap with the yarn tail along the base of the toes.

ASSEMBLY

Place the Tummy over the front of the Body, with the top edge lined up with Rnd 8 of the Body. Pin in place with straight pins and carefully sew all around the shape with the yarn tail, sewing through the back loop of each stitch around the Tummy.

Pin the Back Legs to the sides of the Body and sew in place with yarn tail. Pin the Front Legs to either side of the Tummy and sew in place with a tail.

With **C** embroider the mouth across the top curve of the Tummy. With **C** and **B** embroider spots all over the back and the dip between the eyes.

FLUFFY

Designed by Amy Ting
Skill Level: ⚡ ⚡ ⚡

When a staircase Harry, Ron, and Hermione are ascending suddenly moves during the events of *Harry Potter and the Sorcerer's Stone*, it leaves them on the third floor of Hogwarts, which is forbidden to first-year students. Just as they recognize where they've landed, they notice Mrs. Norris, Argus Filch's cat, and run, as the caretaker is probably close behind. Harry spots a door, and after Hermione unlocks it, they hide, only to realize they're not the only ones in the room. There's a dog in there with them—a twelve-foot-tall, three-headed dog named Fluffy.

Fluffy's size and multiple heads are not initially apparent, as the visual effects crew wanted to fool the audience. At first, Harry, Ron, and Hermione see the head of a sleeping canine. Then the camera moves to show the second head, and then moves again to show the third head. Finally, as Fluffy begins to stand, the camera follows him up, and up, until the trio is confronted by a twelve-foot-tall dog.

This amigurumi Fluffy resembles a Staffordshire Bull Terrier in stature. With his powerful stance and strong, square jaws, he is always ready to take watch—that is, until he hears some delectable music. Crafted and designed with chocolate brown cotton yarn, this amigurumi three-headed guardian of the Sorcerer's Stone brings a playful and endearing spin to the character's fearsome qualities. Fluffy's beady safety eyes emit curiosity, sweetness, and camaraderie, making him irresistibly cute and charming.

"Fluffy? That thing has a name?"
"Well, of course he's got a name. He's mine."

Hermione Granger and Rubeus Hagrid,
Harry Potter and the Sorcerer's Stone

FINISHED MEASUREMENTS
Length: 8 in. / 20.32 cm
Height: 6.5 in. / 15.24 cm
Width: 5 in. / 12.7 cm

YARN
DK weight (#3 light) yarn, shown in Hobbii *Friends Cotton 8/8*, (100% cotton, 82 yd. / 75 m per 1.75 oz. / 50 g ball).
Color A: #20 Americano, 3 balls
Color B: #123 Charcoal, 1 ball

HOOK
• US C-2 / 2.75mm crochet hook

NOTIONS
• Stitch markers
• Three pairs of 12mm black safety eyes
• Three 15mm black safety noses
• Polyester stuffing
• Straight pins
• Textile glue (like UHU)
• Bendable wire, 12 in. / 30.5 cm
• Tapestry needle

GAUGE
Gauge is not critical for this project. Ensure your stitches are tight so the stuffing won't show through.

SPECIAL ABBREVIATIONS
Blo: Work through the back loop only
Flo: Work through the front loop only
Dec (Invisible decrease): Insert hook into front loop of indicated stitch, insert hook into front loop of next stitch (3 loops on hook). Yarn over, pull through 2 loops. Yarn over, pull through remaining 2 loops on hook.
Bo (bobble stitch): Yarn over, insert hook into stitch, yarn over, draw loop back through stitch, yarn

over and pull through 2 loops. Repeat this 3 more times until you have 5 loops on your hook. Yarn over and pull through all 5 loops.

NOTES

- Fluffy is worked in several pieces and requires heavy assembly to ensure the details in his body are exact. There are no shortcuts for this part; expect to spend 2 to 3 hours assembling this project. The body parts are constructed separately and sewn together, with added wire used for structure.
- I highly advise to use the yarn under method of crocheting rather than yarn over. Doing so will result in tighter stitches which is desirable for amigurumi. Yarning over will make a larger piece that may result in a slightly different outcome. The only stitches used in this pattern that will be an exception to this is the bobble stitch (bo) and the invisible decrease (dec)—yarn over for these.
- Pieces worked in the round are continuous rounds with the exception of the neck.

BEHIND THE MAGIC

Fluffy's heads had three distinct personalities. The head on the far left is the shrewd leader, the head on the far right is quick to attack, and the middle head is a bit slow on the uptake of what's happening around him.

HEAD (MAKE 3)

With **A**, make a magic ring.
Rnd 1: 8 sc in magic ring—8 sc.
Rnd 2: Inc around—16 sc.
Rnd 3: (2 sc, 4 inc, 2 sc) x 2—24 sc.
Rnds 4–7: Sc around—24 sc.
Rnd 8: 8 sc, (sc, inc) x 4, 8 sc— 28 sc.
Rnd 9: (3 sc, inc) x 7—35 sc.
Rnd 10: Sc around—35 sc.
Rnd 11: 10 sc, (2 sc, inc) x 5, 10 sc—40 sc.
Rnds 12–15: Sc around—40 sc.
Rnd 16: (8 sc, dec) x 4—36 sc.
Rnd 17: Sc around—36 sc.
Rnd 18: (2 sc, dec, 2 sc) x 6—30 sc.
Rnd 19: (3 sc, dec) x 6—24 sc.
Locate the center of the face with the Head right side up. (The start of the rounds should be at the bottom of the piece.) Insert a safety nose between Rnds 2 and 3. Insert a pair of safety eyes between Rnds 8 and 9, leaving 8 stitches in between.
Rnd 20: Sc around—24 sc.
Rnd 21: (Sc, dec, sc) x 6—18 sc.
Begin stuffing the Head.
Rnd 22: (Sc, dec) x 6—12 sc.
Rnd 23: (Dec) x 6—6 sc.
Fasten off and leave a short tail to weave in. Stuff a little more right before closing up. Thread the needle with the yarn tail and work through the front loops only to cinch the hole closed.

FOREHEAD CREASE

Note: The forehead crease and the eyelids are worked with the same strand of yarn. The forehead crease is created by a series of indentations, similar to making eye indentations in amigurumi.

Step 1: Locate the midline of the face and mark the stitches to be looped over to create the forehead crease with straight pins between every 2 rounds, starting between Rnds 8 and 9 and ending between Rnds 12 and 13.
Step 2: Cut a 20 in. / 50 cm strand of yarn in **A** and thread a needle with it. Insert the needle from the bottom of the Head and out of the stitch marked between Rnds 8 and 9.
Step 3: Go up one round to create a loop and insert your needle back into the Head. Come back out of the same stitch we entered through and tug. This creates the first "indentation."
Step 4: Repeat Step 3 for the other two stitches marked with straight pins.
Step 5: At the end, use your fingers to "pinch" the sides of the forehead to make the crease more pronounced. Without cutting the yarn, continue on to creating the eyelids.

EYELIDS

Step 1: Weave the needle to the inner corner of either eye.
Step 2: Apply a tiny dab of fabric glue over the top of the eye to hold the yarn in place and go back into the Head where the outer corner of the eye is.
Step 3: Repeat Steps 1 and 2 to create a thicker eyelid to make Fluffy's intimidating stare.
Step 4: Do the same process for the other eye.
Weave in and bury the tails.

EARS (MAKE 6)

With **A**, make a magic ring.
Rnd 1: 6 sc in ring—6 sc.
Rnd 2: (Sc, inc) x3—9 sc.
Rnd 3: Sc around—9 sc.
Rnd 4: (2 sc, inc) x 3—12 sc.
Rnd 5: Sc around—12 sc.
Flatten the piece and make 6 sc
   through both layers to crochet
   it closed. Fasten off and leave
   a 12 in. / 30 cm tail for sewing.

ASSEMBLY

Step 1: Position each Ear against
   the Head with the right side
   of the sc edge facing down so
   that the back bumps are facing
   up. This will make assembly
   much smoother.
Step 2: Sew each Ear between
   Rnds 16 and 17, 4 stitches
   apart.
Step 3: Pinch the tip of the Ear
   to shape them in a curve.
Weave in and bury the tails.

BODY

With **A**, make a magic ring.
Rnd 1: 6 sc in ring—6 sc.
Rnd 2: Inc around—12 sc.
Rnd 3: (Sc, inc) x 6—18 sc.
Rnd 4: (Sc, inc, sc) x 6—24 sc.
Rnd 5: (3 sc, inc) x 6—30 sc.
Rnd 6: (2 sc, inc, 2 sc) x 6—36 sc.
Rnd 7: (5 sc, inc) x 6—42 sc.
Rnd 8: Sc around—42 sc.
Rnd 9: 7 sc, (sc, inc) x 5, 8 sc,
   (sc, inc) x 5, 7 sc—52 sc.
Rnds 10—17: Sc around—52 sc.
Rnd 18: (Sc, dec) x 5, 22 sc,
   (sc, dec) x 5—42 sc.
Rnd 19: (5 sc, dec) x 6—36 sc.
Rnds 20—23: Sc around—36 sc.
Rnd 24: (2 sc, inc) x 2, 24 sc,
   (2 sc, inc) x 2—40 sc.
Rnds 25—26: Sc around—40 sc.
Rnd 27: (2 sc, inc) x 2, 28 sc,
   (2 sc, inc) x 2—44 sc.

Rnds 28—29: Sc around—44 sc.
Rnd 30: (20 sc, dec) x 2—42 sc.
Begin stuffing and continue to
   stuff as you work.
Rnd 31: (5 sc, dec) x 6—36 sc.
Rnd 32: Sc around—36 sc.
Rnd 33: (2 sc, dec, 2 sc) x 6—
   30 sc.
Rnd 34: Sc around—30 sc.
Rnd 35: (3 sc, dec) x 6—24 sc.
Rnd 36: (Sc, dec, sc) x 6—18 sc.
Rnd 37: (Sc, dec) x 6—12 sc.
Rnd 38: (Dec) x 6—6 sc.

Fasten off and leave a short tail
   to weave in. Stuff a little more
   right before closing. Thread
   the needle with the yarn tail
   and go through the front loops
   only to cinch the hole closed.
Fluffy's back is the straighter side
   of the Body, and the belly
   side of the Body is the more
   curved. Mark it accordingly
   before assembling the pieces.

NECK (MAKE 3)

Note: This is the only Body part that will be worked in joined rounds and the ch 1 will count as the first stitch. When looking at the piece, Rnds 2 and 3 will appear as one round. Leave 18 in. of yarn for sewing before starting your initial chain.

Starting with **A**.

Rnd 1: Ch 26, sl st into the first ch to create a loop. *Make sure that the chain isn't twisted.* Ch 1 (counts as the first st), 25 sc, sl st into the first st in **B** to join the rnd—26 sc.

Rnd 2: Ch 1, (blo), sl st loosely around, sl st into the first st to join the rnd—26 sc.

Rnd 3: Ch 1, (blo), sc around, sl st into the first st in **A** to join the rnd—26 sc.

Rnd 4: Ch 1, (blo), sl st loosely around, sl st into the first st to join the rnd—26 sc.

Leave 18 in. of yarn for sewing and fasten off.

ASSEMBLY

Note: Don't be afraid to rearrange the positioning until you're happy with it! I personally like to create a more realistic pose with each Head facing a slightly different direction versus three neat and symmetrical Heads all lined up perfectly. Sewing each Head at a slight angle makes Fluffy appear to be scanning his surroundings suspiciously.

Step 1: Position each Head on the Body so that they're looking up. Keep in mind that the Body we are sewing onto is rounded. Mark where the Head will be attached to the Neck with straight pins.

Step 2: Working through both loops, sew the Neck to the Head using the yarn tail attached to the foundation chain.

Center Head: Between Rnds 19 and 20.

Left Head: Spanning Rnds 13 and 20.

Right Head: Spanning Rnds 14 and 21.

Step 3: Working through both loops of the sl sts, sew the Necks onto the Body with the other yarn tail. When you have a few stitches remaining, stuff the piece well to create a bulky, strong Neck.

Center Head: Between Rnds 4 and 5.
Left Head: Spanning Rnds 6 and 14.
Right Head: Spanning Rnds 5 and 13.

FRONT LEGS (MAKE 2)

With **A**, make a magic ring.
Rnd 1: 8 sc in ring—8 sc.
Rnd 2: Inc around—16 sc.
We will create the toes in the next round. Be sure to make the sc in between each toe very tight to make each toe pop out.
Rnd 3: (Bo, sc) x 4, 8 sc—16 sc.
Rnd 4: (Sc, dec) x 3, 7 sc—13 sc.
Rnd 5: Sc, 3 dec, 6 sc—10 sc.
Rnds 6−8: Sc around—10 sc.
Cut 6 inches of wire and fold it in half. Twist the tips so that they don't stick out and insert it into the foot. Stuff as you go.
Rnd 9: (2 sc, inc) x 3, sc—13 sc.
Rnds 10−12: Sc around—13 sc.
Next, we will create the "bend" in the Front Legs. Depending on your tension, the start of your round may have shifted. Add or undo a few sc as necessary to start at the side of your piece with the toes pointing to your left.
Rnd 13: Sc, (sc, inc) x 3, (sc, dec) x 2—14 sc.
Rnds 14−16: Sc around—14 sc.
For the right Leg, undo 3 stitches to get to the back of the Leg (aligned with the heel). For the left Leg, add 5 stitches to get to the front of the Leg (aligned with the toes). The next round will make the outer side of each Front Leg a bit longer

so that it fits around Fluffy's rounded chest.
Rnd 17 (partial rnd): Hdc, dc, dc, hdc, sc—no st count.
Stuff well. Fasten off and leave a tail for sewing.

ASSEMBLY

Step 1: Use straight pins to position each Front Leg against the Body with the toes facing forward.
Step 2: Sew them to the Body spanning Rnds 10 to 15, 12 sts apart on the belly side.
Step 3: Shape the Front Legs to bend with a boxy, intimidating stance.
Step 4: Weave in and bury the excess tails.

HIND LEGS (MAKE 2)

With **A**, make magic ring.
Rnd 1: 8 sc in ring—8 sc.
Rnd 2: Inc around—16 sc.
We will create the toes in the next rnd. Be sure to make the sc in between each toe very tight to make each toe pop out.
Rnd 3: (Bo, sc) x 4, 8 sc—16 sc.
Rnd 4: (Sc, dec) x 3, 7 sc—13 sc.
Rnd 5: Sc, 3 dec, 6 sc—10 sc.
Rnds 6−8: Sc around—10 sc.
Cut 6 inches of wire and fold it in half. Twist the ends so that they don't stick out and insert it into the foot. Stuff as you go.
Rnd 9: (2 sc, inc) x 3, sc—13 sc.
Rnds 10−11: 8 sl st, 5 hdc—13 sc.
Rnd 12: (2 sc, inc) x 4, inc—18 sc.
Rnd 13: Sc around—18 sc.
Rnd 14: (Sc, inc, sc) x 6—24 sc.
Rnds 15−16: Sc around—24 sc.
Rnd 17: (Sc, dec, sc) x 6—18 sc.

Rnd 18: (Sc, dec) x 6—12 sc.
Stuff the thigh (Rnds 12 to 18) very lightly because it will be sewn flat against the Body.
Rnd 19: (Dec) x 6—6 sc.
Fasten off and leave a long tail for sewing. Thread the needle with the yarn tail and go through the front loops only to cinch the hole closed.

ASSEMBLY

Note: Assembly for the Hind Legs will be crucial in helping Fluffy to stand upright without tilting over!
Step 1: Use straight pins to position each Hind Leg against the Body with the toes facing forward.
Step 2: Position the center of Rnd 19 of the Hind Leg to fall between Rnds 26 and 27 of the Body. Sew the Hind Legs onto the Body spanning Rnds 25 to 32, 12 sts apart. The Legs should appear to be "lurching forward."
Step 3: Weave in and bury the excess tails.

TAIL

With **A**, make a magic ring.
Rnd 1: 6 sc in ring—6 sc.
Rnd 2: Sc around—6 sc.
Fasten off and leave a yarn tail for sewing.

ASSEMBLY

Sew the Tail spanning Rnds 35 and 36 of the Body. Bury the excess yarn tail.

NORBERT

Designed by Aaron Hayden
Skill Level: ✚ ✚

There is nothing Hogwarts groundskeeper Rubeus Hagrid wants more than a dragon, and in *Harry Potter and the Sorcerer's Stone*, he gets his wish, having acquired a dragon egg. Since doing this is frowned upon, Hagrid tries to keep it a secret—and then Harry, Ron, and Hermione come to see him, just as the dragon egg is about to hatch.

Hagrid sets the dragon egg on a small table, where it begins to judder and rock. Suddenly, the egg cracks, and emerging from an explosion of green gas, a dragonet appears. Hagrid names the Norwegian Ridgeback "Norbert." The tiny dragon is adorable, until it sneezes out its first flame and singes Hagrid's beard (with a digital fire).

The filmmakers decided the just-born Ridgeback wouldn't have a developed ridge, but he does have leathery, bat-shaped wings; a bony rib cage; wrinkly skin; horns on his head; and a body like a lizard's. His large head, feet, and wings are out of proportion to the rest of his body, which is true for any baby mammal.

A symbol of the bonds formed in unexpected places, this delightful amigurumi of Norbert, the Norwegian Ridgeback dragon, is a tribute to the heartwarming tale of how Hagrid came to acquire him. The endearing amigurumi dragon is crocheted with olive green yarn, and measures approximately 10 inches in length, reflecting the small size of the baby dragon as portrayed in the story. Norbert is worked in multiple pieces sewn together. With intricate detailing and the gentle curve of its wings, every stitch brings to life the magical creature Hagrid desires to secretly raise in his hut on the grounds of Hogwarts castle.

"Isn't he beautiful? Oh, bless him, look, he knows his mummy. Hello, Norbert."

Rubeus Hagrid, *Harry Potter and the Sorcerer's Stone*

FINISHED MEASUREMENTS
Height: 4 in. / 10 cm
Width: 7 in. / 18 cm
Length: 10 in. / 25 cm

YARN
Worsted weight (#4 medium) yarn, shown in Lion Brand *Basic Stitch* (100% acrylic, 185 yd. / 170 m per 3.5 oz. / 100 g skein) in #202-132
Color: Olive, 1 skein.

HOOK
• US E-4 / 3.5mm crochet hook

NOTIONS
• Stitch markers
• Pair of 12mm safety eyes
• Polyester fiberfill
• Tapestry needle

GAUGE
Gauge is not critical for this project. Ensure your stitches are tight so the stuffing won't show through.

WING SECTIONS (MAKE 4)

Row 1: Ch 3 and turn—3 ch.
Row 2: 2 inc, ch 1 and turn—4 sc.
Row 3: 1 inc, 2 sc, 1 inc, ch 1 and turn—6 sc.
Row 4: 1 inc, 4 sc, 1 inc, ch 1 and turn—8 sc.
Row 5: 1 inc, 6 sc, 1 inc, ch 1 and turn—10 sc.
Row 6: 1 inc, 8 sc, 1 inc, ch 1 and turn—12 sc.
Row 7: 1 inc, 10 sc, 1 inc, ch 1 and turn—14 sc.
Row 8: 1 inc, 12 sc, 1 inc, ch 1 and turn—16 sc.
Row 9: 1 inc, 14 sc, 1 inc, ch 1 and turn—18 sc.
Row 10: 1 inc, 16 sc, 1 inc, ch 1 and turn—20 sc.
Fasten off.
TO ASSEMBLE: Place two of the Wing sections together centered on top of each other and connect them to form one Wing by working around the outside edges to join them.

BEHIND THE MAGIC

A prop dragon egg set on Hagrid's table had air jets blowing underneath it to make it wobble before it hatched. Norbert himself, however, was a digital creation.

1. Ch 1 and turn, 1 sc through both of the Wing Sections, 1 hdc, 2 dc, 1 hdc, 1 sc, 1 sl st, 1 sc, 1 hdc, 2 dc, 1 hdc, 1 sc, 1 sl st, 1 sc, 1 hdc, 2 dc, 1 hdc, 1 sc—20 st.
2. Continue up the side of the Wing, 9 sc—9 sc.
3. Once you reach the top tip of the Wing, ch 4, turn and in the second loop from the hook, place 1 sl st and repeat twice more down the chain to create a finger—3 st.
4. Sc in the next stitch at the Wing tip and ch 4, turn and in the second loop from the hook, place 1 sl st and repeat twice more down the chain to create another finger—3 st.
5. 9 sc down the remaining side of the Wing closing the opening. Make sure to stuff the loose threads inside before closing completely. Do not stuff. Fasten off, leaving a long tail for sewing to the Body.
Repeat these steps a second time to complete both Wings.

LEGS (MAKE 2)

Make a magic ring.
Rnd 1: 8 sc in ring—8 sc.
Rnd 2: Inc x 8—16 sc.
Rnd 3: (1 sc, inc) x 8—24 sc.
Rnd 4: (2 sc, dec) x 6—18 sc.
Rnd 5: (4 sc, dec) x 3—15 sc.
Rnd 6: 15 sc—15 sc.
Rnd 7: 15 sc—15 sc.
Rnd 8: (4 sc, inc) x 3—18 sc.
Rnd 9: (2 sc, inc) x 6—24 sc.
Rnd 10: 24 sc—24 sc.
Fasten off, leaving a long tail for sewing to the Body.

LITTLE HORNS (MAKE 2)

Make a magic ring.
Rnd 1: 6 sc in ring—6 sc.
Rnds 2−4: 6 sc—6 sc.
Fasten off, leaving a long tail for sewing to the Body.

BIG HORNS (MAKE 2)

Make a magic ring.
Rnd 1: 6 sc in ring—6 sc.
Rnds 2−6: 6 sc—6 sc.
Fasten off, leaving a long tail for sewing to the Body.

BODY

Make a magic ring. Start stuffing as you go.
Rnd 1: 6 sc in ring—6) sc.
Rnd 2: Inc x 6—12 sc.
Rnd 3: (1 sc, inc) x 6—18 sc.
Rnd 4: (2 sc, inc) x 6—24 sc.
Rnds 5−6: 24 sc—24 sc.
Rnd 7: (3 sc, inc) x 6—30 sc.
Rnd 8: (4 sc, inc) x 6—36 sc.
Rnds 9−11: 36 sc—36 sc.
Rnd 12: (8 sc, inc) x 4—40 sc.
Rnd 13: (4 sc, inc) x 8—48 sc.
Rnds 14−16: 48 sc—48 sc.
Continue stuffing firmly as you go, insert the eyes between Rnds 9 and 10 with 14 stitches between them.
Rnd 17: (4 sc, dec) x 8—40 sc.
Rnd 18: (8 sc , dec) x 4—36 sc.
Rnd 19: (4 sc, dec) x 6—30 sc.
Rnd 20: (3 sc, dec) x 6—24 sc.
Rnd 21: (4 sc, dec) x 4—20 sc.
Rnd 22: (4 sc, inc) x 4—24 sc.
Rnd 23: (3 sc, inc) x 6—30 sc.
Rnd 24: (5 sc, inc) x 5—35 sc.
Rnds 25−27: 35 sc—35 sc.
Rnd 28: (6 sc, inc) x 5—40 sc.
Rnds 29−36: 40 sc—40 sc.

Rnd 37: (3 sc, dec) x 8—32 sc.
Rnd 38: (2 sc, dec) x 8—24 sc.
Rnd 39: (2 sc, dec) x 6—18 sc.
Rnds 40—43: 18 sc—18 sc.
Rnd 44: 16 sc, dec—17 sc.
Rnds 45—46: 17 sc—17 sc.
Rnd 47: 2 dec, 13 sc—15 sc.
Rnds 48—51: 15 sc—15 sc.
Rnd 52: (3 sc, dec) x 3—12 sc.
Rnds 53—54: 12 sc—12 sc.
Rnd 55: (2 sc, dec) x 3—9 sc.
Rnds 56—57: 9 sc—9 sc.
Rnd 58: (1 sc, dec) x 3—6 sc.
Rnds 59—60: 6 sc—6 sc.
Fasten off, leaving a short tail and
   close the opening.

FINISHING

Lay the Body down on a flat
   surface and mark the center
   front and center back with a
   stitch marker, this will make it
   easier to sew the Body parts
   on symmetrically. Sew the
   parts to the Body as follows.
Wings: Between Rnds 25 and 29
   with 4 or 5 stitches between
   them centered on the back of
   the Body.
Legs: Between Rnds 29 and 37
   with 6 or 7 stitches between
   them centered on the
   underside of the Body.
Big Horns: Between Rnds 15
   and 16 with 5 or 6 stitches
   between them centered with
   the eyes on top of the head.
Little Horns: between Rnds 16
   and 17 with 14 or 15 stitches
   between them centered with
   the eyes on top of the head.

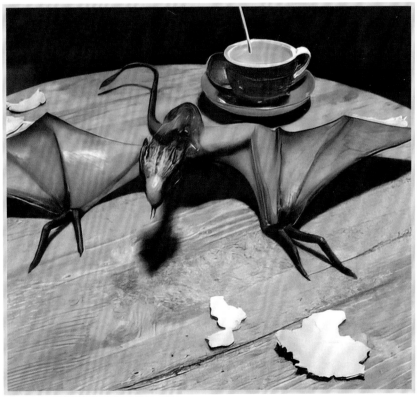

BUCKBEAK

Designed by Laura Rook
Skill level: ⚡ ⚡

In *Harry Potter and the Prisoner of Azkaban*, Rubeus Hagrid is named the new Care of Magical Creatures professor, and for his first lesson, brings out the magnificent Hippogriff named Buckbeak. A Hippogriff is a mythical creature who is part horse and part eagle. Unlike many of the mixed species in the Harry Potter films, the Hippogriff has a definite divide between his two aspects.

The visual and digital designers visited both bird sanctuaries and horse stables to observe how each animal's body was structured for its movements. However, director Alfonso Cuarón specified that while Buckbeak would be graceful in the air, he would be clumsy on the ground, with the gawkiness of a "sloppy teenager."

There were three life-sized Buckbeak models in addition to his digital version. One Hippogriff stood in the background of shots. The second, seen sitting in the pumpkin patch at Hagrid's hut, could move his wings, eyes, neck, tongue, and nostrils. The third could spread his wings, curl his claws, and move his right foreleg and left hind leg to bow.

This is a masterpiece of amigurumi artistry inspired by the majestic Hippogriff, Buckbeak. The fusion of creativity and craftsmanship captures the essence of this beloved creature in every curve and detail. This magical creature is worked from the bottom up with Buckbeak's head crocheted separately. Some of the delicate feathers are worked into the stitches, and others are lovingly sewn on. The wings are crocheted separately to help form the iconic feature of Buckbeak's magnificent silhouette.

FINISHED MEASUREMENTS
Height: 8 in. / 20.5 cm tall
Length: 6.4 in. / 16.25 cm

YARN
Worsted weight (#4 medium) shown in Redheart *Super Saver* (100% acrylic, 364 yd. / 333 m per 7 oz. / 198 g skein).
Color G: #640340 Dusty Gray, 1 skein
Color A: #640313 Aran, 1 skein

HOOK
• US C-2 / 3.0mm crochet hook

NOTIONS
• Stitch markers
• Pair of 8mm safety eyes
• Polyester fiberfill
• Tapestry needle

GAUGE
Gauge is not critical for this project. Ensure your stitches are tight so the stuffing won't show through.

SPECIAL ABBREVIATIONS
Back Loop Only (blo): Work through back loop only
Front Loop Only (flo): Work through front loop only

"Isn't he beautiful? Say hello to Buckbeak."
Rubeus Hagrid, *Harry Potter and the Prisoner of Azkaban*

BACK LEGS (MAKE 2)

With **G**, make a magic ring.
Rnd 1: Sc 6 in ring—6 st.
Rnd 2: Sc in blo of each st—6 st.
Rnd 3: Sc in each st—6 st.
Rnd 4: Sc in each st—6 st.
Rnd 5: (Sc x 2, inc) x 2—8 st.
Rnd 6: Sc in each st—8 st.
Rnd 7: Sc in each st—8 st.
Rnd 8: (2 hdc) x 2, sc, (dec) x 2, sc—8 st.
Rnd 9: Sc in each st—8 st.
Rnd 10: Sc in each st—8 st.
Rnd 11: (Sc x 3, inc) x 2—10 st.
Rnd 12: (Sc x 4, inc) x 2—12 st.
Rnd 13: Sc in each st—12 st.
Rnd 14: Sc in each st—12 st.
Leg 1: Flatten the Leg, and with the bend of the Leg on the left, mark the front middle stitch. This is where you will join to the Body.
Leg 2: Flatten the Leg, and with the bend of the Leg on the right, mark the middle of the side of the Leg. This is where you will join to the Body.
Stuff Legs firmly.

FRONT LEGS (MAKE 2)

With **G**, make a magic ring, and work the first 3 rounds loosely.
Rnd 1: Sc 6 in ring—6 st.
Rnd 2: Join with sl st. Do not ch. In flo, sl st in 1st st (mark open loop so it's easy to find for the next round) (ch 3, sl st in back bump of 2nd and 3rd ch, sl st in next st) 3 times. This forms the talons. Flo sc in last 2 st.
Rnd 3: Sc in each of the open loops from Rnd 2.
Rnds 4–6: Sc in each st—6 st.
Rnd 7: (Sc x 2, inc) x 2—8 st.
Rnd 8: Sc in each st—8 st.
Rnd 9: (Sc x 3, inc) x 2—10 st.
Rnd 10: Sc in each st, **on last st change to A**—10 st.
Rnds 11–13: Sc in each st—10 st.
Rnd 14: (Sc x 4, inc) x 2—12 st.
Front Leg 1: Fasten off and mark Stitch 5.
Front Leg 2: Do not fasten off. Mark Stitch 4. Continue from Front Leg 2 into the Body.

BODY

Note: Mark the first stitch of each round.
From Front Leg 2, ch 2, and join to Front Leg 1 in marked st.
Rnd 1: Sc 9 on Front Leg 1, ch 12, join in marked st of Back Leg 1, sc 9 on Back Leg 1, ch 2, join Back Leg 2 in marked st, sc 9 on Back Leg, ch 12, join to Front Leg in marker, sc 9 on last Leg. This rnd should end before the first ch 2 made—64 st.
Rnd 2: Sc in each ch and each st around—64 st.
Rnds 3–4: Sc in each st—64 st.
Rnd 5: Sc, dec, sc x 6, dec, sc x 11, dec, sc x 2, inc, sc x 5, dec x 2, sc x 4, inc, sc x 2, dec, sc x 11, dec, sc x 6—59 st.
Rnd 6: Sc x 10, dec, sc x 10, dec, (sc dec) x 4, sc x 10 dec, sc x 11—52 st.
Rnd 7: Dec, sc x 10, dec, sc x 11, dec, sc x 11, dec, sc x 12—48 st.
Rnd 8: (Sc x 3, dec) x 2, sc x 4, dec, (sc x 2, dec) x 2, dec, (sc x 2, dec) x 2, (sc x 4, dec) x 2, sc x 2—38 st.
Rnd 9: Sc x 17, dec x 2, sc x 17—36 st.
Rnd 10: Sc x 12, dec, sc x 3, dec x 2, sc x 3, dec, sc x 10—32 st.
Rnd 11: Sc x 8, skip 17 st, sc x 7. **Change to G in last st.** This makes the start of the neck. Leave the back open. The neck and head have color changes.
Rnd 12: (Sc G, sc A) x 3, sc 5 G, sc 2 A, sc G, sc A—15 st.
Rnd 13: Sc 4 G, sc A, sc 8 G, sc A, sc G—15 st.
Rnd 14: Sc 15 G.
Rnd 15: Sc 15 G, **attach A in last st**.
Rnd 16: Sc A, inc G, sc A, inc G, sc A, sc 9 G, sc A—17 st.
Rnd 17: Sc 2 A, inc x 3 A, sc 4 A, sc 4 G, sc 3 A—19 st.
Rnd 18: Sc 9 A, sc 8 G, sc 2 A—19 st.
Rnd 19: With A, inc, (sc, inc) x 3, inc, sc, with G, sc x 10—24 st.
Rnds 20–21: Sc 14 A, sc 10 G—24 st.

BEHIND THE MAGIC

Every feather on the three life-size models of Buckbeak was individually inserted and glued on by hand.

Rnd 22: With **A** sc x 6, dec, 6 sc, with **G**, dec, sc x 6, dec—21 st.

Rnd 23: With **G** (sc x 5, dec) x 3—1 8 st.

Insert safety eyes between Rnds 21 and 22, with about 6 to 7 st in between.

Rnd 24: With **G** (sc x 4, dec) x 3—15 st.

Stuff neck and head firmly. Sew head opening closed.

BELLY

With **A**, ch 3.

Row 1: Sc 2—2 st.

Row 2: Sc 2—2 st.

Row 3: Sc, inc—3 st.

Row 4: Inc, sc, inc—5 st.

Rows 5–16: Sc 5—5 st.

Row 17: Dec, sc, dec—3 st.

Row 18: Dec, sc—2 st.

Rows 19–20: Sc 2—2 st.

Fasten off, leaving a long tail for sewing.

WINGS (MAKE 2)

With **G**, ch 3.

Row 1: Sc 2—2 st.

Row 2: Sc, inc—3 st.

Row 3: Inc, sc, inc—5 st.

Rows 4–9: sc in each st—5 st.

Row 10: Dec, sc, dec—3 st.

Row 11: Sc, dec—2 st.

Fasten off, do not weave in ends yet.

Wing 1 FEATHERS

Row 1: With beginning and tail end of yarn on the bottom of your work, join yarn in the top corner. Sc 10 st evenly along the long side of the Wing, sc 2 in the corner, then sc one more st on the short side of Wing, before the knot of the other tail—13 st.

Row 2: Turn your work. Ch 1 (sc in next st, ch 2, sl st in back bump in 2nd ch from hook, sc) in same st. Repeat 13 x leaving a long tail for sewing.

Wing 2 FEATHERS

Row 1: With beginning and tail end of yarn on the bottom of your work, join the yarn in the bottom right corner. Sc, sc 2 in the corner, sc 10 evenly down the long side of the Wing.

Row 2: Repeat Row 2 from other Wing.

Attach both Wings to the opposite sides of the Body.

BEAK

With **G**, ch 7.

Row 1: Sc 6 in back bumps of chain.

Row 2: Sc, hdc, 2dc in the next st, ch 2 sl in back bump of ch, 2dc in the next st, hdc, sc.

Fasten off. Fold the Beak and sew in the tops of the stitches from Row 2 with the exception of the middle dcs and ch stitch. This will leave the sides and the first row not sewn. Mold to the front of the head, 1 row below the eyes.

HEAD FEATHERS (MAKE 2)

With **G**, sc 6 and fasten off. Attach each one close by an eye so it covers it a little, giving Buckbeak a little bit of a squint.

MIDDLE HEAD FEATHERS

With **G**, ch 6, sc x 5, ch 1, turn. (sc, ch 2, slip st in back bump in 2nd ch from hook, sc) x 5. Fasten off with long tail for sewing. Attach to the top of the head, right on top of where you closed the head and stretching to meet the two Head Feathers.

TAIL

Cut six strands of **G** and six strands of **A** about 10 in. long. Fold in half and knot in four-strand sections to the rear of Buckbeak.

CORNISH PIXIE

Designed by Amanda Molloy
Skill Level: ✎ ✎

Cornish pixies are mischievous creatures, who gleefully cause destruction given the opportunity. Professor Gilderoy Lockhart, the new Defense Against the Dark Arts professor in *Harry Potter and the Chamber of Secrets*, uses them in a demonstration for his first class. Just before lifting the cover from their bell-shaped cage, Lockhart asks the class not to scream, for it might provoke them! Instead of screaming, when the cover is removed, most of the class laugh at the eight-inch-tall creatures with wings and pointed faces who rattle the cage while giggling and sticking their arms through the bars.

Cornish pixies are colored an electric blue. Cornwall in England is known for its Cornish Blue pottery, Cornish Blue roosters, and an award-winning Cornish Blue cheese.

This Cornish Pixie amigurumi captures the spirit of the mischievous little creatures that wreak havoc in Professor Lockhart's Defense Against the Dark Arts class. Don't be fooled by his small size and big smile—Cornish pixies have a reputation for causing mayhem. To construct your Cornish pixie, the legs, body, and head are worked up in one piece from the bottom to the top. The arms, pointy ears, antennae, and delicate wings are crocheted separately and sewn on at the end.

"Cornish pixies?"

"Freshly caught Cornish pixies. Laugh if you will, Mr. Finnigan. But pixies can be devilishly tricky little blighters."

Seamus Finnigan and Professor Gilderoy Lockhart,
Harry Potter and the Chamber of Secrets

FINISHED MEASUREMENTS
Height: 6 in. / 15.25 cm (from head to feet)
Width: 4 in. / 10 cm (from wingtip to wingtip)

YARN
Worsted weight (#4 medium) yarn, shown in WeCrochet *Brava*, (100% acrylic, 218 yd. / 200 m per 3½ oz. / 100 g skein).
Color A: #28422 Cornflower, 1 skein (approx. 90 yd. required)
Color B: #28455 White, 1 skein (approx. 20 yd. required)

HOOK
• US E-4 / 3.5mm crochet hook

NOTIONS
• Stitch markers
• Polyester stuffing
• Small amount of black embroidery thread for eyelashes and mouth (optional)
• Pair of 9mm safety eyes (optional, eyes can also be embroidered)
• Tapestry needle

GAUGE
Gauge is not critical for this project. Ensure your stitches are tight so the stuffing won't show through between stitches.

SPECIAL ABBREVIATION
Invisible Decrease (inv dec): Insert hook into front loop of indicated stitch, insert hook into front loop of next stitch (3 loops on hook). Yarn over, pull through 2 loops. Yarn over, pull through remaining 2 loops on hook.

NOTES
• Pattern is worked in continuous rounds without joining. Use a stitch marker to keep track of the rounds.

- Legs, body, and head are worked in one piece from bottom to top. Arms, ears, antennae, and wings are worked up separately and sewn on at the end.
- The legs, arms, head, antennae, and ears are worked in color A (Cornflower).
- The wings are worked in color B (White).

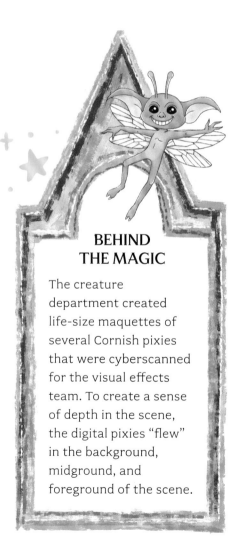

BEHIND THE MAGIC

The creature department created life-size maquettes of several Cornish pixies that were cyberscanned for the visual effects team. To create a sense of depth in the scene, the digital pixies "flew" in the background, midground, and foreground of the scene.

LEGS, BODY, HEAD

FIRST LEG

With **A**, make a magic ring.
Rnd 1: 6 sc in ring—6 sc.
Rnd 2: 2 sc in each st around—12 sc.
Rnds 3–10: Sc in each st around—12 sc.
Fasten off.

SECOND LEG

Repeat instructions for first Leg. Do not fasten off. Continue to instructions below to join the two Legs.

JOIN LEGS

Rnd 11: Ch 2 on second Leg then join Legs with a sc in the next sc on first Leg (after where you fastened off). Sc in next 11 sts around first Leg, sc in each of the 2 ch sts, sc in next 12 sts around second Leg, sc in each of the 2 ch sts (this will be on the other side of the chain)—28 sc.
Stuff the Legs. Continue working up the Body, stuffing as work progresses.

BODY

Rnd 12: *2 sc in first st, sc next 13 sts, repeat from * around—30 sc.
Rnds 13–15: Sc in each st around—30 sc.
Rnd 16: *Inv dec, sc next 8 sts, repeat from * around—27 sc.
Rnds 17–18: Sc in each st around—27 sc.
Rnd 19: *Inv dec, sc next 7 sts, repeat from * around—24 sc.
Rnd 20: Sc in each st around—24 sc.

Rnd 21: *Inv dec, sc next 6 sts, repeat from * around—21 sc.
Rnd 22: Sc in each st around—21 sc.
Rnd 23: *Inv dec, sc next 5 sts, repeat from * around—18 sc.
Rnd 24: Sc in each st around—18 sc.
Rnd 25: *Inv dec, sc next st, repeat from * around—12 sc.
Rnd 26: Sc in each st around—12 sc.
Next, increases will be worked again to form the Head.

HEAD

Rnd 27: *2 sc in first st, sc next st, repeat from * around—18 sc.
Rnd 28: *2 sc in first st, sc next 2 sts, repeat from * around—24 sc.
Rnd 29: *2 sc in first st, sc next 3 sts, repeat from * around—30 sc.
Rnd 30: *2 sc in first st, sc next 4 sts, repeat from * around—36 sc.
Rnds 31–39: Sc in each st around—36 sc.
Insert safety eyes between Rnds 36 and 37 approximately 7 stitches apart in the center of the face. If adding eyelashes, stitch them using the embroidery thread before securing the safety eyes in place. Also use the embroidery thread to stitch a mouth. Then use a small amount of **B** to make two downward stitches below the mouth to form the teeth.
Rnd 40: *Inv dec, sc next 4 sts, repeat from * around—30 sc.
Start stuffing the Head. Continue stuffing throughout the next rounds making sure enough stuffing has been added before the opening is too small.

Rnd 41: *Inv dec, sc next 3 sts, repeat from * around—24 sc.

Rnd 42: * Inv dec, sc next 2 sts, repeat from * around—18 sc.

Rnd 43: * Inv dec, sc next st, repeat from * around—12 sc.

Rnd 44: Inv dec in each st around—6 sc.

Fasten off. Sew top of Head closed. Weave in all ends and cut yarn. Set aside for assembly later.

ARMS (MAKE 2)

With **A**, make a magic ring.

Rnd 1: 6 sc in ring—6 sc.

Rnd 2: *2 sc in first st, sc next st, repeat from * around—9 sc.

Rnds 3–11: Sc in each st around—9 sc.

Fasten off. Stuff the bottom half of the Arm, flatten the top and sew closed. Leave a tail to sew Arms to the Body. Repeat instructions for second Arm. Set Arms aside for assembly.

ANTENNAE (MAKE 2)

With **A**, make a magic ring.

Rnd 1: 4 sc in ring—4 st.

Rnd 2: *2 sc in first st, sc next st, repeat from * around—6 st.

Rnds 3–6: Sc in each st around—6 st.

Fasten off leaving a tail to sew onto Head. Repeat instructions for the second Antenna. Set Antennae aside for assembly.

EARS (MAKE 2)

With **A**, make a magic ring.

Rnd 1: 6 sc in ring—6 sc.

Rnd 2: Sc in each st around—6 sc.

Rnd 3: *2 sc in first st, sc next st, repeat from * around—9 sc.

Rnd 4: Sc in each st around—9 sc.

Rnd 5: *2 sc in first st, sc next 2 sts, repeat from * around—12 sc.

Rnds 6–7: Sc in each st around—12 sc.

Rnd 8: *2 sc in first st, sc next 3 sts, repeat from * around—15 sc.

Rnd 9: Sc in each st around—15 sc.

Rnd 10: *Inv dec, sc next 3 sts, repeat from * around—12 sc.

Rnd 11: *Inv dec, sc next 2 sts, repeat from * around—9 sc.

Fasten off, leaving a tail for sewing onto Head. Repeat instructions for second Ear. Set aside for assembly.

WINGS

LARGE WINGS (MAKE 2)

With **B**, make a magic ring.

Rnd 1: 6 sc in ring—6 sc.

Rnd 2: 2 sc in each st around—12 sc.

Rnd 3: *2 sc in first st, sc next st, repeat from * around—18 sc.

Rnd 4: *2 sc in first st, sc next 2 sts, repeat from * around—24 sc.

Rnd 5: Sc first 10 sts, 2 hdc in next st, (dc, ch 1, dc) in next, 2 hdc in next, sc last 11 sc.

Fasten off, leaving a tail for sewing onto the Body. Repeat instructions for second Wing. Set Wings aside for assembly.

SMALL WINGS (MAKE 2)

With **B**, make a magic ring.

Rnd 1: 6 sc in ring—6 sc.

Rnd 2: 2 sc in each st around—12 sc.

Rnd 3: *2 sc in first st, sc next st, repeat from * around—18 sc.

Rnd 4: *2 sc in first st, sc next 5 sts, repeat from * around—21 sc.

Rnd 5: Sc first 9 sts, 2 hdc in next st, (dc, ch 1, dc) in next, 2 hdc in next, sc last 9 sc.

Fasten off, leaving a tail for sewing onto the Body. Repeat instructions for second Wing. Set Wings aside for assembly.

ASSEMBLY

Referring to photograph as a guide to placement, sew the pieces together.

1. Sew Arms to Body, one on each side, lined up with the top of the Body below the neck.
2. Sew Antennae to Head across from each other lined up approximately 4 to 6 rounds from the top of the Head.
3. Sew Ears to Head, one on each side directly below the Antennae.
4. Sew Large Wings to the top of the back. Wings should meet in the center of the back and angle upward to be visible from the front.
5. Sew Small Wings to the back layered partially on top of the Large Wings. Wings should meet in the center and angle slightly downward to be visible from the front.

Weave in and cut all yarn tails.

MERPERSON

Designed by Chanel Beauchamp-Snyder
Skill Level: ⚡ ⚡ ⚡

For the second task of the Triwizard Tournament in *Harry Potter and the Goblet of Fire*, the four champions must retrieve someone dear to them—one of four students secured with a spell under the waters of the Black Lake. When Harry finds them, he rescues Ron, his best friend, then realizes champion Fleur Delacour is not coming for her sister, Gabrielle. He starts to release her as well before he's stopped by a merperson. The merpeople are supervising this task, allowing no one to break the rules and rescue more than one.

The merpeople are a true shift from traditional underwater creatures as there is no break between their human and fish parts. Instead, the concept designers brought their "fishiness" into their human aspect by having scales run the length of their bodies. They also have large fishlike eyes, a fishlike mouth, and hair like the floating strands of sea anemones. Their tail moves from side to side instead of the conventional up and down.

Starting from the thoughtfully designed tail, this amigurumi merperson captures the essence of these aquatic beings in every stitch. Each fin and spine is crocheted separately, allowing for intricate detailing that brings this creature to life. The gills are delicately embroidered onto these merpeople of the Black Lake, making them fierce and vicious rather than beautiful and alluring. A metal frame embedded in this amigurumi allows for creative and expressive poses that mirror the fluidity of underwater life.

*"Come and seek us where our voices sound.
We cannot sing above the ground."*

Merpeople's song with the second task clue,
Harry Potter and the Goblet of Fire

FINISHED MEASUREMENTS
Height: 16 in. / 41 cm
Width: 4 in. / 10 cm

YARN
Worsted weight (#4 medium) yarn, shown in WeCrochet's *Wool of the Andes Worsted*, (100% wool, 110 yd. / 100 m per 1.75 oz. / 50 g skein).
Color A: #24076 Onyx Heather, 1 skein
Color B: #25992 Icicle Heather, 1 skein
Color C: #25647 Fjord Heather, 1 skein
Color D: #23430 Pumpkin, 1 skein

Lace weight (#0 lace) crochet thread, shown in WeCrochet's *Curio #10*, (100% mercerized cotton, 721 yd. / 659 m per 3.5 oz. / 100 g skein).
Color E: #26267 Sagebrush, small amount

HOOKS
• US C / 3.00mm crochet hook
• US B / 2.50mm crochet hook

NOTIONS
• Stitch markers
• Pair of 12mm safety eyes
• Polyester stuffing
• Tapestry needle
• Straight pins
• Embroidery thread, small amount of black
• Optional: Cloth stem wire 18 gauge, two 18 in. long lengths

GAUGE
26 sc and 28 sc rows = 4 in. / 10 cm worked in the round with larger hook.
Gauge is not critical for this project. Ensure your stitches are tight so the stuffing won't show through.

SPECIAL ABBREVIATIONS

Picot (picot): Ch 3, sl st into first ch of ch 3.

Back Loop Single Crochet (BLsc): Single crochet in the back loop

Back Post Single Crochet (bpsc): Insert your hook into the next st by first going through the WS of both loops of st; going around the post of the st; and second, insert your hook going through the RS of both loops of the same st. Yo, and pull up a loop through both insertion points of the hook. Yo, pull through both loops on hook.

Front Post Single Crochet (fpsc): Insert hook around the front of the post (from front to back to front), yo and draw up a loop, yo and draw through both loops to complete the st.

Half Double Crochet Decrease (hdc dec): Yo, insert the hook into the indicated st, yo, pull through, yo, pull through 1 loop, insert the hook into the next st, yo, pull through, yo, pull through all the loops on the hook—1 st decreased.

Decrease (dec): Insert hook in the front loop of the indicated st, insert hook into the front loop of the next st, yo, pull through, yo, pull through the remaining 3 loops on the hook—1 st decreased.

BEHIND THE MAGIC

Several different fish were referenced for the merpeople's design: sturgeons provided proportions and the shield-like plates, called scutes, that run down their bodies. Their tails were based on a tuna's.

CHIN

With **C** and the larger hook, make a magic ring and work 6 sc into it.

Place a stitch marker in the first sc created to mark the start of your round. Move this stitch marker up each round.

Rnd 1: Inc 6 times—12.

Fasten off with a short tail. Use a tapestry needle to weave the yarn tails in.

BREASTS (MAKE 2)

With **C** and the larger hook, make a magic ring and work 6 sc into it.

Place a stitch marker in the first sc created to mark the start of your round. Move this stitch marker up each round.

Rnd 1: Inc 6 times—12.

Rnd 2: [Inc, sc] 6 times—18.

Fasten off with a short tail. Use a tapestry needle to weave the yarn tails.

ARM FINS (MAKE 2)

With **B** and smaller hook, ch 3.

Row 1: (RS) starting in the second ch from the hook, 2 BLsc, ch 1—3.

Row 2: (WS) ch 1, turn, starting in the second ch from the hook, 3 BLsc—3.

Row 3: (RS) ch 1, turn, 3 BLsc, ch 1—4.

Row 4: (WS) ch 1, turn, starting in the second ch from the hook, 4 BLsc—4.

Row 5: (RS) ch 1, turn, 4 BLsc, ch 1—5.

Row 6: (WS) ch 1, turn, starting in the second ch from the hook, 5 BLsc—5.

Row 7: (RS) ch 1, turn, 4 BLsc—4. Leave the last st unworked.

Row 8: (WS) ch 1, turn, 4 BLsc—4.

Row 9: (RS) ch 1, turn, 3 BLsc—3. Leave the last st unworked.

Row 10: (WS) ch 1, turn, 3 BLsc—3.

Row 11: (RS) ch 1, turn, 2 BLsc—2. Leave the last st unworked.

Row 12: (WS) ch 1, turn, 2 BLsc—2.

Fasten off with a long tail (about 8 to 10 in.) for sewing later.

SIDE FINS (MAKE 2)

With **A** and the larger hook, make a magic ring and work 6 sc into it.

Place a stitch marker in the first sc created to mark the start of your round. Move this stitch marker up each round.

Rnd 1: Inc 6 times—12.

Rnd 2: [Inc, sc] 6 times—18.

Rnd 3: [Sc, inc, sc] 6 times—24.

Rnd 4: [Inc, 3 sc] 6 times—30.

Rnd 5: [2 sc, inc, 2 sc] 6 times—36.

Rnd 6: 12 sc, sk 12 sts, 12 sc—24.

Rnd 6 splits the piece into 2 parts: one with 24 sts around and one with 12 sts around. Continue working the remaining rounds on the larger of the two sections.

Rnd 7: Sc in each st around—24.

Rnd 8: 10 sc, dec 3 times, 8 sc—21.

Rnd 9: Dec 2 times, 15 sc, dec—18.

Rnd 10: 7 sc, dec 3 times, 5 sc—15.

Rnd 11: Dec 2 times, 9 sc, dec—12.

Rnd 12: Sc in each st around—12.

Rnd 13: [Sc, dec, sc] 3 times—9.

Rnd 14: [Dec, sc] 3 times—6.

Rnd 15: Sc in each st around—6.

Fasten off with a long tail (10 to 12 in.) for sewing later. Don't stuff. Press the Fin flat.

BACK FINS (MAKE 2)

For this section, the picots at the end of rows will be counted as a single stitch. Do not ch 1 when you turn unless it is specifically noted.

With **B** and smaller hook, ch 10.

Place a stitch marker in the front loop of the 9th ch to mark the spot where the yarn will be attached again later.

Row 1: (RS) starting in the second ch from the hook, 9 sc, picot—10.
Row 2: (WS) turn, sl st, 8 FPsc—9.
Row 3: (RS) ch 1, turn, 7 sc, picot—8.
Row 4: (WS) turn, sl st, 6 FPsc—7.
Row 5: (RS) ch 1, turn, 5 sc, picot—6.
Row 6: (WS) turn, sl st, 4 FPsc—5.
Row 7: (RS) ch 1, turn, 3 sc, picot—4.
Row 8: (WS) turn, sl st, 2 FPsc—3.
Row 9: (RS) ch 1, turn, sc, picot—2.
Row 10: (WS) turn, sl st—1.

Fasten off with a short tail and weave the yarn tails in. With the WS facing you, return to the marked st and attach a new strand of **B** with a ch 1. This ch 1 does not count as a st, so work the first sc in the same space.

Row 11: (WS) 9 sc, picot—10.
Row 12: (RS) turn, sl st, 8 BPsc—9.
Row 13: (WS) ch 1, turn, 7 sc, picot—8.
Row 14: (RS) turn, sl st, 6 BPsc—7.
Row 15: (WS) ch 1, turn, 5 sc, picot—6.
Row 16: (RS) turn, sl st, 4 BPsc—5.
Row 17: (WS) ch 1, turn, 3 sc, picot—4.
Row 18: (RS) turn, sl st, 2 BPsc—3.
Row 19: (WS) ch 1, sc, picot—2.
Row 20: (RS) turn, sl st—1.

Fasten off with a 10 to 12 in. long tail for sewing later.

LONG TAIL FIN

With **A** and larger hook, make a magic ring and work 6 sc into it.

Place a stitch marker in the first sc created to mark the start of your round. Move this stitch marker up each round. Do not ch 1 when you turn unless it is specifically noted.

Rnds 1–2: Sc in each st around—6.
Rnd 3: [Inc, sc] 3 times—9.
Rnds 4–5: Sc in each st around—9.
Rnd 6: Sc, inc 3 times, 5 sc—12.
Rnds 7–8: Sc in each st around—12.
Rnd 9: 4 sc, inc 3 times, 5 sc—15.
Rnd 10: Sc in each st around—15.
Rnd 11: Sc, dec, 2 sc, inc 3 times, 2 sc, dec, sc, dec—15.

Rnd 12: 6 sc, inc 3 times, 6 sc—18.

Rnd 13: Sc in each st around—18.

Row 14: 5 sc—5. Leave the remaining sts unworked. Remove the stitch marker.

Row 15: Turn, 9 sc—9. Leave the remaining sts unworked.

Row 16: Turn, 8 sc—8. Leave the last st unworked.

Row 17: Turn, 7 sc—7. Leave the last st unworked.

Row 18: Turn, 6 sc—6. Leave the last st unworked.

Rnd 19 is worked in the round (down the sides of the short rows, across the unworked sts of Rnd 8, and back up the other side of the short rows. Place a stitch marker in the first st of the round. When working down the sides of short rows, work into the unworked sts.

Rnd 19: Sc in each st around—18.

Rnd 20: 5 sc, inc 3 times, 10 sc—21.

Row 21: 3 sc—3. Leave the remaining sts unworked. Remove the stitch marker.

Row 22: Turn, 10 sc—10. Leave the remaining sts unworked.

Row 23: Turn, 9 sc—9. Leave the last st unworked.

Rnd 24 is worked in the round (down the sides of the short rows, across the unworked sts of Rnd 20, and back up the other side of the short rows. Place a stitch marker in the first st of the round. When working down the sides of short rows, work into the unworked sts.

Rnd 24: Sc in each st around—21.

Rnd 25: 4 sc, inc 3 times, 14 sc—24.

Row 26: Sc—1. Leave the remaining sts unworked. Remove the stitch marker.

Row 27: Turn, 12 sc—12. Leave the remaining sts unworked.

Row 28: Turn, 11 sc—11. Leave the last st unworked.

Rnd 29 is worked in the round (down the sides of the short rows, across the unworked sts of Rnd 25, and back up the other side of the short rows. Place a stitch marker in the first st of the round. When working down the sides of short rows, work into the unworked sts.

Rnds 29–30: Sc in each st around—24.

Row 31: Sc—1. Leave the remaining sts unworked. Remove the stitch marker.

Row 32: Turn, 12 sc—12. Leave the remaining sts unworked.

Row 33: Turn, 11 sc—11. Leave the last st unworked.

Rnd 34 is worked in the round (down the sides of the short rows, across the unworked sts of Rnd 30, and back up the other side of the short rows. Place a stitch marker in the first st of the round. When working down the sides of short rows, work into the unworked sts.

Rnd 34: Sc in each st around—24.

Rnd 35: 18 sc, [inc, sc] 3 times—27.

Fasten off with a 10 to 12 in. tail. Press the Fin flat and don't stuff. Use the yarn tail to sew the open end of the Fin shut. Leave the remaining yarn tail loose for sewing later.

SHORT TAIL FIN

With **A** and larger hook, make a magic ring and work 6 sc into it.

Place a stitch marker in the first sc created to mark the start of your round. Move this stitch marker up each round. Do not ch 1 when you turn unless it is specifically noted.

Rnd 1: Sc in each st around—6.

Rnd 2: Inc 3 times, 3 sc—9.

Rnd 3: Sc in each st around—9.

Rnd 4: Sc, inc 3 times, 5 sc—12.

Rnd 5: Sc in each st around—12.

Rnd 6: 3 sc, inc 3 times, 6 sc—15.

Rnd 7: Dec, 3 sc, inc 3 times, 3 sc, dec 2 times—15.

Rnd 8: 6 sc, inc 3 times, 6 sc—18.

Rnd 9: Sc in each st around—18.

Rnd 10: 7 sc, inc 3 times, 8 sc—21.

Rnd 11: Sc in each st around—21.

Rnd 12: 9 sc, inc 3 times, 9 sc—24.

Rnd 13: Dec 2 times, 7 sc, inc 3 times, 8 sc, dec—24.

Row 14: 6 sc—6. Leave the remaining sts unworked. Remove the stitch marker.

Row 15: Turn, 12 sc—12. Leave the remaining sts unworked.

Row 16: Turn, 11 sc—11. Leave the last st unworked.

Rnd 17 is worked in the round (down the sides of the short rows, across the unworked sts of Rnd 13, and back up the other side of the short rows). Place a stitch marker in the first st of the round. When working down the sides of short rows, work into the unworked sts.

Rnd 17: Sc in each st around—24.

Row 18: Sc—1. Leave the remaining sts unworked. Remove the stitch marker.

Row 19: Turn, 12 sc—12. Leave the remaining sts unworked.

Row 20: Turn, 11 sc—11. Leave the last st unworked.

Rnd 21 is worked in the round (down the sides of the short rows, across the unworked

sts of Rnd 17, and back up the other side of the short rows). Place a stitch marker in the first st of the round. When working down the sides of short rows, work into the unworked sts.

Rnd 21: Sc in each st around—24.

Rnd 22: 17 sc, [inc, sc] 3 times, sc—27.

Fasten off with a 10 to 12 in. tail. Press the Fin flat and don't stuff. Use the yarn tail to sew the open end of the Fin shut. Leave the remaining yarn tail loose for sewing later.

HAIR CAP

With **D** and larger hook, make a magic ring and work 6 sc into it.

Place a stitch marker in the first sc created to mark the start of your round. Move this stitch marker up each round. Do not ch 1 when you turn unless it is specifically noted.

Rnd 1: Inc 6 times—12.

Rnd 2: [Inc, sc] 6 times—18.

Rnd 3: [Sc, inc, sc] 6 times—24.

Rnd 4: [Inc, 3 sc] 6 times—30. Place a stitch marker in the 4th st of Rnd 4 to mark the spot where the yarn will be attached again later. Remove the stitch marker that marks the start of the round.

Row 5: Turn, 4 sc—4. Leave the remaining sts unworked.

Row 6: Turn, 3 sc—3. Leave the last st unworked.

Row 7: Turn, 2 sc—2. Leave the last st unworked.

Fasten off with a short tail and weave in the tails. With the RS facing you, return to the marked st of Rnd 4 and attach a strand of **D** using a ch 1.

This ch 1 does not count as a st, so work the first sc in the same space.

Row 8: 4 sc—4. Leave the remaining sts unworked.

Row 9: Turn, 3 sc—3. Leave the last st unworked.

Row 10: Turn, 2 sc—2. Leave the last st unworked.

Rnd 11 is worked in the round (down the sides of the short rows, across the unworked sts of Rnd 4, and back up the other side of the short rows). Place a stitch marker in the first st of the round. When working down the sides of short rows, work into the unworked sts.

Rnd 11: Sc in each st around—30.

Fasten off with a 10 to 12 in. long tail for sewing later.

BODY

With **A** and larger hook, make a magic ring and work 6 sc into it. Place a stitch marker in the first sc created to mark the start of your round. Move this stitch marker up each round.

Rnds 1−6: Sc in each st around—6.

Rnd 7: [Inc, sc] 3 times—9.

Rnds 8−10: Sc in each st around—9.

Rnd 11: [Sc, inc, sc] 3 times—12.

Rnds 12−14: Sc in each st around—12.

Rnd 15: [Inc, 3 sc] 3 times—15.

Rnds 16−18: Sc in each st around—15.

Rnd 19: [2 sc, inc, 2sc] 3 times—18.

Rnds 20−22: Sc in each st around—18.

Rnd 23: [Inc, 5 sc] 3 times—21.

Rnds 24−26: Sc in each st around—21.

Insert wire into the center of the tail making sure the end of the wire reaches all the way down into the tip of the tail. Begin lightly stuffing the tail, keeping the wire in the center.

Rnd 27: [3 sc, inc, 3 sc] 3 times—24.

Rnds 28−30: Sc in each st around—24.

Rnd 31: [Inc, 7 sc] 3 times—27.

Rnds 32−34: Sc in each st around—27.

Rnd 35: [4 sc, inc, 4 sc] 3 times—30.

Rnds 36−38: Sc in each st around—30.

Rnd 39: [Inc, 9 sc] 3 times—33.

Rnds 40−42: Sc in each st around—33. Continue adding stuffing.

Rnd 43: [5 sc, inc, 5sc] 3 times—36.

Rnds 44−46: Sc in each st around—36.

Rnd 47: [Inc, 11 sc] 3 times—39.

Rnds 48−50: Sc in each st around—39.

Rnd 51: [6 sc, inc, 6 sc] 3 times—42.

The next 6 rounds will transition between **A**, **B**, and **C**. Always change colors by finishing the previous stitch in the new color.

Rnd 52: A: 3 sc, [**B**: sc, **A**: 6 sc] 5 times, **B**: sc, **A**: 3 sc—42.

Rnd 53: A: sc, **B**: sc, [**A**: 3 sc, **B**: sc, **A**: 2 sc, **B**: sc] 4 times, **A**: 3 sc, **B**: sc, **A**: sc—42.

Rnd 54: B: 3 sc, [**A**: sc, **B**: 6 sc] 5 times, **A**: sc, **B**: 3 sc—42.

Cut **A** and weave the yarn tail into the interior of the project.

Rnd 55: B: sc, **C**: sc, [**B**: 3 sc, **C**: sc, **B**: 2 sc, **C**: sc] 5 times, **B**: 3 sc, **C**: sc, **B**: sc—42.

Rnd 56: C: sc, [**B**: 2 sc, **C**: sc, **B**: 3 sc, **C**: sc] 5 times, **B**: 2 sc, **C**: sc, **B**: 3 sc—42.

Rnd 57: **C**: 5 sc, [**B**: sc, **C**: 6 sc] 5 times, **B**: sc, **C**: sc—42.

Cut **B** and weave the yarn tail into the interior of the project. Continue working in **C** only. Continue stuffing.

Rnd 58: [6 sc, dec, 6 sc] 3 times—39.

Rnd 59: Sc in each st around—39.

Rnd 60: [Dec, 11 sc] 3 times—36.

Rnd 61: Sc in each st around—36.

Rnd 62: [5 sc, dec, 5 sc] 3 times—33.

Rnd 63: Sc in each st around—33.

Rnd 64: [Dec, 9 sc] 3 times—30.

Rnd 65: Sc in each st around—30.

Rnd 66: [4 sc, dec 4 sc] 3 times—27.

Rnd 67: Sc in each st around—27.

Rnd 68: [Dec, 7 sc] 3 times—24.

Rnds 69−71: Sc in each st around—24.

Rnd 72: 6 sc, inc, 11 sc, inc, 5 sc 26.

Rnd 73: Sc in each st around—26.

Rnd 74: 7 sc, inc, 12 sc, inc, 5 sc—28.

Rnd 75: Sc in each st around—28.

Rnd 76: 8 sc, inc, 13 sc, inc, 5 sc—30.

Rnd 77: Sc in each st around—30.

In Rnd 78, the Breasts will be attached to the Body using sc. To attach them, hold the Breast with the WS (inside) facing up with one edge parallel to the Body. Insert the hook into the st of the Breast (from inside out). Then insert the hook into the next st of the Body, yo, pull through, yo and pull through both loops on the hook.

Rnd 78: 11 sc, connect the first Breast to the Body with 4 sc, 3 sc, connect the second Breast to the Body with 4 sc, 8 sc—30.

In Rnd 79, the 4 connecting sc for each Breast will be ignored. Instead, work from the Body around the outside edges of the Breasts and back. Also note that the hdc dec sts will be worked half into the Body and half into the Breast and vice versa.

Rnd 79: 9 sc, hdc, hdc dec, 12 sc, hdc dec, hdc, hdc dec, 12 sc, hdc dec, hdc, 6 sc—46.

Rnd 80: 9 sc, sc 3 tog, 4 sc, dec, 4 sc, dec 3 times, 4 sc, dec, 4 sc, sc3tog, 5 sc—37.

Rnd 81: 6 sc, dec, sc, dec, 4 sc, dec, 2 sc, sc3tog, 2 sc, dec, 4 sc, dec, sc, dec, 2 sc—29.

Rnd 82: 4 sc, dec, sc, dec, 7 sc, dec, 6 sc, dec, sc, dec—24.

As you stuff the chest section of the Body, be sure to stuff the Breasts as well and keep the wire running up the center of the project.

In Rnd 83, the round will be extended on both sides to create holes where the Arms will later be worked.

Rnd 83: 7 sc, ch 9, 15 sc, ch 9, 2 sc—42.

Rnd 84: Sc in each st and ch around—42.

Rnd 85: Sc in each st around—42.

Rnd 86: 9 sc, dec, sc, dec, 6 sc, dec, 4 sc, dec, 6 sc, dec, sc, dec, 3 sc—36.

Rnd 87: [2 sc, dec, 2 sc] 6 times—30.

Rnd 88: [Dec, 3 sc] 6 times—24.

Rnd 89: [Sc, dec, sc] 6 times—18.

Rnd 90 marks the base of the neck. As you continue, firmly stuff the neck and keep the wire in the center.

Rnd 90: [Dec, sc] 6 times—12.

Rnds 91−95: Sc in each st around—12.

Rnd 96: [Inc, sc] 6 times—18.

In Rnd 97, the Chin is attached to the head section of the Body using sc. To attach it, hold the Chin with the WS (inside) facing up with one edge parallel to the Body. Insert the hook into the st of the Chin (from inside out). Then insert the hook into the next st of the Body, yo, pull through, yo and pull through both loops on the hook.

Rnd 97: 3 sc, [inc, sc] 3 times, 4 sc, connect the Chin to the Body with 3 sc, 2 sc—21.

In Rnd 98, the 3 connecting sc of the Chin will be ignored. Instead, work from the Body around the outside edges of the Chin and back. Note that the dec sts will be worked half into the head and half into the Chin and vice versa.

Rnd 98: 3 sc, inc, 6 sc, inc, 4 sc, dec, 7 sc, dec, sc—27.

Rnd 99: 5 sc, [inc, 2 sc] 3 times, 13 sc—30.

Rnds 100−103: Sc in each st around—30.

Rnd 104: 22 sc, [dec, sc] 2 times, dec—27.

Rnd 105: Sc in each st around—27.

Rnd 106: Dec, 19 sc, dec, sc, dec, sc—24.

Rnd 107: Sc in each st around—24.

Place the eyes on the front of the face (using the Chin as a centerline) between Rnds 104 and 105 with 5 sts in between. Use wire cutters to cut any excess wire and fold the end down into a "U" shape so it sits inside the head. After placing the backs on the eyes, cut a length of **C** about 12 in. long and embroider eyelids over the top edges of each eye. Tie off the excess yarn and stuff it into the head and firmly stuff the head section of the Body.

Rnd 108: [Sc, dec, sc] 6 times—18.

Rnd 109: [Dec, sc] 6 times—12.

Rnd 110: Dec 6 times—6.

Fasten off with a 6 to 8 in. short tail and sew the remaining hole closed. Weave in the remaining yarn tail.

ARMS (MAKE 2)

Optional: Cut a length of floral wire (about 12 in. long) and push it through the armhole, across the chest, and through the other armhole so there is an equal amount of wire for each Arm.

Hold your project with the tail up, head down, and the front of the Body facing away from you. In each hole created earlier for the Arms, there are 9 bottom chains and a small gap between where the chain started and connected. In that gap there are 2 horizontal bars. To start each Arm, attach a strand of **C** to the rightmost bar in the gap with a ch 1. This ch 1 does not count as a st, so work the first sc in the same space.

Rnd 1: Work into the next bar in the gap, sc, work into the bottom chains, 9 sc—11. Lightly add stuffing into the Arm as you go, keeping the wire in the center.

Rnds 2–12: Sc in each st around—11.

Rnd 13: 3 sc, dec, 6 sc—10.

Rnd 14: 7 sc, dec, sc—9.

Rnds 15–24: Sc in each st around—9.

If you're using wire, don't stuff the Arm past Rnd 24, otherwise lightly add stuffing.

Rnd 25: [Dec, sc] 3 times—6.

Rnd 26: Sc in each st around—6.

Use wire cutters to cut the excess wire so that only about 0.75 in. is protruding from the wrist. Fold the end of the wire in half to form a "U" shape. Continue working the hand around the wire.

Rnd 27: Inc 6 times—12.

Rnds 28–30: Sc in each st around—12.

Rnd 31: [Dec, 2 sc] 3 times—9.

Rnd 32: Sc in each st around—9.

Rnd 33: [Dec, sc] 3 times—6.

Rnd 34: Sc in each st around—6.

Fasten off with a 6 to 8 in. tail and sew the remaining hole closed. Weave in the remaining yarn tail. Repeat for the second Arm.

ASSEMBLY

ARM FINS

Pin the longest, flat edge of each Arm Fin to the back of each Arm between Rnds 4 and 16. Use the leftover yarn tail to sew the flat edge of each Fin to the back of the Arm. Weave in any excess yarn tails.

BACK FIN

Take the two Back Fins and place them flush with each other with the ridged stitches facing out on both sides. Use one of the yarn tails to sew the two pieces together, working first along the bottom edge and then along the top curve. Be sure to leave the picot sts loose. Weave in the yarn tail.

Then pin the long edge to the back of the Body between Rnds 56 and 84. The natural point of the long edge of the Back Fin should sit flush with the dip of the waist on the Body. Use the leftover yarn tail to sew the flat edge of the Fin to the back of the Body. Weave in any excess yarn tails.

TAIL FINS

Pin the flat edge of the Long Tail Fin to the tail part of the Body between Rnds 1 and 12, making sure it's centered and in line with the Back Fin. Use the leftover yarn tail to sew the flat edge of the Fin to the tail part of the Body. Weave in any excess yarn tails.

Then pin the flat edge of the Short Tail Fin between Rnds 1 and 12, making sure it's centered and in line with the face on the front of the Body. When viewed from the side, the two Tail Fins should be completely vertical. Use the leftover yarn tail to sew the flat edge of the Fin to the tail. Weave in any excess yarn tails.

SIDE FINS

Pin the Side Fins to the sides of the tail part of the Body between Rnds 19 and 26. Use the leftover yarn tail to sew the open edge of each Fin to the sides of the tail part of the Body. Weave in any excess yarn tails.

HAIR CAP

Pin the Hair Cap to the head with the "U" shaped part created by the short rows toward the face. Using the yarn tail, sew the edges of the Hair Cap to the head. Weave in the remaining yarn tail.

Cut several lengths of **D** (you can wrap the yarn several times around a phone case and then cut one end of the loop when you pull the yarn off). Use a crochet hook to attach a strand of yarn to each st around the edge of the Hair Cap. Then continue adding strands to the sts on the Hair Cap to fill out any spots that look too flat or gappy. (You don't have to put a strand of yarn in every st on the Hair Cap.)

GILLS

Cut a length of **E** about 14 in. long and embroider 3 lines (for gills) on each side of the neck. Weave in the remaining crochet thread.

FACE

Cut a length of black embroidery thread about 14 in. long and embroider a mouth onto the face. Use pins to set the placement before you stitch. Weave the remaining embroidery thread into the head.

Cut a length of **C** about 10 in. long and embroider a nose onto the face 1 to 2 rounds above the mouth. Weave in the remaining yarn.

Optional: *If you want to give your mermaid a more pronounced upper lip, cut a length of C about 12 in. long and embroider the same mouth shape just above where you embroidered before. Weave in the remaining yarn.*

TROLL

Designed by Nicole Rogowski
Skill Level: ⚡ ⚡ ⚡

The Halloween celebration in *Harry Potter and the Sorcerer's Stone* is interrupted by Professor Quirinus Quirrel running into the Great Hall shouting "Troll in the dungeon!" before he faints onto the floor. Immediately, the students rise up, screaming and struggling to exit the hall, until Headmaster Dumbledore tells them not to panic, and to return to their dormitories. Hermione Granger is not among these students as she's upset, and secluded herself in the girls' bathroom. When Harry and Ron see the troll heading in that direction, they race to save her.

The concept artists checked out medical photographs to inspire the troll's green, saggy skin covered in grime and spots. Its warty feet end in two toes, and its head is topped by clumps of tatty hair. There's also hair on its saggy belly and in its armpits. The troll's legs, feet, and hands were created practically, at full size, for the actors to work against. The digital troll was based on an actor filmed wearing a full-size mountain troll costume.

Beware of this crocheted troll as seen in the first Harry Potter film making an appearance at your next Halloween feast! This sizable amigurumi, brandishing a club and measuring approximately 12 inches tall, possesses brute strength and a somewhat clumsy demeanor just like his character. This troll wears an orange-brown crocheted vest over his broad shoulders and muscular arms. French knots are added to the troll's mottled gray skin to create the appearance of warts, contributing to his unique appearance.

> "Not many first year students could take on a fully grown mountain troll and live to tell the tale!"
>
> Minerva McGonagall,
> *Harry Potter and the Sorcerer's Stone*

FINISHED MEASUREMENTS
Height: 12 in. / 30 cm
Width: 11.2 in. / 28 cm

YARN
Worsted weight (#4 medium) yarn shown in Lion Brand *Heartland* (100% acrylic, 251 yd. / 230 m per 5 oz. / 140 g skein).
Color A: #136-154J Petrified Forest, 2 skeins

Worsted weight (#4 medium) yarn shown in Lion Brand *Basic Stitch Skein Tones* (100% acrylic, 185 yd. / 170 m per 3½ oz. / 100 g skein).
Color B: #202-122T Hazelnut, 1 skein
Color C: #202-125AA Truffle, 1 skein
Color D: #202-129B Cocoa, 1 skein

HOOK
• US F-5 / 3.75mm crochet hook

NOTIONS
• Stitch markers
• Pair of 8mm safety eyes
• Polyester stuffing
• Tapestry needle

GAUGE
Gauge is not critical for this project. Ensure your stitches are tight so the stuffing won't show through.

SPECIAL ABBREVIATIONS
Back Post Single Crochet (bpsc): Insert your hook into the next st by first going through the WS of both loops of st; going around the post of the st; and second insert your hook going through the RS of both loops of the same st. Yo and pull up a loop through both insertion points of the hook. Yo pull, through both loops on hook.
Picot (picot): Ch 2, sl st into the front loop of last st made.

Popcorn St (pc): [Yo, insert your hook into indicated st, yo, pull up loop, yo, pull through 2 loops on hook] 5 times, yo, pull through 6 loops on hook.

Back Loop Only (blo): Work through back loop only.

NOTE

All rounds are worked continuously, unless noted otherwise—use a st marker as needed to keep track of the beginning of each round. The torso is created first. The body parts are created next, and joined after they are made. The vest, loincloth, and club are made last, and each attached to the troll after they are completed. A French knot, an embroidery stitch, is used to create the individual warts on the troll's legs.

EMBROIDERY STITCH

French Knot: Thread the tapestry needle with an 18 in. strand of color **A** yarn. Insert the needle through any point in the base of the leg and come out where you want to place a wart—leaving at least 3 in. of a tail hanging out of the base of the leg. With your less dominant hand, hold the needle down flat on top of the place you want your wart. While the needle is held in place, use your dominant hand to wrap the needle 4 or 5 times with the yarn. Keeping the wraps in place, insert the needle back into the leg ½ a st-width away from your wart. Push the needle through the leg to the next place you would like to have a wart and pull the yarn taut to complete the wart. Repeat until you have very little left of your yarn strand. Weave the end into the leg. Snip off the original tail from the base of the leg. Repeat all steps as desired.

TORSO

With **A**, make a magic ring and ch 1.

Rnd 1: 8 sc in the ring, pull tail tightly to close the ring and knot the tail—8 sts.

Rnd 2: [Inc] eight times—16 sts.

Rnd 3: [Sc, inc] eight times—24 sts.

Rnd 4: [Sc 2, inc] eight times—32 sts.

Rnd 5: [Sc 3, inc] eight times—40 sts.

Rnd 6: [Sc 4, inc] eight times—48 sts.

Rnd 7: Sc 2, inc, [sc 5, inc] seven times, sc 3—56 sts.

Rnds 8—13: Sc around.

Rnd 14: [Sc 5, dec] eight times—48 sts.

BEHIND THE MAGIC

The digital crew imagined the troll moved like a four-year-old, knocking down everything in his way, like a walking bulldozer.

Rnds 15—17: Sc around.

Rnd 18: Sc 16, dec, [sc 4, dec] five times—42 sts.

Rnd 19: Sc around.

Rnd 20: Sc 15, dec, [sc 3, dec] five times. At the end of this round, pause to add stuffing to the piece before it narrows too much—36 sts.

Rnds 21—30: Sc around.

Rnd 31: [Sc 2, dec] nine times—27 sts.

Rnd 32: [Sc, dec] nine times. At the end of this round, pause to add some more stuffing to your piece—18 sts.

Rnd 33: [Dec, sc 7] two times—16 sts.

Rnd 34: [Dec] eight times—8 sts.

Fasten off, leaving a 10 in. long tail, finish stuffing the Torso, and set aside for assembly.

HEAD

With **A**, make a magic ring and ch 1.

Rnd 1: Sc 5 in ring, pull tail tightly to close the ring, and knot the tail—5 sts.

Rnd 2: Inc five times—10 sts.

Rnd 3: [Sc, inc] five times—15 sts.

Rnd 4: Sc around.

Rnd 5: [Sc 2, inc] five times—20 sts.

Rnd 6: Sc around.

Rnd 7: [Sc 3, inc] five times—25 sts.

Rnd 8: Sc around.

Rnd 9: [Sc 4, inc] five times—30 sts.

Rnd 10: Sc 15, pc, sc 14, pause to add the eyes—placing one between the 15th sts of Rnds 8 and 9, and one between the 17th sts of Rnds 8 and 9—29 sc sts, 1 popcorn st.

Rnds 11—13: Sc around.

Rnd 14: [Sc, dec] ten times, pause to stuff the inside of the Head before moving on to the next round—20 sts.

Rnd 15: Dec ten times—10 sts.

Rnd 16: [Sc 3, dec] two times—
8 sts.

Fasten off and finish stuffing the Head firmly, then set aside for assembly

UNIBROW

With **A**, ch 7 and fasten off with 6 in. long tail. Set aside for assembly.

EARS (MAKE 2)

With **A**, make a magic ring and ch 1.

Row 1: [Hdc, dc 2, ch 2, sl st] in ring, do NOT pull tail to close ring. Ch 1 and turn.

Row 2: Sc into first ch, inc into next ch, inc, sc 2, ch 1 and join ring.

Fasten off with a 6 in. long tail, pull the magic ring tail tightly

to close the ring and knot tail. Set aside for assembly.

ASSEMBLY (HEAD PIECES)

Attaching the Unibrow: Thread the tapestry needle with the 6 in. long tail. First tack the end of the Unibrow to the Head two or three sts away from one of the eyes—aligned horizontally with the eye. Then continue to use the tail to tack the 4th ch of the ch-7 of the Unibrow down to the space in between the eyes. Then use the remaining length of the tail to tack down the slip knot end of the Unibrow two or three sts away from the other eye—aligned horizontally with the second eye. Weave the remaining length of the tail into the

Head, and weave in the original tail from the slip knot.

Attaching the Ears: Thread the tapestry needle with the 6 in. tail of one of the Ears. Turn the Head on its side so that you have access to the profile side. Locate the 9th round of the Head—which is the same round that you used in the placement of the eyes. Tack the Ear down to the side of the Head using the tail, weaving it in a couple times to the base of the Ear. Weave any remaining length of the tail into the Head. Thread the tapestry needle with the beginning of the magic ring tail. Tack the other side of the Ear down two rounds directly below the first tacking spot (Rnd 11). Weave any remaining

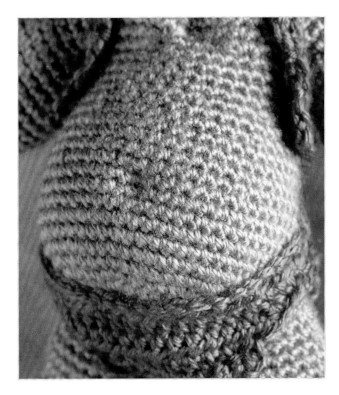

length of the magic ring tail into the Head. Repeat the same process for the other Ear, on the other side of the Head.

ASSEMBLY (HEAD TO TORSO)

Before attaching the Head to the Torso, weave in the Head's tail so that it is out of the way. Thread the tapestry needle with the 10 in. long tail of the Torso. Line up the Head and Torso so that the nose points in the same direction

as the belly. Use a couple of st markers to keep the Head in place, connecting the Head stitches to the Torso stitches. Use the 10 in. tail to sew the tops of the stitches of the last round of the Head, to the matched tops of the stitches of the last round of the Torso. Weave any remaining length of the tail.

Extra Shaping of the Torso: This step is entirely optional. It is recommended at this point to add shaping to the Torso, such

as the belly button and chest splitting. There is no science to this step, just trial and error.

LEGS (MAKE 2)

With **A**, make a magic ring and ch 1.

Rnd 1: 8 sc in ring, pull tail tightly to close the ring and knot the tail—8 sts.

Rnd 2: [Inc] eight times—16 sts.

Rnd 3: [Sc, inc] eight times—24 sts.

Rnd 4: [Sc 2, inc] eight times—32 sts.

Rnd 5: [Sc 3, inc] eight times, join to the first st made and ch 1—40 sts.

Rnd 6: Bpsc around.

Rnds 7–12: Sc around.

Rnd 13: [Sc 6, dec] five times—35 sts.

Rnds 14–15: Sc around. At the end of Rnd 15, pause to stuff the base of the Leg.

Rnd 16: [Sc 5, dec] five times—30 sts.

Rnds 17–18: Sc around.

Rnd 19: [Sc 4, dec] five times—25 sts.

Rnds 20–25: Sc around.

Rnd 26: [Sc 3, dec] five times—20 sts.

Rnds 27–31: Sc around.

Fasten off with an 18 in. long tail, finish stuffing the Leg, and set aside for assembly.

BIG TOES (MAKE 2)

With **A**, ch 5.

Row 1: Sk the first ch from the hook, sc into the back bumps of the next 3 chs, 3 sc into the back bump of the last ch. Rotate work to have access to the unworked loops of the foundation ch. Sc across the

unworked loops of the first 3 chs. Ch 1 and turn—9 sts.

Row 2: Sc 3, [inc] three times, sc 3, ch 1 and turn—12 sts.

Row 3: Blo sc, bpsc 10, blo sc, ch 1 and turn.

Rows 4−7: Sc across, ch 1 and turn.

Row 8: [Dec, sc 2, dec] two times, ch 1 and turn—8 sts.

Row 9: Sc across, ch 1 and turn.

Row 10: Dec, sc 4, dec, ch 1 and turn—6 sts.

Row 11: [Sc3tog] two times—2 sts.

Fasten off with 12 in. long tail and set aside for assembly.

SMALL TOES (MAKE 2)

With **A**, ch 4.

Row 1: Sk the first ch from the hook, sc into the back bumps of the next 2 chs, 3 sc into the back bump of the last ch. Rotate work to have access to the unworked loops of the foundation ch. Sc across the unworked loops of the first 2 chs. Ch 1 and turn—7 sts.

Row 2: Sc 2, [inc] three times, sc 2, ch 1 and turn—10 sts.

Row 3: Blo sc, bpsc 8, blo sc, ch 1 and turn.

Rows 4−7: Sc across, ch 1 and turn.

Row 8: [Dec, sc 2] two times, dec, ch 1 and turn—7 sts.

Row 9: Sc across, ch 1 and turn.

Row 10: Dec, sc3tog, dec—3 sts.

Fasten off with 12 in. long tail and set aside for assembly.

BIG TOENAILS (MAKE 2)

With **B**, ch 5.

Row 1: Sk the first ch from the

hook, sc into the back bumps of the next 3 chs, 3 sc into the back bump of the last ch. Rotate work to have access to the unworked loops of the foundation ch. Sc across the unworked loops of the first 3 chs. Ch 1 and turn—9 sts.

Row 2: Sc 3, [inc] three times, sc 3—12 sts.

Fasten off with a 6 in. long tail and set aside for assembly.

SMALL TOENAILS (MAKE 2)

With **B**, ch 4.

Row 1: Sk the first ch from the hook, sc into the back bumps of the next 2 chs, 3 sc into the back bump of the last ch. Rotate work to have access to the unworked loops of the foundation ch. Sc across the unworked loops of the first 2 chs. Ch 1 and turn—7 sts.

Row 2: Sc 2, [inc] three times, sc 2—10 sts.

Fasten off with a 6 in. long tail and set aside for assembly.

ASSEMBLY

TOENAILS TO TOES: Match the Small Toenails up with the Small Toes, and the Big Toenails with the Big Toes. For placement, the raw edges of the toenails will always line up with the bottom edge (bpsc row) of the toes. For alignment, the centerline of the Toenail will always line up with the center of the front of the Toe. Use the 6 in. long tails of the Toenails to sew the Toenails onto their matched-up Toes. Stuff the remaining tails into the inside of the Toes—the tails will be

concealed once the Toes are connected to the Legs. Make sure all Toenails are sewn on before moving on to the next assembly section.

TOES TO LEGS: Each Leg gets one Small Toe and one Big Toe. The finished Toe attachment to the Legs will be a mirrored look. Grab four st markers and attach each one to the middle point of the raw edges (Rows 1 and 2) of the Small and Big Toes.

Attaching the Small Toes: The top of the Toe (Row 10) should line up with Rnd 13 of the Leg. Locate the "join to the first st made and ch 1 . . ." spot from Rnd 5 of the Leg. Use the attached marker to connect the raw edge of the Small Toe the top of the 38th st of Rnd 5 (counting 3 sts backwards from the "join to the first st made and ch 1 . . ." spot). Use the 12 in. tail of the Small Toe to sew the entire edge of the Toe onto the Leg—lightly stuff the Toe before completing the seam. Weave in any remaining length of tail. Repeat the same steps to attach the other Small Toe to the other Leg—however you MUST connect the Toe (using the st marker) to the 3rd st of Rnd 5. That way it is mirrored to the first Leg.

Attaching the Big Toes: The top of the Toe (Row 11) should line up with Rnd 15 of the Leg. Start with the first Leg you attached a Small Toe to. Locate the same "join to the first st made and ch 1 . . ." spot from Rnd 5 of the Leg. Use the attached st marker to connect the raw edge of the Big Toe to the top of the

3rd st of Rnd 5 (counting 3 sts forward from the "join to the first st made and ch 1 . . ." spot). Use the 12 in. long tail of the Big Toe to sew the entire edge of the Toe onto the Leg—lightly stuff the Toe before completing the seam. Use the remaining length of the tail to create a couple of French Knot Warts on the Leg and hide the rest of the tail inside the Leg. Repeat the same steps to attach the other Big Toe to the other Leg—however you must connect the Toe (using the st marker) to the 38th st of Rnd 5. That way it is mirrored to the first Leg.

Leg Warts (see Embroidery Stitch note on French Knot): Using **A** create the Warts on the Legs before the next assembly section. The number of knots that are needed to be added to the Legs is completely up to you.

ASSEMBLY (LEGS TO TORSO):
You will be attaching one Leg at a time to the base of the Torso, using st markers to help align and keep the Leg in place while sewing it on. The placement of the Legs should be at the back-half of the Torso base, away from the belly. The inner side of the Leg should be placed at least 2 sts from the centerline of the bottom of the Torso. First, secure the placement of the Leg onto the bottom of the Torso using at least two st markers—the Toes of the Leg should be pointing forward like the belly of the Torso. Thread the tapestry needle with the 18 in. long tail of the Leg. Use the tail to sew

the Leg onto the bottom of the Torso—checking halfway through to make sure that the Toes are still pointing forward like the belly. Once attached, weave in any remaining length of the tail. Repeat these same steps to attach the second Leg to the bottom of the Torso.

ARMS (MAKE 2)

With **A**, create a slip knot with an 18 in. long tail and ch 3.

Row 1: Sk the first ch from the hook, inc across the last two chs, ch 1 and turn—4 sts.

Row 2: Inc, sc 2, inc, ch 1 and turn—6 sts.

Row 3: Sc across, ch 1 and turn.

Row 4: Inc, sc 4, inc, ch 1 and turn—8 sts.

Rows 5—6: Sc across, ch 1 and turn.

Row 7: Sc 8, ch 8. Without twisting ch-8, join to the first st made, ch 1 and do NOT turn work. *You will be working in the round from here*—8 sts, 8 chs.

Rnd 1: Sc into the same st as joining, sc 7, blo sc across each ch. *Work continuously from here*—16 sts.

Rnds 2—4: Sc around.

Rnd 5: [Sc, inc] eight times—24 sts.

Rnds 6—10: Sc around.

Rnd 11: [Sc 4, dec] four times—20 sts.

Rnds 12—13: Sc around.

Rnd 14: [Sc 3, dec] four times—16 sts.

Rnds 15—16: Sc around.

Rnd 17: [Sc 2, dec] four times—12 sts.

Rnd 18: [Sc, dec] four times. Before moving on to the hand base, stuff inside of the Arm—8 sts.

Rnd 19 *(Begin hand base):* [Inc] seven times, sc—15 sts.

Rnds 20—21: Sc around. At the end of Rnd 21, join to the first st made and ch 4, sk 4, join to the next st and ch 1. The last step at the end of Rnd 21 created a thumbhole, and the next round will continue from this new joining point.

Rnd 22: Sc into the same st as joining, sc 10, blo sc across each ch. *Work continuously from here.*

Rnd 23: Sc around.

Rnd 24: *We will be using four st markers in this round to help form the fingers.* Sc, pm, sc 5, pm, sc 3, pm, sc 5 pm, sc— 15 sts, of which four sts are given markers.

Rnd 25 *(Begin middle finger):* Ch 1, sk 5, sc into 2nd marked st, sc 2, sk 5, sc into 4th marked st, sc—5 sts, 1 ch.

Rnd 26: Sc into the ch-1 space, sc 5—6 sts.

Rnds 27—30: Sc around.

Rnd 31 *(Middle fingernail round):* Sc 3. Join to the next st, pulling up a loop of **B** to change colors. Flo [ch 1, sc, picot, ch 1, sl st] into the same st as joining. Fasten off both colors. *Make a slip knot on your hook with* **A** *to begin the first finger*—4 sts, 1 picot.

Rnd 25 *(Begin first finger):* Join to the first marked st and ch 1. Sc into the same st as joining, sc 4, ch 1. *Work continuously from here*—5 sts, 1 ch.

Rnd 26: Sc 5, sc into the ch-1 space—6 sts.

Rnds 27—28: Sc around.

Rnd 29 *(First fingernail round):* Sc 5. Join to the next st, pulling up a lp of **B** yarn to change colors. Flo [ch 1, sc, picot, ch 1, sl] into the same st as joining. FO both yarn colors. *You will now create a slip knot on your hook with A to begin the 3rd finger—6 sts, 1 picot.*

Rnd 25 *(Begin third finger):* Join to the 4th marked st, and ch 1. Sc into the same st as joining, sc 4, ch 1. *Work continuously from here—5 sts, 1 ch.*

Rnd 26: Sc 5, sc into the ch-1 space—6 sts.

Rnds 27−29: Sc around.

Rnd 30 *(Third fingernail round):* Sc. Join to the next st, pulling up a loop of **B** to change colors. Flo [ch 1, sc, picot, ch 1, sl] into the same st as joining. FO both yarn colors. *Create a new slip knot with A to begin the thumb—6 sts, 1 picot.*

Rnd 22 *(Begin thumb): Before working the thumb, pause to very lightly stuff the inside of the hand base through the thumbhole.* Join to the first skipped st at the end of Rnd 21 and ch 1. Sc into the same st as joining, sc across the next three skipped sts. Rotate piece to have access to the unworked loops of the ch-4. Sc across the four unworked loops. *Work continuously from here—8 sts.*

Rnds 23−26: Sc around.

Rnd 27 *(Thumbnail round):* Sc 2. Join to the next st, pulling up a loop of **B** to change colors. Flo [ch 1, sc, picot, ch 1, sl] into the same st as joining. Fasten off both yarn colors.

CLEAN UP THE HANDS: *Before attaching the Arms to the Torso, you will need to clean up all the tails from the fingers and thumbs of the hands. First, use the A tails of each finger*

to close up the opening at the top of each finger, then weave the remaining lengths of the tails into the fingers. From there, you can weave in the **B** tails from the nails of each finger.

ASSEMBLY (ARMS TO TORSO): The top of the shoulders (foundation ch of Row 1) should line up to Rnd 34 of the Torso. The centerline of the Arms should line up with the side of the Ears. Thread a tapestry needle with the 18 in. long tail of the Arm. First sew down the top of the shoulder (foundation ch of Row 1) to base of the neck (Rnd 34 of the Torso). Next sew down the remainder of the edge of the Arm opening, including the bottom edge of the ch-8 from Rnd 7—be sure to lightly stuff the inside of the shoulder for sewing down the last length of the edge. Weave any remaining length of the tail into the Torso. Repeat the same steps to attach the other Arm to the other side of the Torso.

VEST FRONT (MAKE 2)

With **C**, ch 5.

Row 1: Sk the first ch from the hook, hdc across the next 4 chs, ch 1 and turn—4 sts.

Rows 2−3: Hdc across, ch 1 and turn.

Row 4: [Hdc dec] two times, ch 1 and turn—2 sts.

Rows 5−12: Hdc across, ch 1 and turn. At the end of Row 12, fasten off and set aside for assembly.

VEST BACK

With **C**, ch 21.

Row 1: Sk the first ch from the hook, hdc across the next 20 chs, ch 1 and turn—20 sts.

Row 2: Hdc across, ch 1 and turn.

Row 3: Hdc dec, hdc 16, hdc dec, ch 1 and turn—18 sts.

Row 4: Hdc across, ch 1 and turn.

Row 5: Hdc dec, hdc 14, hdc dec, ch 1 and turn—16 sts.

Row 6: Hdc across, ch 1 and turn.

Row 7: Hdc dec, hdc 12, hdc dec, ch 1 and turn—14 sts.

Row 8: Hdc across, ch 1 and turn.

Row 9: Hdc dec, hdc 10, hdc dec, ch 1 and turn—12 sts.

Row 10: Hdc across, ch 1 and turn.

Row 11: Hdc dec, hdc 8, hdc dec, ch 1 and turn—10 sts.

Row 12: Hdc across. Fasten off, and gather the two front pieces of the vest for assembly.

ASSEMBLY (SEW VEST PIECES TOGETHER): *You will be attaching one front piece of the Vest to the back piece of the Vest at a time. The WS and RS of the pieces do not matter in this section, because the Vest is meant to look "homemade" as if the troll made his own clothes. Thread the tapestry needle with a 10 in. long strand of* **D**. *First, sew together the top of the Front Vest piece (Row 12), to the last two sts of Row 12 of the Back Vest piece— working the seaming sts in the direction "outside to inside." Second, work crude running sts in a vertical line moving down the front piece of the Vest—just inside the inner edge of the front piece. Third, work a couple of running sts horizontally along the bottom* edge of the front piece of the Vest until you reach the other long side of the front piece—again just inside the bottom edge of the front piece of the Vest. Line up the raw edges of the first three rows of the Front and Back Vest pieces together. Use the tail to sew together the raw edges of the first three rows. Weave in any remaining length of the tail to the inside of the Vest and grab the other Front Vest piece. Repeat the same sewing instructions to attach the second Front Vest piece to the other side of the Back Vest piece—attaching the top of the Front Vest piece (Row 12) to the first two sts of Row 12 of the Back Vest piece.

LOINCLOTH (MAKE 2)

With **C**, ch 24.

Row 1: Sk the first ch from the hook, hdc across the next 23 chs, ch 1 and turn—23 sts.

Row 2: Hdc across, ch 1 and turn.

Row 3: Sl st 3, hdc 17, ch 1 and turn—17 hdc sts, 3 sl sts, 3 skipped sts.

Row 4: Sl st 2, hdc 13, ch 1 and turn—13 hdc sts, 2 sl sts, 2 skipped sts.

Row 5: Sl st 2, hdc 9, ch 1 and turn—9 hdc sts, 2 sl sts, 2 skipped sts.

Row 6: Sl st 2, hdc 5, ch 1 and turn—5 hdc sts, 2 sl sts, 2 skipped sts.

Row 7: Sl st, [sl st, ch2], [2 tr, picot, ch 3], sl. *Fasten off and set aside for assembly—3 sl sts, 2 tr sts, 1 picot st, 1 ch-2, 1 ch-3.*

ASSEMBLY (SEW LOINCLOTH PIECES TOGETHER): *You will be seaming up just ONE side of the Loincloth for this section. Once again, the WS and RS of the pieces do not matter in this section, because the Loincloth is meant to look "homemade" as if the troll made his own clothes.* Thread the tapestry needle with a 20 in. long strand of **D**. Gather both Loincloth pieces, and line up the raw edges of Rows 1–3 of one side of the pieces. Sew the lined up raw edges together using at least three or four sts. Pick a Loincloth side as your "front side" and sew crude running stitches along the triangular edge—just inside the bottom edge. Once you reach the other raw edge side of the front Loincloth, weave the remaining length of the yarn into the inside.

ASSEMBLY (LOINCLOTH TO TORSO): *The placement of the Loincloth onto the Torso—how low it is hanging off the belly of the troll—is up to you. Be sure to line the picot points of the Loincloth (Row 7) with the centerline of the belly of the Torso.* Thread the tapestry needle with another 20 in. long strand of **D**. Line up the other raw edges of Rows 1–3 of the Loincloth pieces, and sew the raw edges together. Leaving the tapestry needle threaded, carefully pull the Loincloth onto the troll Legs first. Use st markers to keep the Loincloth in place and use the threaded tapestry needle to tack it onto the bottom of the Torso, just beneath the belly at the widest part of the belly. Weave any remaining length of the yarn into the inside of the torso. At this point you may put the Vest on the troll.

WOODEN CLUB

With **D**, create a slip knot with a 12 in. long tail and ch 26.

Row 1: Sk the first ch from the hook, hdc into the next 8 chs, sc into the next 17 chs, ch 1 and turn—17 sc sts, 8 hdc sts.

Row 2: Blo sc 17, blo hdc 8, ch 1 and turn—17 sc sts, 8 hdc sts.

Row 3: Blo hdc 14, blo sc 11, ch 1 and turn—14 hdc sts, 11 sc sts.

Row 4: Blo sc 15, blo hdc 10, ch 1 and turn—15 sc sts, 10 hdc st.

Row 5: Blo hdc 13, blo sc 12, ch 1 and turn—13 hdc sts, 12 sc sts.

Row 6: Blo sc 11, blo hdc 14, ch 1 and turn—14 hdc sts, 11 sc sts.

Row 7: Blo sc across, ch 1 and turn—25 sts.

Row 8: Blo sc 12, blo hdc 13, ch 1 and turn—13 hdc sts, 12 sc sts.

Row 9: Blo hdc 14, blo sc 11, ch 1 and turn—14 hdc sts, 11 sc sts.

Row 10: Blo sc 18, blo hdc 7, ch 1 and turn—18 sc sts, 7 hdc sts.

Row 11: Blo hdc 8, blo sc 17, ch 1 and turn—17 sc sts, 8 hdc sts.

Row 12 *(Seaming row):* Fold the long sides together to line up the tops of the sts of Row 11 with the unworked loops of the foundation ch from Row 1. Work sl sts across each set of matched sts and unworked loops to seam the long sides together. Ch 1 and rotate your piece so you have access to the nearest raw edges of Rows 1–11. *Pause here to stuff the inside of the club before moving on to the last two rounds—25 seaming sl sts.*

Rnd 1 *(End of club):* Work 11 sc evenly around the raw edges of the end of the club. *Work continuously from here for the last round*—11 sts.

Rnd 2: Blo sc, [blo dec] five times. Fasten off with a 6 in. long tail and set aside for assembly—6 sts.

ASSEMBLY (CLUB TO HAND): *The skinnier end of the Club will be the end that is placed in the troll's hand. It does not matter which hand the troll holds the Club in.* Before attaching the Club to the hand, thread the tapestry needle with the 6 in. long tail and close the opening of the Club from Rnd 2. Weave in any remaining length of the tail into the Club. Next, thread the tapestry needle with the beginning 12 in. long tail and close the other opening. Weave the tail into the Club, pushing the needle back out to any spot ¾"–1" up from the bottom of the Club. Use the rest of the tail to tack the Club onto the inside of one of the hands. Weave the remaining length of the tail into the Club.

PYGMY PUFF

Designed by Christina Marie
Skill level: ✎ ✎

As she passes out copies of *The Quibbler* on the Hogwarts Express in *Harry Potter and the Half-Blood Prince*, Luna Lovegood comes upon Ginny Weasley and her current boyfriend, Dean Thomas, chatting in the aisle. Ginny has a puffy pink creature perched on her shoulder that bobbles and purrs, with a small snout and large eyes—a Pygmy Puff.

Pygmy Puffs are the miniature version of a Puffskein, and are sold by Ginny's twin brothers, Fred and George, at their joke shop in Diagon Alley, Weasleys' Wizard Wheezes. They come in either pink or purple, and are part of their bestselling WonderWitch line of products for young witches.

This delightful Pygmy Puff amigurumi is sure to captivate hearts with its adorable charm. Its wide, glistening eyes radiate playfulness and its button-like nose adds an extra touch of cuteness. Using soft and fluffy yarn, this Pygmy Puff is made for cuddles. The luxurious body invites fingers to explore its cloud-like texture. Crocheted with a sprinkle of your own magic, this Pygmy Puff makes for a popular companion.

> "He's lovely. They've been known to sing on Boxing Day, you know."
>
> Luna Lovegood,
> *Harry Potter and the Half-Blood Prince*

FINISHED MEASUREMENTS
Height: 4 in. / 10.16 cm
Width: 3.75 in. / 9.5 cm

YARN
Worsted weight (#4 medium) yarn, shown in Lion Brand *Feels Like Butta* (100% polyester, 218 yd. / 199 m per 3½ oz. / 100 g skein).
Color A: #215-101A Pink, 1 skein

Note: The following two yarns are held and worked together.
Chunky weight (#5 bulky) yarn, shown in Scheepjes *Sweetheart Soft* (100% polyester, 167 yd / 153 m per 3½ oz. / 100 g skein).
Color B: #9 Bright Pink, 1 skein
Fingering weight (#1 super fine) yarn, shown in Scheepjes *Catona* (100% cotton, 136 yd. / 125 m per 1¾ oz. / 50 g skein).
Color C: #519 Freesia, 1 skein

HOOKS
• US F-5 / 3.75mm crochet hook
• US 7 / 4.5mm crochet hook

NOTIONS
• Polyester stuffing
• Pair of 8mm safety eyes
• Straight pins
• Tapestry needle
• Embroidery thread, small amount in dark pink

GAUGE
Gauge is not critical for this project. Ensure your stitches are tight so the stuffing won't show through.

NOTES
• All pieces are worked in the round. Pieces are worked in continuous rounds unless noted otherwise.

- Use straight pins to move and adjust the placement of pieces before sewing.
- All items are crocheted using the yarn under method: Insert your hook under the top two loops, yarn under, pull up a loop, yarn over and pull through both loops. This creates an "x" stitch.

BEHIND THE MAGIC

Concept artist Rob Bliss imagined the Pygmy Puff, the miniature form of a Puffskein, in its less furry form, and then exploding with cuddly fluff.

HEAD AND BODY

With **A** and smaller hook, make a magic ring.

Rnd 1: 6 sc in ring; do not join—6 sc.

Rnd 2: Inc in each sc around—12 sc.

Rnd 3: Sc around.

Rnd 4: [Sc in next sc, inc in next sc] around—18 sc.

Rnd 5: Sc in next sc, inc in next sc, [sc in next 2 sc, inc in next sc] around, sc in last sc—24 sc.

Rnd 6: Sc around.

Rnd 7: [Sc in next 3 sc, inc in next sc] around—30 sc.

Rnd 8: Sc around.

Stuffing as you go, insert eyes between Rnds 5 and 6 with 7 stitches in between.

Start working the Body with **B** and **C** held together and larger hook.

Rnd 9: Sc in next 2 sc, inc in next sc, [sc in next 4 sc, inc in next sc] repeat around, sc in next 2 sc—36 sc.

Rnd 10: [Sc in next 5 sc, inc in next sc] around—42 sc.

Rnd 11: Sc in next 3 sc, inc in next sc, [sc in next 6 sc, inc in next sc] around, sc in next 3 sc—48 sc.

Rnd 12: [Sc in next 7 sc, inc in next sc] around—54 sc.

Rnds 13−22: Sc around. (10 rounds)

Rnd 23: [Sc in next 7 sc, dec in next 2 sc] around—48 sc.

Rnd 24: Sc around.

Rnd 25: Sc in next 3 sc, dec in next 2 sc, [sc in next 6 sc, dec in next 2 sc] around, sc in next 3 sc—42 sc.

Rnd 26: Sc around.

Rnd 27: [Sc in next 5 sc, dec in next 2 sc] around—36 sc.

Rnd 28: Sc in next 2 sc, dec in next 2 sc, [sc in next 4 sc, dec in next 2 sc] around, sc in next 2 sc—30 sc.

Rnd 29: [Sc in next 3 sc, dec in next 2 sc] around—24 sc.

Rnd 30: [Sc in next sc, dec in next 2 sc] around—16 sc.

Rnd 31: Decrease around.

Finish stuffing firmly. Fasten yarn and leave a tail for sewing. Weave end through the remaining front loops. Pull tight to close and weave in end. Cut your yarn.

EARS (MAKE 2)

With **A** and smaller hook, make a magic ring.
Rnd 1: 6 sc in ring; do not join—6 sc.
Fasten yarn and leave a tail for sewing. Pull your magic ring tight. You won't be closing the magic ring.

LEGS (MAKE 4)

With **A** and smaller hook, make a magic ring.
Rnd 1: 8 sc in ring; do not join—8 sc.
Fasten yarn and leave a tail for sewing. Pull your magic ring tight. You won't be closing the magic ring.

ASSEMBLY

1. Sew Ears between Rnds 8 and 9 with approximately 6 stitches in between.
2. Sew Front Legs between Rnds 11 and 12 with approximately 6 stitches in between.
3. Sew Back Legs between Rnds 21 and 22 with approximately 6 stitches in between.
4. With the dark pink embroidery thread, embroider a nose over Rnd 1.

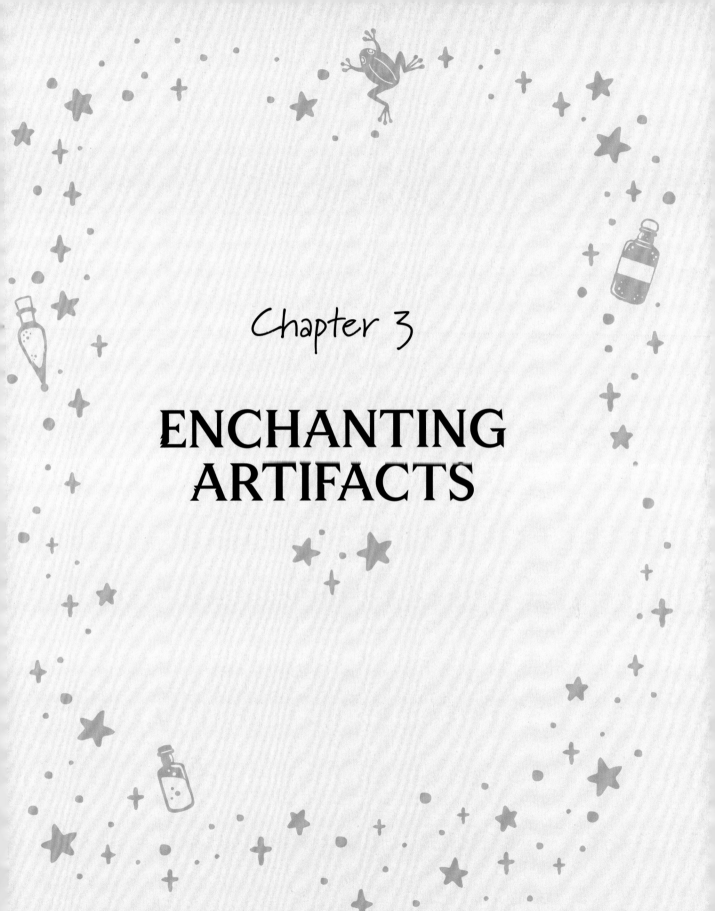

Chapter 3

ENCHANTING ARTIFACTS

CHOCOLATE FROG

Designed by Jacki Donhou
Skill Level: ⚡ ⚡

While Harry Potter and Ron Weasley introduce themselves on the Hogwarts Express in *Harry Potter and the Sorcerer's Stone*, the trolley witch comes by with a cart bursting with wizarding confections and candies. Well, nothing could be better for starting a lifelong friendship than a sweet treat?

One of these treats is one of the most popular in the wizarding world: Chocolate Frogs. Chocolate Frogs come in a gold-trimmed purple box with five sides. When Harry opens the box, the chocolate frog inside leaps up, which results in it flying out the train's window. Ron sympathizes about Harry's rotten luck, as each chocolate frog has "only one good jump in them to begin with."

The packaging for the Chocolate Frogs confection was created by Ruth Winick, who used the Gothic architecture prevalent in Hogwarts castle's design for inspiration. The overall design was based on suggestions by production designer Stuart Craig, who drew the shape of a pentagon for her, and told her to think "classical." The Chocolate Frog box is, indeed, classic, and an unforgettable part of the wizarding world.

This amigurumi Chocolate Frog is a slightly oversized version of the iconic treat from the wizarding world. The adorable frog itself is crocheted with meticulous care and exhibits a playful charm with a touch of blush under its eyes. The Chocolate Frog sits gracefully inside his crocheted purple box adorned with beautiful delicate yellow lacing around the edges, adding an extra touch of authenticity to the packaging seen in the films.

> "These aren't real frogs, are they?"
> "It's just a spell."
>
> Harry Potter and Ron Weasley,
> *Harry Potter and the Sorcerer's Stone*

FINISHED MEASUREMENTS
Frog
Height: 5 in. / 12.7 cm
Box
Height and Width: 6 in. / 15.24 cm

YARN
DK Weight (#3 light) yarn shown in Universal Yarn *Bamboo Pop*, (50% cotton, 50% bamboo, 292 yd. / 266 m per 3.5 oz. / 100 g ball).
Color A: #152 Chocolate, 1 ball
Color B: #141 Bubblegum, 1 ball
Color C: #101 White, 1 ball
Color D: #112 Black, 1 ball
Color E: #116 Royal, 1 ball
Color F: #139 Sundae, 1 ball

HOOK
• US-0 / 2.00mm crochet hook

NOTIONS
• Stitch markers
• Pair of 20mm safety eyes
• Polyester stuffing
• Tapestry needle
• Embroidery needle
• Straight pins
• Fabric stiffening spray
• Blocking mat
• Plastic canvas

GAUGE
Gauge is not critical for this project. Ensure your stitches are tight so the stuffing won't show through.

SPECIAL ABBREVIATIONS
Back Loop Only (blo): Work through back loop only
Front Loop Only (flo): Work through front loop only
Single Crochet 2 Tog (sc2tog): Decrease by working 2 single crochets together
Double Crochet 2 tog (dc2tog): Decrease by working 2 double crochets together

NOTES

- Each of the frog's pieces is crocheted separately and in continuous rounds. Both the head and the body are worked from the bottom of the piece to the top. It is also recommended to begin stuffing the head, body, and legs at the midpoint of the work and not wait until the end rounds.
- The box pieces are crocheted flat and then joined at the end of each round. To attach the pieces together, the mattress stitch and whip stitch will be used.

BEHIND THE MAGIC

Director Chris Columbus remembers actor Rupert Grint [Ron] "thought this was the greatest day of his acting career, because we were letting him eat chocolate and candy all day" while filming his scene eating sweets inside the train compartment in *Harry Potter and the Sorcerer's Stone.*

HEAD

With **A**, make a magic ring.

Rnd 1: 6 sc in ring—6 sc.

Rnd 2: 2 sc in each sc around—12 sc.

Rnd 3: [Sc in next sc, 2 sc in next sc] 6 times—18 sc.

Rnd 4: [Sc in next sc, 2 sc in next sc, sc in next sc] 6 times—24 sc.

Rnd 5: [Sc in next 3 sc, 2 sc in next sc] 6 times—30 sc.

Rnd 6: [Sc in next 2 sc, 2 sc in next sc, sc in next 2 sc] 6 times—36 sc.

Rnd 7: [Sc in next 5 sc, 2 sc in next sc] 6 times—42 sc.

Rnd 8: [Sc in next 3 sc, 2 sc in next sc, sc in next 3 sc] 6 times—48 sc.

Rnd 9: [Sc in next 7 sc, 2 sc in next sc] 6 times—54 sc.

Rnd 10: Sc around.

Rnd 11: [Sc in next 4 sc, 2 sc in next sc, sc in next 4 sc] 6 times—60 sc.

Rnds 12–14: Sc around.

Rnd 15: Sc in next 11 sc, [sc2tog over next 2 sc, sc in next sc] twice, sc2tog over next 2 sc, sc in the next 21 sc, [sc2tog over next 2 sc, sc in next sc] twice, sc2tog over next 2 sc, sc in the next 12 sc—54 sc.

Rnd 16: [Sc in next 7 sc, sc2tog over next 2 sc] 6 times—48 sc.

Rnds 17–18: Sc around.

Rnd 19: [Sc in next 15 sc, ch 2, sk next 2 sc] twice, sc in next 16 sc—48 sc.

Note: The chain spaces with the skips in Rnd 19 will be where you place the safety eyes later in the pattern.

Rnds 20–22: Sc around.

Note: On Rnd 23, the increases (or 2 sc in the next sts) need to be lined up above each of the safety eyes. If they are not, start the rnd over and adjust the starting stitch marker by 1 to 3 sts to make sure those increases are parallel with each of the safety eyes.

Rnd 23: Sc in next 11 sc, [2 sc in next sc] 8 times, sc in the next 9 sc, [2 sc in next sc] 8 times, sc in the next 12 sc—64 sc.

Rnd 24: Sc around.

Add the safety eyes in the chain spaces on Rnd 19. Make sure the backs are fastened as far as they will push down on the stem of the safety eye. This will ensure that they will not move and will be tight enough for the details later.

Rnd 25: Sc in next 11 sc, [sc2tog over next 2 sc] 8 times, sc in the next 9 sc, [sc2tog over next 2 sc] 8 times, sc in the next 12 sc—48 sc.

Rnd 26: Sc in next 11 sc, [sc2tog over next 2 sc, sc in next sc] twice, sc2tog over next 2 sc, sc in the next 9 sc, [sc2tog over next 2 sc, sc in next sc] twice, sc2tog over next 2 sc, sc in the next 12 sc—42 sc.

Rnd 27: [Sc in next 5 sc, sc2tog over next 2 sc] 6 times—36 sc.

Rnd 28: Sc around.

Stuff the Head firmly.

Rnd 29: [Sc in next 2 sc, sc2tog over next 2 sc, sc in next 2 sc] 6 times—30 sc.

Rnd 30: [Sc in next 3 sc, sc2tog over next 2 sc] 6 times—24 sc.

Rnd 31: [Sc in next sc, sc2tog over next 2 sc, sc in next sc] 6 times—18 sc.

Rnd 32: [Sc in next sc, sc2tog over next 2 sc] 6 times—12 sc.

Finish stuffing the Head firmly.

Rnd 33: [Sc in next sc, sc2tog over next 2 sc] 4 times—8 sc.

Fasten off. Weave yarn under all flo, pull tight to close and hide the yarn tail inside the Head.

Stuff the Body gently. Pinch the Body closed and work through both sides with 15 sc to close the opening.

Fasten off. Leave a long tail for attaching.

TOES (MAKE 12)

With **A**, make a magic ring.

Rnd 1: 10 sc in ring—10 sc.

Rnds 2—3: Sc around.

Rnd 4: Sc2tog around—5 sc.

Rnds 5—6: Sc around.

Do not stuff the Toes. Fasten off. Hide the yarn tails inside the Toes.

FRONT LEGS (MAKE 2)

With **A**, attach three Toes together and work Front Leg as follows:

Rnd 7: Attach the yarn to the first Toe with a ch and sc in next 2 stitches, leaving the 2 stitches on the back side of the Toe unworked. Next, attach the second Toe with a sc in next 3 stitches, leaving the 2 stitches on the back side of the Toe unworked. Then, sc in next 5 stitches around the third Toe, sc in next 2 unworked stitches on the back side of the second Toe and then sc in the 2 unworked stitches on the back side of the first Toe. This will complete Rnd 7 of the Front Leg—15 sc.

Rnds 8—10: Sc around.

Rnd 11: [Sc in next sc, sc2tog over next 2 sc] 5 times—10 sc.

Rnds 12—15: Sc around.

Rnd 16: Sc2tog over next 2 sc, sc in next 2 sc, [2 sc in next sc] twice, sc in next 2 sc, sc2tog over next 2 sc—10 sc.

BODY

With **A**, make a magic ring.

Rnd 1: 6 sc in ring—6 sc.

Rnd 2: 2 sc in each sc around—12 sc.

Rnd 3: [Sc in next sc, 2 sc in next sc] 6 times—18 sc.

Rnd 4: [Sc in next sc, 2 sc in next sc, sc in next sc] 6 times—24 sc.

Rnd 5: [Sc in next 3 sc, 2 sc in next sc] 6 times—30 sc.

Rnd 6: [Sc in next 2 sc, 2 sc in next sc, sc in next 2 sc] 6 times—36 sc.

Rnd 7: [Sc in next 5 sc, 2 sc in next sc] 6 times—42 sc.

Rnds 8—10: Sc around.

Rnd 11: [Sc in next 3 sc, 2 sc in next sc, sc in next 3 sc] 6 times—48 sc.

Rnds 12—16: Sc around.

Rnd 17: [Sc in next 3 sc, sc2tog over next 2 sc, sc in next 3 sc] 6 times—42 sc.

Rnds 18—19: Sc around.

Rnd 20: [Sc in next 5 sc, sc2tog over next 2 sc] 6 times—36 sc.

Rnds 21—22: Sc around.

Rnd 23: [Sc in next 2 sc, sc2tog over next 2 sc, sc in next 2 sc] 6 times—30 sc.

Rnd 24: Sc around.

Rnd 17: Hdc in next sc, sc in next 8 sc, hdc in next sc—10 st.

Rnd 18: Hdc in next sc, sc in next 9 sc—10 st.

Rnds 19—26: Sc around.

Gently stuff both of the Front Legs. Add 1 or 2 extra sc after Rnd 26 if the last stitch isn't parallel to the bottom of the foot. Pinch the Leg closed and work through both sides with 5 sc to close the opening. Fasten off. Leave a long yarn tail for attaching.

BACK LEGS (MAKE 2)

With **A**, attach three Toes together and work Back Leg as follows:

Rnd 7: Attach the yarn to the first Toe with a ch and sc in next 2 stitches, leaving the 2 stitches on the back side of the Toe unworked. Next, attach the second Toe with a sc in next 3 stitches, leaving the 2 stitches on the back side of the Toe unworked. Then, sc in next 5 stitches around the third Toe, sc in next 2 unworked stitches on the back side of the second Toe and then sc in next 2 unworked stitches on the back side of the first Toe. This will complete Rnd 7 of the Back Leg. [15]

Rnds 8—10: Sc around.

Rnd 11: [Sc in next sc, sc2tog over next 2 sc] 5 times—10 sc.

Rnds 12—25: Sc around.

Rnd 26: [Sc in next sc, 2 sc in next sc] 5 times—15 sc.

Rnds 27—30: Sc around.

Gently stuff both of the Back Legs. Add 2 or 3 extra sc after Rnd 30 if the last stitch isn't parallel to the bottom of the foot. Pinch the Leg closed, and work through both sides

with 7 sc to close the opening. Fasten off. Leave a long yarn tail for attaching.

FACE DETAILS

Using **C** and embroidery needle push the needle through the side of the Head and out at the bottom of the first eye (I prefer a smaller embroidery needle with a sharp tip for this). Then, insert your needle through the top center of the eye. Pull the yarn through the Head and out the same stitch or near where you entered. This adds a stripe to the outside portion of the eye. Do not pull too tight, otherwise the yarn may slip under the eye. Secure this yarn in place by having the needle come back up and circle the middle of the yarn strand on the outside of the eye. Take the needle back through the side of the Head at the starting point, tie it off, and hide the yarn tail inside the Head. Then, repeat the steps for the second eye.

To add the cheeks, push the embroidery needle and **B** yarn through the bottom of the Head and out a stitch below the start of **C** on the bottom of the first eye. Then, insert your needle 3 stitches away on the same round, and parallel to the outside of the eye. Bring the needle up through the same starting stitch and repeat these steps 3 times by wrapping the yarn around the 3 stitches creating a cheek. Once complete, bring the needle back through the bottom of the Head at the starting point, tie it off, and hide the yarn tails inside the Head. Then, repeat the steps for the second cheek.

With the pins, mark the width of the nose in the center of the face at Rnd 16. Each pin should be 3 to 4 stitches away from each eye. Adjust to the right or left by 1 stitch if the pins are not centered on the face. Once even, enter the embroidery needle with **D** through the bottom of the Head and out at the first marked pin on the right. Enter the needle into the next stitch toward the eye on the same rnd and back up through the first stitch you entered. Repeat these steps once more, wrapping the yarn around the 1 stitch twice to create a nostril. Once complete, exit the yarn back through the same stitch on the bottom of the Head, knot the two ends, and hide the yarn tails inside the Head. Repeat these steps for the left nostril, but after entering through the stitch marked with the pin, bring the needle down through the stitch to the left toward the safety eye on that side of the face.

Like the steps for the nostrils, use pins to mark the mouth before sewing the details. Mark both mouth corners 3 stitches directly below the start of the cheeks. Then mark the center of the mouth on Rnd 14, 2 rnds below the nostrils, and centered on the face. Enter the embroidery needle with **D** through the bottom of the Head and out at the right-marked corner of the mouth. Then, enter the needle through the left-marked corner of the mouth. Then, bring the needle up through the top-centered pin circling the yarn and pushing the needle back through the same stitch. This secures the yarn in that position. Exit the needle back through the bottom of the Head at the starting point, tie off the two yarn tails, and hide the yarn inside the Head.

ASSEMBLY

Pin the Body to the back of the Head, centered between Rnds 13 and 14. The Head should push down onto the front of the Body giving the look of a round belly. Once the placement is to your liking, sew together. Add 3 to 4 whip stitches on both sides of the Head and the sides of the Body just below the sewn corners. This prevents the Head from flopping back and forth. When complete, hide the yarn tails inside the Body.

The Front Legs are sewn using whip stitches to the sides of the Body starting between the 3 to 4 whip stitches that secured the side of the Head to the Body. Angle them toward the front of the Body so one Toe on each foot is touching. Add a few extra whip stitches to the inside and middle portion of the Arms to secure them to the Body.

Bend the Back Legs so one end of the closed seam is touching the bottom of the foot. With a long piece of yarn and the needle, add a few whip stitches to the Legs just below the curve to create permanently bent Legs. Tie off the yarn ends and hide them inside the Legs.

Pin the seams of the Back Legs near Rnds 6 and 7 of the bottom of the Body with at least 1 stitch between them. Once the Frog is sitting on his own, whip stitch the Back Legs in place. Add a few extra whip stitches to the bend portion of the Legs to secure them to the Body just

under the front Arms. Tie off the yarn ends and hide them inside the Body.

BOX (MAKE 4 PENTAGON-SHAPED PIECES)

Note: The 2 chs starting each rnd does not count as a dc. Join the end of each rnd with a sl st in the first dc.

With **E**, make a magic ring.

Rnd 1: Ch 2, dc in ring 15 times, join rnd— 15 dc.

Rnd 2: Ch 2, (dc, tr, dc) together in same dc as the previous chs, dc in next 2 dc, [(dc, tr, dc) together in next dc, dc in next 2 dc] 4 times, join—20 dc, 5 tr.

Rnd 3: Ch 2, dc in same dc as the previous chs, [(dc, tr, dc) together in next dc, dc in next 4 dc] 4 times, (dc, tr, dc) together in next dc, dc in next 3 dc, join—30 dc, 5 tr.

Rnd 4: Ch 2, dc in same dc as the previous chs, dc in next dc [(dc, tr, dc) together in next dc, dc in next 6 dc] 4 times, (dc, tr, dc) together in next 4 dc, join—40 dc, 5 tr.

Rnd 5: Ch 2, dc in the same dc as the previous chs, dc in next 2 dc, [(dc, tr, dc) together in next dc, dc in next 8 dc] 4 times, (dc, tr, dc) together in next dc, dc in next 5 dc, join—50 dc, 5 tr.

Rnd 6: Ch 2, dc in the same dc as the previous chs, dc in next 3 dc, [(dc, tr, dc) together in next dc, dc in next 10 dc] 4 times, (dc, tr, dc) together in next dc, dc in next 6 dc, join—60 dc, 5 tr.

Rnd 7: Ch 2, dc in the same dc as the previous chs, dc in next 4 dc, [(dc, tr, dc) together in next

dc, dc in next 12 dc] 4 times, (dc, tr, dc) together in next dc, dc in next 7 dc, join—70 dc, 5 tr.

Rnd 8: Ch 2, dc in the same dc as the previous chs, dc in next 5 dc, [(dc, tr, dc) together in next dc, dc in next 14 dc] 4 times, (dc, tr, dc) together in next dc, dc in next 8 dc, join—80 dc, 5 tr.

Rnd 9: Ch 2, dc in the same dc as the previous chs, dc in next 6 dc, [(dc, tr, dc) together in next dc, dc in next 16 dc] 4 times, (dc, tr, dc) together in next dc, dc in next 9 dc, join—90 dc, 5 tr.

Rnd 10: Ch 2, dc in the same dc as the previous chs, dc in next 7 dc, [(dc, tr, dc) together in next dc, dc in next 18 dc] 4 times, (dc, tr, dc) together in next dc, dc in next 10 dc, join—105 dc, 5 tr.

Fasten off. Weave the yarn tails inside the Box pieces.

Using the blocking mat and pins, secure each of the Box pieces in place, but first wet them with water and wring them out. Make sure the four Box pieces are stretched to 5½ x 5½ inches. Let them dry for twenty-four hours.

Lay two of the Box pieces face down on the plastic canvas and with a pencil trace an outline of each piece. Cut the two pentagons out and trim them to fit the two crocheted Box pieces. Stack the third and fourth crocheted Box pieces on top of the other Box pieces with the plastic canvas pieces sandwiched between.

Cut a piece of **E** about 24 inches long and attach it to the corner blo of the bottom Box piece with a ch. Then, using the mattress stitch, sew around the outside of both of the Box pieces to secure the plastic canvas in place. Fasten off. Weave the yarn tails inside the pieces.

Attach **F** to the flo of the stitch before the right corner of the top Box piece facing upward with a sc. Leaving the bottom flo alone for details later.

Rnd 11: Ch 2, (then work this rnd only in all flo) dc in the same dc as chs, dc in next 19 dc, [(dc, tr, dc) together in next dc, dc in next 20 dc] 4 times, (dc, tr, dc) together in next dc, join—120 dc, 5 tr.

Rnd 12: Ch 2, dc in the same dc as the chs, dc in next 20 dc, [dc2tog over next 2 dc, dc in next 21 dc] 4 times, dc2tog over next 2 dc, join—110 dc.

Fasten off. Leave a long yarn tail for attaching. Repeat Rnds 11 and 12 for the other piece. Using a blocking mat and pins, re-secure the two Box pieces in place at the corners. Spray with the fabric stiffening spray around the two pieces and the sides to stiffen them. Repeat as many times as needed.

BOX TOP DETAIL: Flip one of the Box pieces over with the **F** edging face down. Attach **F** to the flo of the dc in the bottom right corner.

Rnd 1: Ch 2, sk the next flo, [sc in next flo, ch 2, sk the next flo] 9 times, (sc in next 2 flo, ch 2) to make the corner, then repeat all steps 4 times to complete the 5 sides, join with a sl st to the first sc—60 sc, 100 ch, 55 sk.

Note: Scallops on Rnd 2 are made of 5 treble crochets with a picot at the top of each, then 1 more treble without a picot. To create the picot, ch 2 then

sc in the top side of the treble crochet just below the chs.

Note: All the stitches made on Rnd 2 will be crocheted around the ch loops.

Rnd 2: Ch, [sk first loop, scallop in next loop, sk next loop, sc in the next loop, (dc, picot, dc) together in next loop, sc in next loop, sk next loop, scallop in next loop, sk next loop, sc in next loop, sc2tog over next 2 sc] 4 times, join with a sl st to the first sc—60 tr, 10 dc, 20 sc, 20 sk.

Fasten off. Leave a long yarn tail for attaching. With the long yarn tail and the needle, sew down the center tip of the scallops (treble 3 out of the 5) and the extra middle picot. Weave the needle under the **E** dc's to reach the next scallop tip. Fasten off. Hide the yarn tails inside the pieces.

BOX ASSEMBLY: Stand the top Box piece upright, with the details facing away from you. Place the bottom piece up against the inside of the Box so the edging of the top is underneath it and use pins to secure them together. Once in place, use the needle and the yarn tail on the bottom Box piece to whip stitch the two pieces together. Making sure to only go through one layer of the pentagon, starting at the corner work your way around the bottom of the Box first, then continue whip stitching around to the inside. Once finished, weave the yarn tails inside the Box pieces to hide them.

Spray the stiffening spray once more around the Box including the sides and top details. Let dry.

GOLDEN SNITCH

Designed by Christina Marie
Skill level: ✔

Quidditch is the most popular game in the wizarding world, played while flying on brooms. There are seven players, a Quaffle, two Bludger balls, and one Golden Snitch, which is the size of a walnut and, if caught, is worth 150 points—enough to win the game. The Golden Snitch flies quickly and unpredictably, challenging the Seekers on both sides to catch it. Harry Potter is Seeker for the Gryffindor Quidditch team.

Coming up with the design of the Golden Snitch for the first game in *Harry Potter and the Sorcerer's Stone* was also a challenge, as its fluttering gold wings needed to expand when it was flying, but retract into the ball and be hidden when it was at rest. And so two narrow and deep channels are carved across the Snitch's surface, part of its Art Nouveau—style exterior. The tiny prop was electroformed in copper and then plated with gold. Whenever it was seen near Harry, the computer artists created a reflection of the Golden Snitch in his glasses.

Whether you're a Seeker at heart or simply admire the enchanting game of Quidditch, this amigurumi Golden Snitch captures the excitement and wonder of the wizarding world. Made with golden yellow yarn, this Golden Snitch gleams and shimmers. Its delicate wings are crocheted with care and capture the Snitch's swift movements.

"But you're a Seeker. The only thing I want you to worry about is this . . . the Golden Snitch."

Gryffindor Quidditch captain Oliver Wood to Harry Potter, *Harry Potter and the Sorcerer's Stone*

FINISHED MEASUREMENTS
Height: 1.5 in. / 3.81 cm
Width: 7.5 in. / 19.05 cm

YARN
Worsted Weight (#4) yarn, shown in Lion Brand's *Feels Like Butta*, (100% polyester, 218 yd. / 199 m per 3½ oz. / 100 g skein).
Color A: #215-159U Golden Sunshine, 1 skein

HOOKS
• US F-5 / 3.75mm crochet hook, for Snitch
• US D / 3mm crochet hook, for Wings

NOTIONS
• Polyester stuffing
• Straight pins
• Tapestry needle

GAUGE
Gauge is not critical for this project. Ensure your stitches are tight so the stuffing won't show through.

NOTES
• Some items are worked in the round, and some are worked in rows. Items worked in rounds are continuous rounds; do not join.
• Use straight pins to move and adjust the placement of pieces before sewing.
• All items are crocheted using the yarn under method: Insert your hook under the top two loops, yarn under, pull up a loop, yarn over and pull through both loops. This creates an "x" stitch.

SNITCH

With **A** and larger hook, make a magic ring.

Rnd 1: 6 sc in ring; do not join—6 sc.

Rnd 2: Inc in each sc around—12 sc.

Rnd 3: [Sc in next sc, inc in next sc] around—18 sc.

Rnd 4: Sc in next sc, inc in next sc, [sc in next 2 sc, inc in next sc] around, sc in last sc—24 sc.

Rnd 5: Sc around.

Rnd 6: [Sc in next 3 sc, inc in next sc] around—30 sc.

Rnd 7: Sc in next 2 sc, inc in next sc, [sc in next 4 sc, inc in next sc] around, sc in next 2 sc—36 sc.

Rnds 8–13: Sc around. (6 rounds)

Rnd 14: Sc in next 2 sc, dec over next 2 sc, [sc in next 4 sc, dec over next 2 sc] around, sc in next 2 sc—30 sc.

Rnd 15: [Sc in next 3 sc, dec over next 2 sc] around—24 sc.

Rnd 16: Sc around.

Rnd 17: Sc in next sc, dec over next 2 sc, [sc in next 2 sc, dec over next 2 sc] around, sc in next sc—18 sc.

Rnd 18: [Sc in next sc, dec over next 2 sc] around—12 sc.

Rnd 19: Decrease around.

Stuff firmly and fasten off, leaving a tail for sewing. Weave end through the remaining front loops. Pull tight to close and weave in the end.

BEHIND THE MAGIC

Harry wins his first Quidditch game by catching the Golden Snitch in his mouth! Director Chris Columbus remembers reading this and laughing out loud. "It was so completely unexpected," he says.

WINGS (MAKE 2)

With **A** and smaller hook, ch 3.

Row 1: Sc in the 2nd ch from the hook (you will leave the very first chain unworked)—1 sc.

Row 2: Ch 1 and turn. Inc in next sc—2 sc.

Row 3: Ch 1 and turn. Inc in next sc, sc in next sc—3 sc.

Row 4: Ch 1 and turn. Inc in next sc, sc in next 2 sc—4 sc.

Row 5: Ch 1 and turn. Inc in next sc, sc in next 3 sc—5 sc.

Row 6: Ch 1 and turn. Inc in next sc, sc in next 4 sc—6 sc.

Row 7: Ch 1 and turn. Inc in next sc, sc in next 5 sc—7 sc.

Row 8: Ch 1 and turn. Inc in next sc, sc in next 6 sc—8 sc.

Row 9: Ch 1 and turn. Inc in next sc, sc in next 7 sc—9 sc.

Row 10: Ch 1 and turn. Inc in next sc, sc in next 8 sc—10 sc.

Row 11: Ch 1 and turn. Inc in next sc, sc in next 9 sc—11 sc.

Rows 12–14: Ch 1 and turn. Sc in next 11 sc. [11] (3 rows)

Row 15: Ch 1 and turn. Dec in next 2 sc, sc in next 9 sc—10 sc.

Row 16: Ch 1 and turn. Dec in next 2 sc, sc in next 8 sc—9 sc.

Row 17: Ch 1 and turn. Dec in next 2 sc, sc in next 7 sc—8 sc.

Row 18: Ch 1 and turn. Dec in next 2 sc, sc in next 6 sc—7 sc.

Row 19: Ch 1 and turn. Dec in next 2 sc, sc in next 5 sc—6 sc.

Row 20: Ch 1 and turn. Dec in next 2 sc, sc in next 4 sc—5 sc.

Row 21: Ch 1 and turn. Dec in next 2 sc, sc in next 3 sc—4 sc.

Row 22: Ch 1 and turn. Dec in next 2 sc, sc in next 2 sc—3 sc.

Row 23: Ch 1 and turn. Dec in next 2 sc, sc in next sc—2 sc.

Row 24: Ch 1 and turn. Dec in next 2 sc. Ch 1. [1]

Fasten off and leave a tail for sewing.

ASSEMBLY

Sew the Wings between Rnds 8 and 9 on either side of the Snitch with approximately 16 stitches in between. If needed, sew multiple times across the same few stitches to secure the Wings. Weave in all yarn ends.

WINGED KEYS

Designed by Sam Savalle
Skill Level: ⚡ ⚡

As Harry, Ron, and Hermione race to find the Sorcerer's Stone to prevent it from getting into the wrong hands, they are challenged by several tests created by professors to protect it. Once they make it past the twelve-foot-tall three-headed dog, and untangle themselves from a huge clump of Devil's Snare, they find themselves in a room holding only a broom and many keys with wings. It's soon realized the only way to get out of the room is to fly on the broom and catch the key that will unlock the door.

The design of the keys needed to be scary and wild, but "not *too* scary or *too* wild," says visual effects supervisor Robert Legato. "The more beautiful you make something, the more nonthreatening it becomes." Legato and his team also needed to design the way the keys moved within the room—their inspiration was to have them move in concert, like a flock of birds. "They are in essence tied together," Legato explains. "The way they move affects the way they'll look on-screen."

These amigurumi Winged Keys unlock a world of possibilities. Variety reigns when you can mix and match your keys' bow, shaft, and pins. Each key is unique, crocheted in the form of rectangles that are subsequently transformed into cylindrical tubes and then artfully shaped to look like genuine keys. The magic comes to life when these amigurumi Winged Keys are suspended on a fishline to make them appear to flutter and soar through the air.

"They're not birds. They're keys!"

Harry Potter, *Harry Potter and the Sorcerer's Stone*

FINISHED MEASUREMENTS
Height: 7 in. / 18 cm
Width: 6 in. / 15 cm

YARN
Worsted weight (#4 medium) yarn, shown in Caron *Simply Soft*, (100% acrylic, 315 yd. / 288 m per 6 oz. / 170 g skein).
Color A: Autumn Maize, 1 skein
Color B: White, 1 skein

HOOK
• US E-4 / 3.5mm crochet hook

NOTIONS
• Stitch marker
• Tapestry needle
• Pipe cleaners
• Optional: Fishing line or clear thread, to make your winged keys fly!

GAUGE
21 sc and 22 sc rows = 4 in. / 10 cm worked flat
Gauge is not critical for this project. Ensure your stitches are tight so the pipe cleaner won't show through.

NOTES
• Many pieces are created with a flat rectangle, then sewn down the side to create a very thin key. A pipe cleaner is inserted to shape each piece.
• Mix and match each element from each key—the head, body, teeth and wings—to create your perfect keys!

ORNATE KEY

BODY

With **A**, ch 21.
Row 1: Sc in 2nd ch from hook and each ch across, turn—20 sc.
Row 2: Ch 1 (does not count as first sc), sc across, turn—20 sc.
Rows 3–4: Ch 1 (does not count as first sc), sc across, turn—20 sc.
Fasten off leaving a 12 in. tail.

BEHIND THE MAGIC

The wings of the key that opens the door, which is old-fashioned and rusty, was crafted in an iridescent shot silk.

HEAD

With **A**, ch 16.
Row 1: Sc in 2nd ch from hook and each ch across, turn—15 sc.
Row 2: Ch 1 (does not count as first sc), sc across, turn—15 sc.
Rows 3–4: Ch 1 (does not count as first sc), sc across, turn—15 sc.
Fasten off leaving a 6 in. tail.

HEADPINS (MAKE 3)

With **A**, Ch 14.
Row 1: Sc in 2nd ch from hook and each ch across, turn—13 sc.
Row 2: Ch 1 (does not count as first sc), sc across, turn—13 sc.
Rows 3–4: Ch 1 (does not count as first sc), sc across, turn—13 sc.
Fasten off leaving a 6 in. tail.

ASSEMBLE THE TUBES

For each of the five pieces above:
Using needle, thread tail and whip stitch the starting chain row to the front loops of the last row. Tie off. Do not cut extras.
Cut a pipe cleaner twice as long as each piece. Fold in half and tightly twist. This will create more structure and keep the Key from bending with the weight of the Wings. Insert into each of the five pieces.

SEW THE KEY

Using needle, thread the tail of Head. Attach open sides to create a doughnut shape and sew shut and together. Fasten off.
Using needle, thread the tail of the Body. Sew onto the doughnut shape of the Head. Fasten off. In the same manner, attach the three Headpins.

DECORATIVE BODY PIECE (MAKE 3)

With **A**, ch 8. Fasten off leaving a long tail for sewing. Sew onto the top of the Body near the Head. Repeat two more times.

TEETH

With Color **A**.
Row 1: Ch 3, sc in 2nd st and across. Turn—2 sc.
Row 2: Sc. Leave the last st unworked. Ch 2. Turn—1 sc and 2 ch.
Row 3: Sc in 2nd ch. Sc in st. Turn—2 sc.
Now sc around the border. To do this:
Border Row: Sc 2, ch, sc, ch, sc, ch, sc, ch, sc, ch, sc, ch, sc 2 in starting 2 ch, ch, sc 7 around back side, sl st to first st and fasten off.
Now you are making the thin part of the Teeth that attaches to the Body. Insert your hook in the 3rd st on the back from right. Pull up a loop, ch 1, then place a sc in the 3rd, 4th, and 5th stitch along the back. Turn. Ch 1, and sc 3. Fasten off, then sew to the Body.

FRONT WINGS (MAKE 2)

With **B**, make a magic ring.
Rnd 1: 6 sc in ring—6 sc.
Rnd 2: *Sc, inc* x 3—9 sc.
Rnd 3: *Sc 2, inc* x 3—12 sc.
Rnd 4: *Sc 3, inc* x 3—15 sc.
Rnds 5–7: Sc around—15 sc.
Rnd 8: *Sc 4, inc* x 3—18 sc.
Rnds 9–10: Sc around—18 sc.
Rnd 11: *Sc, dec* x 6—12 sc.
Rnd 12: Fold in half so open stitches are lined up in two rows of six. Crochet across the work, going into both stitches. Sc 3, hdc 3. Fasten off and leave a long tail for sewing.

BACK WINGS (MAKE 2)

With **B**, make a magic ring.
Rnd 1: 6 sc in ring—6 sc.
Rnd 2: *Sc, inc* x 3—9 sc.
Rnd 3: *Sc 2, inc* x 3—12 sc.
Rnd 4: *Sc 3, inc* x 3—15 sc.
Rnds 5—7: Sc around—15 sc.
Rnd 8: *Sc 4, inc* x 3—18 sc.
Rnds 9—10: Sc around—18 sc.
Rnd 11: *Sc 5, inc* x 3—21 sc.
Rnds 12—13: Sc around—21 sc.
Rnd 14: Sc 9, inc* x 3, sc 9—
  24 sc.
Rnds 15—16: Sc around—24 sc.
Rnd 17: Dec, sc 6, dec x 5, sc
  6—18 sc.
Rnd 18: *Sc 4, dec* x 3—15 sc.
Rnd 19: *Sc 3, dec* x 3—12 sc.
Rnd 20: Fold in half so open
  stitches are lined up in two
  rows of six. You will crochet
  across the work, going into
  both stitches.

FINISHING

Lay Back Wings on top of each
  other. Attach a 24 in. strand of
  yarn and sew onto the Body
  going through both Wings
  when sewing. Continue in this
  manner for the Front Wings.
  If desired, sew in between the
  Front and Back Wings for extra
  support. You may also want
  to sew the Wings shut so they
  don't move. Weave in all ends.
  Trim all tails.

SUSPENDING

Depending on how you are
  using your Wings, you may
  want your Wings to fly. To
  do this, attach a clear fishing
  line to the end of the Body
  by the Teeth and Head piece.
  Additional strands may be tied
  to the Wings to keep them in
  the position you'd like them.

THE DRAGONFLY KEY

HEAD

OUTER RING

With **A**, ch 20.
Row 1: Sc in 2nd ch from hook and
  each ch across, turn—19 sc.
Row 2: Ch 1 (does not count as
  first sc), sc across, turn—19 sc.
Row 3: Ch 1 (does not count as
  first sc), sc across, turn—19 sc.
Fasten off leaving a 6 in. tail.
With needle and the tail of
  the Head, sew short ends
  together to create a doughnut
  shape. Fasten off and weave
  in the ends.

INNER RING

With **A**, make a magic ring and
  work 4 sc in ring. Sl st to first
  sc. Fasten off.
Sew into the Outer Ring,
  suspending it in the middle.
  Fasten off and weave in
  the ends.

BODY

With **A**, ch 20.
Row 1: Sc in 2nd ch from hook and
  each ch across, turn—19 sc.
Row 2: Ch 1 (does not count as
  first sc), sc across, turn—19 sc.
Row 3: Ch 1 (does not count as
  first sc), sc across, turn—19 sc.
Fasten off leaving a 12 in. tail
  for sewing
Place a pipe cleaner the long way
  in the middle of the Body and
  whip stitch closed. Cut pipe
  cleaner and sew ends shut.

FILIGREE SQUARE

With **A**, ch 4.
Row 1: Sc in 2nd ch from hook
  and each ch across, turn—3 sc.
Row 2: Ch 1 (does not count as

first sc), sc across, turn—3 sc.
Row 3: Ch 1 (does not count as
  first sc), sc across, turn—3 sc.
Sc around perimeter. Sl st to first
  sc. Fasten off leaving a 6 in. tail
  for sewing. Sew onto the Body
  about ¼ in. from the top.

FILIGREE BAND

Ch 6. Fasten off leaving a long
  tail for sewing. Sew onto the
  top of the Body above the
  Square.

TEETH

With **A**, ch 7.
Row 1: Inc in 2nd ch, sc 4, 3 sc
  in last st, then working along
  the back side of the ch, sc
  5 across. Sl st to first st and
  fasten off leaving a long tail to
  sew. Sew onto the base of the
  Body. Weave in ends.

WINGS (MAKE 2)

WING BRACE (MAKE 2)

With **B**, ch 21.
Row 1: Sc in 2nd ch from hook and
  each ch across, turn—20 sc.
Row 2: Ch 1 (does not count as
  first sc), sc across, turn—20 sc.
Fasten off leaving a 12 in. tail
  for sewing.
Place a pipe cleaner the long way
  in the middle of the piece and
  whip stitch closed. Cut pipe
  cleaner and sew ends shut.
  Set aside.

WINGS (MAKE 2)

With **B**, ch 7.
Row 1: Hdc in 2nd ch from hook
  and each ch across, turn—6 sc.
Row 2: Ch 1 (does not count as
  first sc), sc in front loop only
  across, turn—6 sc.
Row 3: Ch 1, sc across, turn—6 sc.
Row 4: Ch 1, hdc across, turn—
  6 hdc.

Row 5: Ch 1, sc in back loop only across, turn—6 sc.
Row 6: Ch 1, sc across, turn—6 sc.
Row 7: Ch 1, hdc across, turn—6 hdc.
Row 8: Ch 1, sc in front loop only across, turn—6 sc.
Row 9: Ch 1, sc across, turn—6 sc.
Row 10: Ch 1, hdc across, turn—6 hdc.
Row 11: Ch 1, sc in back loop only across, turn—6 sc.
Row 12: Ch 1, sc across, turn—6 sc.
Row 13: Right Wing: Ch 1, sc 4, dec, turn. **Left Wing:** Ch 1, dec, sc 4, turn—5 sc.
Row 14: Right Wing: Ch 1, dec, dec, sc, turn. **Left Wing:** Ch 1, sc, dec, dec, turn—3 sc.
Row 15: Right Wing: Ch 1, sc, dec. **Left Wing:** Ch 1, dec, sc—2 sc.
Sc around the perimeter of the Wing. Sl st to starting sc. Fasten off leaving a 12 in. tail.
Sew Wing on top of Wing Brace. Weave in all ends.

FINISHING

Weave in all ends. Trim all tails.

THE ROUND KEY

HEAD

With **A**, ch 25.
Row 1: Sc in 2nd ch from hook and each ch across, turn—24 sc.
Row 2: Ch 1 (does not count as first sc), sc across, turn—24 sc.
Rows 3–4: Ch 1 (does not count as first sc), sc across, turn—24 sc.
Fasten off leaving a 12 in. tail for sewing. Place a pipe cleaner the long way in the middle of the piece and whip stitch closed. Cut pipe cleaner and sew ends together, creating a doughnut shape. Weave in ends.

BODY

With **A**, ch 23.
Row 1: Sc in 2nd ch from hook and each ch across, turn—22 sc.
Row 2: Ch 1 (does not count as first sc), sc across, turn—22 sc.
Rows 3–4: Ch 1 (does not count as first sc), sc across, turn—22 sc.
Fasten off leaving a 12 in. tail for sewing. Place a pipe cleaner the long way in the middle of the piece and whip stitch closed. Cut pipe cleaner and sew ends together. Sew onto Head. Weave in ends.

TEETH

With **A**, ch 4.
Row 1: Sc in 2nd ch from hook and each ch across, turn—2 sc.
Row 2: Ch 1 (does not count as first sc), sc, leave 2nd sc unworked. Ch 3, turn—1 sc and 3 ch.
Row 3: Sc in 2nd ch, sc in next ch, sc in sc.
Fasten off. Sew onto the Body of the Key.

WINGS (MAKE 2)

With Color **B**, ch 16.
Row 1: Sl st in the 2nd st, sl st 2, sc 3, hdc, 2 hdc in the next st, hdc, sc 3, sl st 2, (sl st, ch, sl st) in last ch. Now working on the other side of the starting ch, ch 1, sl st in the same st, sl st 2, sc 3, hdc, 2 hdc in the next st, hdc, sc 3, sl st 2, sl st in last st.
Row 2: Ch 1, sc 3, hdc 3, 2 hdc in each of the next 4 sts, hdc 3, sc 3, skip ch, 2 sc in the next st, skip ch, sc 3, hdc 3, 2 hdc in each of the next 4 sts, hdc 3, sc 3, sl st to starting sc.
Fasten off. Sew onto the Body of the Key.

FINISHING

Weave in all ends. Trim all tails.

HOWLER

Designed by Larissa Soares
Skill Level: ✏ ✏

Among the many enchanting objects from the wizarding world, one stands out with its dramatic and awe-inspiring impact: the infamous Howler. The Howler is a magical letter of extraordinary nature, both feared and revered among the wizarding community. Sent in a red envelope, it reads out its contents in the voice of the sender. Very loudly. Molly Weasley sends her youngest son, Ron, a Howler in *Harry Potter and the Chamber of Secrets*. Ron has driven his father's Ford Anglia car without permission to fly Harry and himself to Hogwarts when they cannot get through Platform 9¾ in time to make the Hogwarts Express. (She does also congratulate daughter Ginny for getting into Gryffindor house at the same time.)

Graphic designer Miraphora Mina didn't want just a face on a letter speaking digitally; she wanted the letter to tell its own story. Mina's inspiration for the Howler came from origami, the Japanese art of folding paper. "There were so many things that lent themselves to that. The ribbon that encircles the letter could turn into a tongue, for example. The white paper inside would turn into teeth within the red mouth." The letter was written on real paper by Mina, then incorporated into its digital form.

Crafted with beginner-friendly stitches, but assembled with meticulous precision, this Howler appears like any ordinary red envelope, but within lies a powerful secret waiting to be unleashed! Use your crochet skills to bring the Howler to life, and it will capture the attention of everyone in its vicinity.

"Ronald Weasley! How dare you steal that car! I am absolutely disgusted! Your father's now facing an inquiry at work, and it's entirely your fault! If you put another toe out of line, we'll bring you straight home!"

Molly Weasley's Howler letter to her son Ron

FINISHED MEASUREMENTS
Length: 7.5 in. / 19 cm
Height: 4 in. / 10 cm closed, 10 in. / 25 cm opened

YARN
DK weight (#3 light) shown in Hobbii *Friends Cotton 8/8* (100% cotton, 82 yd. / 75 m per 1.75 oz. / 50 g skein).
Color A: #40 Tomato, 2 skein

Fingering weight (#1 super fine) shown in Hobbii *Friends Cotton 8/4* (100% cotton, 175 yd. / 160 m per 1.75 oz. / 50 g skein).
Color B: #43 Bordeaux, 1 skein
Color C: #01 White, 1 skein
Color D: #24 Sunflower, 1 skein

HOOKS
• US D-3/ 3mm crochet hook, or size needed to obtain gauge
• US C-2/ 2.5mm crochet hook, or size needed to obtain gauge

NOTIONS
• Stitch markers
• Tapestry needle
• One roll 2mm craft wire

GAUGE
17 sts and 12 rows = 4 in. / 10 cm in hdc

SPECIAL ABBREVIATIONS
Picot stitch: Ch 3, insert your hook in the third chain from the hook, yarn over (yo) and draw the yarn through the stitch and through the loop on the hook.
Front post double crochet (FPdc): Instead of making your stitch through the loops at the top of the stitch, you make it around the stitch.

Yarn over and insert hook from front to back to front of the stitch on the row below, pull up loop, Then finish your double crochet as normal, yo, pull through 2 loops. Yo again, pull through the last 2 loops.

NOTE
- This pattern is mainly worked in rows, unless stated otherwise.

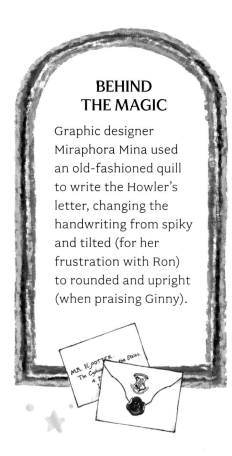

BEHIND THE MAGIC

Graphic designer Miraphora Mina used an old-fashioned quill to write the Howler's letter, changing the handwriting from spiky and tilted (for her frustration with Ron) to rounded and upright (when praising Ginny).

BODY OF LETTER

With **A**, and larger hook.
Row 1: Ch 30, hdc in 3rd ch from hook and in each ch across to last ch, turn—28 hdc.
Rows 2—43: Ch 2, hdc in next 28 hdc, turn—28 hdc.
Do not cut the yarn. Only weave the end at the beginning of the Letter's Body.
Follow the steps shown on the sewing guideline to sew the bottom part of the Letter's Body:
Lay flat the chains of the first row, connecting A to B and sew both parts together with tapestry needle and red yarn.
Push E inside making a diamond shape, sew it inside the Letter's Body.
Sew the middle part of the diamond shape closed.
Lay down the wire on top of the project and work sc over it and around the Letter's Body, so the wire is hidden inside the stitches. The wire will be used to shape the Letter later.

Work as follows: Make 2 sc per row (sides of the Letter), 1 sc in each stitch or chain (bottom and top of the Letter) and 3 sc at each corner. Where the wire tips meet each other, wrap them together with red yarn for around 6 cm. This will secure and hide the wire inside the border.
With stitch markers, mark Rows 31 and 36 on both sides. Bend the top of the Letter until the markers touch each other and sew from Row 31 to 36 together with tapestry needle and red yarn. Be sure to bend the top part of the Letter on the same side as the diamond shape. Leave this aside while we make the other parts.

TONGUE

With **B**, and smaller hook.
Row 1: Ch 9, hdc in 3rd ch from hook and in each ch across to last ch, turn—7 hdc.
Rows 2—14: Ch 2, hdc in next 7 hdc, turn—7hdc.
Row 15: Ch 3, dc in first hdc, [ch

Sewing Guideline

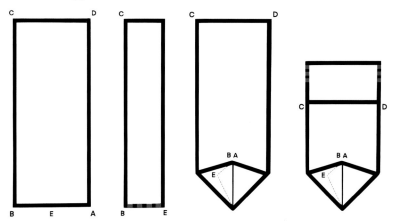

3, insert hook into back bar of the first chain, yo, pull through all loops on hook], hdc in next hdc, sc in next hdc, sl st in next hdc, sc in next hdc, hdc in next hdc, [ch 3, insert hook into back bar of the first chain, yo, pull through all loops on hook], dc in next hdc, ch 3 and sl st in same stitch as the previous dc.

Cut the yarn and weave in the ends. Set aside.

MOUTH AND TEETH

With **C**, and smaller hook.

Row 1: Ch 28, hdc in 3rd ch from hook and in each ch across to last ch, turn—26 hdc.

Rows 2—13: Ch 2, hdc in next 26 hdc, turn—26 hdc.

Next row we will attach the Tongue.

Row 14: Ch 2, hdc in next 9 hdc, crochet the Tongue together in next 8 hdc (including the chains at the beginning of the row), hdc in next 9 hdc, turn—26 hdc.

Rows 15—25: Ch 2, hdc in next 26 hdc, turn—26 hdc.

Row 26: Ch 3, FPdc in next hdc, FPdc in next 4 hdc, ch 2, [sl st in front post of next hdc, ch 2, FPdc in next 4 hdc] x 3, ch 2, FPdc in next 5 hdc, ch 3, sl st in on the 3rd ch of previous row—5 Teeth.

Cut the yarn leaving a long tail for sewing. With the Tongue facing you, attach **C** at the first chain on Row 1 and repeat Row 26. Both sets of Teeth face to the inside of the Mouth.

SEAL

With **D**, and smaller hook, make a magic ring.

Rnd 1: Sc 6 in ring—6 sc.

Rnd 2: 2 sc in next 6 sc—12 sc.

Rnd 3: [sc in next sc, 2 sc in next sc] x 6—18 sc.

Cut the yarn leaving a long tail for sewing.

RIBBON

With **B**, and smaller hook.

Row 1: Ch 9, hdc in 3rd ch from hook and in each ch across to last ch, turn—7 hdc.

Rows 2—25: Ch 2, hdc in next 7 hdc, turn—7 hdc.

Row 26: Ch 2, hdc2tog over next 2 hdc, hdc in next 3 hdc, hdc2tog over next 2 hdc—5 hdc.

Row 27: Ch 2, hdc2tog over next 2 hdc, hdc in next hdc, hdc2tog over next 2 hdc—3 hdc.

Cut the yarn and leave a very long tail for sewing.

RIBBON TAIL (MAKE 2)

With **B**, and smaller hook.

Row 1: Ch 7, hdc in 3rd ch from hook, hdc in next 4 ch, 2ch, turn—5 hdc.

Rows 2—3: Hdc in next 5 hdc—5 hdc.

Row 4: Ch 2, dc in same st, picot stitch, hdc in next st, ch 2, sl st next st, ch 2, hdc in next st, picot stitch, dc in next st, ch 2, sl st in same st.

Cut the yarn and weave the yarn ends. With needle and tail, sew the Ribbon Tails beside Rows 26 and 27 of the Ribbon.

ADDRESS LABEL

With **C**, and smaller hook.

Row 1: Ch 18, hdc in 3rd ch from hook, hdc in next 15 ch, 2ch, turn—16 hdc.

Rows 2—4: Hdc in next 16 hdc—16 hdc.

Work sc around outside edges of the Label: sc 2 beside each row, sc 1 in each ch and hdc—48 sc. Cut the yarn leaving a long tail for sewing.

ASSEMBLY

Pin the top set of Teeth (Teeth-Row 25) on the center of Row 42 of the Letter's Body. Pin the three middle Teeth of the bottom (Teeth-Row 1) on the inside of the diamond shape. Sew them on using **C**, making sure the white yarn doesn't show on the outside of the Letter.

Close the Letter, pin the Ribbon on the outside (Ribbon-Row 27), starting on the diamond shape until the back part of the Letter. Sew it in place using **B**.

Pin the Seal on top of the Ribbon (Ribbon-Row 27) and sew it in place with same color.

Pin the Address Label on the back side of the Letter and sew it in place with same color.

SKELE-GRO BOTTLE

Designed by Tsui-Sie Baker-Wong
Skill Level: ↗ ↗

Quidditch can be a brutal game for the players, but Harry gets into more danger in a game between Gryffindor and Slytherin when a rogue Bludger goes after the Seeker. After a fast pursuit, the iron ball smashes into Harry's arm as he reaches for the Golden Snitch.

Professor Lockhart is one of the first on the scene to help Harry, casting *Brackium Emendo* in an effort to heal his bones. The result of this questionable spell is for Harry's bones to completely disappear.

When Harry is brought to the Hospital Wing after the game, Madam Pomfrey gives him a dose of Skele-Gro, a potion that mends bones or cause bones to regrow if they are missing.

Crocheted from the top down, this amigurumi Skele-Gro potion bottle embodies the essence of a potion that holds the power to mend and restore bones. Its unique shape and carefully textured exterior bear a remarkable resemblance to the bottle Madam Pomfrey poured from to regrow Harry's bones overnight. Portions of the skeleton are crocheted directly onto the bottle's surface. To add a layer of authenticity, the bottle cap is removable.

> "I can mend bones in a heartbeat, but growing them back . . ."
>
> Poppy Pomfrey, *Harry Potter and the Chamber of Secrets*

FINISHED MEASUREMENTS
Height: 7 in. / 18 cm
Width: 2.5 in. / 6 cm

YARN
DK weight (#3 light) yarn, shown in Hobbii *Amigo Yarn* (100% acrylic, 191 yd. / 175 m per 1.8 oz. / 50 g skein).
Color A: #A02 Ecru, 1 skein
Color B: #A03 Sand, 1 skein
Color C: #A12 Black, 1 skein
Color D: #A39 Cognac, 1 skein

HOOK
• US E-4 / 3.5mm crochet hook

NOTIONS
• Stitch markers
• Polyester stuffing
• Tapestry needle
• Embroidery needle
• Cardboard, small scrap
• Embroidery thread, small amount of black

GAUGE
Gauge is not critical for this project. Ensure your stitches are tight so the stuffing won't show through.

SPECIAL ABBREVIATIONS
Back Loop Only (blo): Work through back loop only
Ch2-Picot: Ch 2, starting from 2nd ch from hook, sl st.
Invisible Decrease (dec): Insert hook into the front loop of the first st and insert hook into the front loop of the next st. YO, draw through the first two loops [2 loops on hook]. YO, draw through both loops to complete the st.
Invisible Finish: Sl st into the next stitch. Cut the yarn and pull through the last stitch. Thread the tail onto a tapestry needle, skip the next st, and insert needle

from front to back under both loops of the next st. Next insert the needle through the back loop of the sl st and the back loop of stitch underneath. Pull yarn through to complete the invisible finish.

Standing sc: Create a slip knot on your hook. Insert hook into the first st. YO, draw through both loops to complete the st.

NOTES
- The pattern is worked in continuous rounds, unless otherwise stated.
- The bottle is worked from top down to bottom.

BEHIND THE MAGIC

The prop makers took the name of the potion to heart by crafting a bottle with a skull-shaped stopper. The body of the bottle is wrapped in a human rib cage, with the skeleton's arms creating the handle.

BOTTLE

With **B**, make a magic ring.
Rnd 1: 6 sc in ring—6 sc.
Rnd 2: Inc in each sc around—12 sc.
Rnd 3: [Sc in next sc, inc in next sc] 6 times—18 sc.
Rnd 4: [Sc in next sc, inc in next sc, sc in next sc] 6 times—24 sc.
Rnd 5: [Sc in the next 3 sc, inc in next sc] 6 times—30 sc.
Rnd 6: Blo—[sc in next 2 sc, inc in next sc, sc in the next 2 sc] 6 times—36 sc.
Rnd 7: Sc around—36 sc.
Rnd 8: [Sc in next 5 sc, inc in next sc] 6 times—42 sc.
Rnd 9: [Sc in next 3 sc, {inc/2sc} in next sc, sc in the next 3sc] 6 times—48 sc.
Rnd 10: [Sc in next 7 sc, {inc/2sc} in next sc] 6 times—54 sc.
Rnd 11: Blo—sc around—54 sc.
Rnds 12–24: Sc around for 13 rnds—54 sc.
Rnd 25: [Sc in next 2 sc, dec, sc in next 2 sc] 9 times—45 sc.
Rnd 26: Blo: [Sc in next 4 sc, inc in next sc] 9 times—54 sc.
Rnds 27–40: Sc around for 14 rnds—54 sc.
Rnd 41: Blo—sc around—54 sc.
Stuff the Bottle firmly and cut out a piece of cardboard to fit the base of the Bottle.
Rnd 42: [Sc in next 7 sc, dec] 6 times—48 sc.
Rnd 43: [Sc in next 3 sc, dec, sc in next 3 sc] 6 times—42 sc.
Rnd 44: [Sc in next 5 sc, dec] 6 times—36 sc.
Rnd 45: [Sc in next 2 sc, dec, sc in next 2 sc] 6 times—30 sc.
Rnd 46: [Sc in next 3 sc, dec] 6 times—24 sc.
Rnd 47: [Sc in next sc, dec, sc in next sc] 6 times—18 sc.

Rnd 48: [Sc in next sc, dec] 6 times—12 sc.
Rnd 49: Dec 6 times—6 sc,
Fasten off, leaving approximately 4 in. / 10 cm yarn tail. With the tapestry needle, thread the tail through the front loops of the 6 sts and pull to close. Weave in the tail.

BOTTLE EDGING

With **B**, holding the Bottle upside down, working on the front loops of Rnd 25.
Rnd 1: Sl st around—45 sl st.
Fasten off with an invisible finish and weave in the tail.

BOTTLE NECK

With **B**, holding the Bottle correct way up, working from the front loops of Rnd 5.
Rnd 1: Standing sc in first sc, sc in next 29 sc—30 sc.
Rnds 2–4: Sc around for 3 rnds—30 sc.
Fasten off with an invisible finish and weave in the tail. Set the Bottle aside.

BOTTLE CAP

With **D**, make a magic ring.
Rnd 1: 6 sc in ring—6 sc.
Rnd 2: Inc in each sc around—12 sc.
Rnd 3: Blo—[sc in next sc, inc in next sc] 6 times—18 sc.
Rnd 4: [Sc in next sc, inc in next sc, sc in next sc] 6 times—24 sc.
Rnd 5: [Sc in the next 3 sc, inc in next sc] 6 times—30 sc.
Rnd 6: Blo—[sc in next 2 sc, inc in next sc, sc in next 2 sc] 6 times—36 sc.
Rnds 7–9: Sc around for 3 rnds—36 sc.

Rnd 10*: Blo—sl st around—
36 sl st (*don't sl st the sts
too tightly).
Fasten off with an invisible finish
and weave in the tail.

SKULL NECK

With **A**, working on the front loops
of Rnd 1 of the Bottle Cap.
Rnd 1: Standing sc in first sc, sc in
next 11 sc—12 sc.
Rnds 2–3: Sc around for 2
rnds—12 sc.
Fasten off with an invisible finish
and leave a long tail for
sewing. Stuff the Skull
Neck firmly.
Cut out another piece of
cardboard to fit the underside
of the Bottle Cap. Use fabric
glue or use a hot glue gun to
secure the cardboard. Set the
Bottle Cap aside.

SKULL

With **A**, make a magic ring.
Rnd 1: 6 sc in ring—6 sc.
Rnd 2: Inc in each sc
around—12 sc.
Rnd 3: [Sc in next sc, inc in next
sc] 6 times—18 sc.
Rnd 4: [Sc in next sc, inc in next sc,
sc in next sc] 6 times—24 sc.
Rnd 5: [Sc in the next 3 sc, inc in
next sc] 6 times—30 sc.
Rnd 6: [Sc in next 2 sc, inc in
next sc, sc in next 2 sc] 6
times—36 sc.
Rnd 7: [Sc in next 5 sc, inc in next
sc] 6 times—42 sc.
Rnds 8–13: Sc around for 6
rnds—42 sc.
Rnd 14: [Sc in next 3 sc, inc in
next sc, sc in next 3 sc] 6
times—48 sc.
Rnd 15: Sc around—48 sc.
Rnd 16: Dec 3 times, sc in next 36
sc, dec 3 times—42 sc.
Rnd 17: Sc in next 3 sc, [dec, sc
in next 2 sc] 2 times, dec, sc in
next 3 sc, [ch 10, skip next 10
sc], sc in next 3 sc, [dec, sc in
next 2 sc] 2 times, dec, sc in
next 3 sc—26 sc, 10 ch.
Rnd 18*: [Sc in next 2 sc, dec, sc
in next 2 sc] 6 times—30 sc
(*When working on the ch 10
part, work in the back loops of
the ch).
Rnd 19: [Sc in next 3 sc, dec] 6
times—24 sc.
Rnd 20: [Sc in next sc, dec, sc in
next sc] 6 times—18 sc.
*Start stuffing the Skull firmly,
and continue to stuff for the
remaining rnds.*
Rnd 21: [Sc in next sc, dec] 6
times—12 sc.
Rnd 22: Dec 6 times—6 sc.
Fasten off, leaving approximately
4 in. / 10 cm yarn tail. With the
tapestry needle, thread the tail
through the front loops of the
6 sts and pull to close. Weave
in the tail.

SKULL TEETH

With **A**, working in the skipped 10 sts of Rnd 16 and the front loops of the ch 10 of Rnd 17.

Rnd 1: Standing sc in first sc, sc in next 19 sc, turn—20 sc.

Rnd 2: Ch 1, work through both sts: sc across—10 sc.

Fasten off and weave in the tail.

SKULL EYE SOCKET (MAKE 2)

With **C**, make a magic ring.

Rnd 1: 4 sc in ring—4 sc.

Rnd 2: [Inc in next sc] 2 times, sl st in next 2 sc—4 sc, 2 sl st.

Fasten off with an invisible finish and leave a long tail for sewing.

Sew the Eye Sockets between Rnds 10 and 11 and Rnds 14 and 15, slanting slightly inwards, with approximately five (visible) stitches from top of each Eye.

With **C**, embroider nostrils in between the Eye Sockets, lining up with the bottom of the Eye Sockets. With **C**, stitch vertical lines on the Skull Teeth to create the teeth markings. Each vertical line should be one stitch apart.

With the yarn tail from the Skull Neck, sew the neck onto the skull between Rnds 20 and 21. Set the Bottle Cap aside.

SPINE

With **A**, on the back of the Bottle, use a scrap piece of yarn as a guideline from the base of the Bottle Neck to the Bottle edging of Rnd 25.

Surface crochet the following, working in rows.

Row 1: [Sl st in next st] (approximately) 17 times, turn—17 sl st.

Row 2: Ch 1, alternate: [hdc in next st, sl st in next st]—9 hdc, 8 sl st.

Fasten off and weave in the tail. Set the Bottle aside.

STERNUM

With **A**.

Rnd 1: Ch 7, 2 hdc in 2nd ch from hook, sl st in next ch, sc in next ch, hdc in next 2 ch; {sc, ch2-picot, sc} in last ch, hdc in next 2 ch, sc in next ch, sl st in next ch, 2 hdc in next ch—8 hdc, 4 sc, 2 sl st.

Fasten off with an invisible finish and leave a long tail for sewing. Sew the Sternum onto the Bottle, on the opposite side of the Spine and below the front loops of Rnd 10. The ch2-picot should point downward, so the Sternum spans from Rnds 10 and 11 to Rnds 19 and 20.

PREPARATION FOR THE RIBCAGE

With pins mark the following on the Bottle:

Arms: Mark with a pair of pins equidistant from the Sternum and Spine and in line with the front loops of Rnd 10.

Clavicle: Mark with a pair of pins either side of the top of the Sternum, then another pair of pins behind the Arms (this will be where the Scapula is placed).

Rib 1: Mark with a pair of pins one stitch down from the Clavicle pins on both sides of the Sternum. Mark with a pair of pins both sides of the Spine, between Rnds 8 and 9.

Rib 2: Mark with a pair of pins two visible stitches down from Rib 1 on both sides of the Sternum. Mark with a pair of pins two visible stitches down from Rib 1 on both sides of the Spine.

Rib 3: Mark with a pair of pins two visible stitches down from Rib 2 on both sides of the Sternum. Mark with a pair of pins two visible stitches down from Rib 2 on both sides of the Spine.

Rib 4: Mark with a pair of pins two visible stitches down from Rib 3 on both sides of the Sternum. Mark with a pair of pins two visible stitches down from Rib 3 on both sides of the Spine.

Rib 5: Mark with a pair of pins two visible stitches down from Rib 4 and approximately 3 sts away from both sides of the Sternum. Mark with a pair of pins two visible stitches down from Rib 4 on both sides of the Spine.

RIBS (MAKE 5 ON EACH SIDE)

With **A**, the Ribs will be surface crocheted onto the Bottle.

Using some scrap yarn, pin guidelines for the Ribs from Sternum to Spine.

Start from the Spine and sl st along the guideline. Fasten off when you have reached the Sternum and weave in the tails. Repeat for the other side of the ribcage.

SCAPULAS (MAKE 2) SHOULDER BLADES

With **A**, for the left Scapula, make a magic ring.

Rnd 1: 6 sc in ring—6 sc.

Rnd 2: [Inc in next sc, sc in next sc] 3 times—9 sc.

Rnd 3: [Sc in next sc, 3 sc in next sc, sc in next sc] 3 times—15 sc.

Fasten off with an invisible finish and leave a long tail for sewing. Set the left Scapula aside.

With **A**, for the right Scapula, make a magic ring.

Rnd 1: 6 sc in ring—6 sc.

Rnd 2: [Sc in next sc, inc in next sc] 3 times—9 sc.

Rnd 3: [Sc in next 2 sc, 3 sc in next sc] 3 times—15 sc.

Fasten off with an invisible finish and leave a long tail for sewing.

Sew the Scapulas next to the pin for the Clavicle (on the back of the Bottle).

ARMS (MAKE 2): HUMERUS + FOREARM (ULNA + RADIUS) + HAND

Note: The Arms are worked as one piece.

HUMERUS (UPPER ARM)

With **A**, make a magic ring, leaving a long tail (used to sew the Arms to the Bottle).

Rnd 1: 6 sc in ring—6 sc.

Rnds 2−3: Sc around for 2 rnds—6 sc.

Rnd 4: [Sc in next sc, dec] 2 times—4 sc.

Rnds 5−10: Sc around for 6 rnds—4 sc.

Rnd 11: [Inc in next sc, sc in next sc] 2 times , turn—6 sc.

Rnd 12: Ch 1, work through both sts—sc in 3 paired sc—3 sc.

Do not fasten off.

FOREARM

Rnd 13: Ch 1, turn—sl st in next sc.

ULNA: Ch 11, sl st in 2nd ch from

hook, sl st in the next 9 sc—10 sl st.

Sl st in next st.

RADIUS: Ch 10—10 ch.

Sc into turning ch of the Ulna. Do not fasten off.

HANDS

Working in rows.

Row 1: Ch 1 and turn, 3 sc in next sc—3 sc.

Row 2: Ch 1 and turn, sc in next sc, 3 sc in next sc, sc in next sc—5 sc.

Row 3 (Little Finger): Turn, ch 3, sl st in 2nd ch from hook, sl st in next ch—2 sl st.

Sl st in next st.

Row 3 (Ring Finger): Ch 4, sl st in 2nd ch from hook, sl st in next 2 ch—3 sl st.

Sl st in next st.

Row 3 (Middle Finger): Ch 5, sl st in 2nd ch from hook, sl st in next 3 ch—4 sl st.

Sl st in next st.

Row 3 (Index Finger): Ch 4, sl st in 2nd ch from hook, sl st in next 2 ch—3 sl st.

Sl st in next st.

Row 3 (Thumb): Sl st in next st, ch 2, sl st in 2nd ch from hook—1 sl st.

Fasten off and leave a long tail for sewing. Repeat for the other Arm.

Secure the top of the Humerus (upper Arm) next to the Scapula, so that the Scapula is behind the Arms when looking from front on.

Position the Arms so that the elbow is bent. Then sew the Hands (palm and fingers) to the Bottle placing each Hand on the Bottle edging.

CLAVICLE (MAKE 2) COLLAR BONE

The Clavicles will be surface crocheted onto the Bottle in rows. Using scrap pieces of yarn, pin the guideline for the Clavicle, from the top of the Sternum, pass the top of the Arm and join to the Scapula.

Start from the Sternum with **A**.

Row 1: Sl st along the guideline, turn.

Row 2: Ch 1, sl st into each st.

Fasten off when you reach the Sternum and weave in the tails. Repeat for the other side.

LETTERING

With embroidery thread. Use the chart below to help position and make the Lettering.

ON BOTTLE CAP

Locate the center of the Bottle Cap, the letter "E" will be embroidered here (the second "E" in "Skele-Gro").

ON BOTTLE

Locate the center of the Bottle (in line with the Sternum), count five stitches down from the Bottle edging, and embroider the same lettering as the Bottle Cap.

Lettering Chart

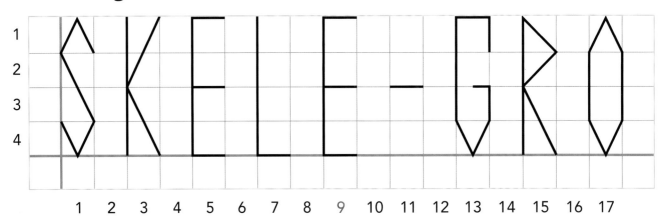

THE MONSTER BOOK OF MONSTERS

Designed by Camery Jacobsen
Skill Level: ◤ ◤

In *Harry Potter and the Prisoner of Azkaban*, Rubeus Hagrid becomes the Care of Magical Creatures professor, and so assigns *The Monster Book of Monsters* for his curriculum. The first challenge with this book is how to even open it. Any attempt elicits growls and biting, which makes studying for class incredibly difficult.

The graphic designers considered many options for a book about monsters that was a monster itself. Concepts included versions with clawed feet or with a tail. One idea was to have the spine of the book made out of spines. It was given two eyes, then four eyes, snaggly teeth, and lots of fur. Similar to the Howler, the book's ribbon became its tongue. Concept artists contributed images of familiar monsters such as Cornish pixies, goblins, and trolls to the pages filling the book. Unfamiliar monsters created by concept artist Rob Bliss were also included, such as a four-limbed snake and plant creatures.

This captivating amigurumi rendition of *The Monster Book of Monsters* is a unique and magical artifact from the wizarding world. It's crafted using luxurious faux fur yarn, making the amigurumi version extremely soft, mirroring the wild nature of the original textbook. The cover is worked in one piece, and the pages are worked in a single strip and then sewn together. The finer details are made using worsted-weight yarn.

"And open your books to page forty-nine."
"Exactly how do we do that?"
"Just stroke the spine, of course. Goodness me."

Rubeus Hagrid and Draco Malfoy,
Harry Potter and the Prisoner of Azkaban

FINISHED MEASUREMENTS
Height: 3 in. / 7 cm
Width: 9 in. / 23 cm

YARN
Bulky weight (#6 super bulky) shown in Knit Picks *Fable Fur* (100% polyester, 61 yd. / 56 m per 3.5 oz. / 100 g skein).
Color A: #28720 Falke, 2 skeins

Worsted weight (#4 medium) shown in Red Heart *Super Saver Yarn* (100% acrylic, 364 yd. / 333 m per 7 oz. / 198 g skein).
Color B: #1501980 Aran, 1 skein
Color C: #3307923 Buff, 1 skein
Color D: #10125730 Cafe, 1 skein
Color E: #5715008 Coffee, 1 skein
Color F: #4210373 Light Raspberry, 1 skein

HOOKS
• US I-9 / 5.5mm crochet hook
• US G-6 / 4mm crochet hook

NOTIONS
• Stitch markers
• One pair each 6mm and 8mm black safety eyes
• Polyester stuffing
• Pipe cleaner in red or black
• Tapestry needle

GAUGE
Gauge is not critical for this project. Ensure your stitches are tight so the stuffing won't show through.

SPECIAL ABBREVIATIONS
Back Loop Only (blo): Work through back loop only
Front Loop Only (flo): Work through front loop only

OUTER COVER

With **A** and larger hook.

Row 1: Ch 26, then in the second ch from your hook, sc in each st, ch 1 and turn your work to work from the back side—25 sc.

Rows 2—50: Sc in each st, ch 1 and turn to work on the back of sts of your work—25 sc.

INSIDE PAGES

With **C** and smaller hook.

Row 1: Ch 106, in second st from your hook, sc in each st—105 sc.

Row 2: Blo sc in each st—105 sc.
Row 3: Flo sc in each st—105 sc.
Row 4: Blo sc in each st—105 sc.
Row 5: Blo sc in each st—105 sc.
Row 6: Blo sc in each st—105 sc.
Row 7: Flo sc in each st—105 sc.
Finish off leaving a 24 in. tail for sewing.

SMALL FANGS

With **D** and smaller hook.

Work a row of Small Fangs along the top and bottom front edges of the Outer Cover of the book. Starting about two inches in from the corner of the right side of the Outer Cover, attach yarn, and sl st in the first 2 sts.

(Ch 3, sl st in 2nd ch from hook, sl st in the next ch (2 sl st), sl st in the next 2 stitches of the book Cover) repeat 2 times.

(Ch 4, sc in 2nd ch from hook, sc in the next 2 ch (3 sc), sl st in the next 2 sts of the book Cover) repeat 2 times.

Ch 5, sc in 2nd ch from hook, hdc in the next 2 ch, sl st in the next ch (4 sts), sl st in the next 12 sts of the book Cover.

(Ch 5, sc in 2nd ch from hook, hdc in the next 2 ch, sl st in the next ch (4 sts), sl st in the next 2 sts of the book Cover) repeat 2 times.

(Ch 4, sc in 2nd ch from hook, sc in the next 2 ch (3 sc), sl st in the next 2 sts of the book Cover) repeat 2 times.

(Ch 3, sl st in 2nd ch from hook, sl st in the next ch (2 sl st), sl st in the next 2 sts of the book Cover) repeat 2 times.

Finish off and weave in tail.

LARGE FANGS

TOP FANGS (MAKE 2)

With **D** and smaller hook make a magic ring.

Row 1: 4 sc in ring—4 sc.
Rows 2—6: Hdc around—4 hdc.
Finish off. Leave tail for sewing.

BOTTOM FANGS (MAKE 2)

With smaller hook and **D**, make a magic ring.

Row 1: 4 sc in ring—4 sc.
Rows 2—5: Hdc around—4 hdc.
Finish off. Leave tail for sewing.
Place a pipe cleaner that is folded in half inside of each Fang. Bend slightly to give arched shape.

BIG EYES (MAKE 2)

With **E** and smaller hook make a magic ring.

Row 1: 8 sc in ring—8 sc.
Rows 2—4: Sc in each st—8 sc.
Insert larger pair of Eyes between Rows 2 and 3 of each. Finish off and leave tail for sewing.

SMALL EYES (MAKE 2)

With **E** and smaller hook make a magic ring.

Row 1: 6 sc in ring—6 sc.
Rows 2—4: Sc in each st—6 sc.
Insert smaller pair of Eyes between Rows 2 and 3 of each.
Finish off and leave tail for sewing.

BEHIND THE MAGIC

Graphic designer Miraphora Mina named the author of the book as Edwardus Limus, which was a tribute to fellow graphic designer Edward Lima.

MOUTH

With **F** and smaller hook

Row 1: Ch 15, starting in the second ch from your hook, sc in each st—14 sc.

Row 2: Dec, 10 sc, dec—12 sc.

Row 3: Sc in each st—12 sc.

Row 4: Dec, 8 sc, dec—10 sc.

*Attach B for first row of Teeth in the flo of Row 4. Do not cut **F**.*

MAKE TEETH

(Ch 3, in the second ch from your hook sl st, sl st—2 st. Sl st in the next st) x 8.

With **F** continue to work the Mouth working in blo of Row 4.

Row 5: Sc in each st—10 sc.

Row 6: Blo sc in each st—10 sc.

Attach **B** for the other row of Teeth working in the flo of Row 6. Do not cut **F**.

(Ch 3, in the second ch from your hook sl st, sl st—2 st. Sl st in the next st) x 8.

With **F** continue to work other part of Mouth in blo of Row 6.

Rows 7—8: Sc in each st—10 sc.

Finish off and leave tail for sewing.

TONGUE

With **F** and smaller hook.

Row 1: Ch 5, from the second chain from your hook, sc in each st, ch 1 and turn your work and work from the back of your sts—4 sc.

Rows 2—9: Sc in each st, ch 1 and turn your work—4 sc.

Row 10: (Ch 3, in the second st from your hook, sc, sc—2 sc. Sl st in the next st) x 2.

Finish off and leave a long tail for sewing. Weave tail on the side of the Tongue to the top.

ASSEMBLY

Line up the Outer Cover with the Pages. Pin together if needed, and simply sew together using the tail from the Pages. Before closing all the way, stuff book enough to keep its cuboid shape.

Sew on Mouth. Stuff the Mouth slightly before sewing closed all the way.

Sew on Large Top and Bottom Fangs. Top Fangs should be bent/arched pointing down, and Bottom Fangs should be bent/arched pointing up.

Sew the Eyes on the top of the book, 2½ inches in from the front edge and centered, with the Big pair on the inside, and Small pair on the outside.

Sew on Tongue to the left of the Mouth.

Weave in all ends. Trim all tails.

GOLDEN EGG

Designed by Mathilde Claiborne
Skill Level: ⚡

The first task of the Triwizard Tournament seen in *Harry Potter and the Goblet of Fire* is to capture a golden egg protected by a dragon. Once opened, the egg will reveal a clue to the second task, which takes place under the waters of the Black Lake. Harry unlocks the egg in front of his fellow Gryffindors, and they are almost deafened when it screeches and shrieks. Thank goodness fellow champion Cedric Diggory gives Harry a clue how to get the clue: open it underwater.

Golden egg designer Miraphora Mina always liked to incorporate the theme of "discovery" in her ideas. "I think, to discover something, you need to work for it," she explains. Mina designed the mechanism that opens the egg as a little owl's head sitting atop three wings. "And it's always interesting to have an uneven number," she adds, "so I knew it would break into three segments. Not like you were cracking an egg in half!" The mechanism to open the egg was a practical effect.

Skillfully designed with attention to detail, this amigurumi golden egg from Harry Potter's second thrilling Triwizard Tournament task gleams with a radiant golden hue and echoes the allure of the original magical object. Just like its cinematic counterpart, this golden egg amigurumi opens and closes. With careful manipulation, you can unlock the secrets held within.

"These represent four very real dragons, each of which has been given a golden egg to protect. Your objective is simple: Collect the egg. This you must do, for each egg contains a clue without which you cannot hope to proceed to the next task."

Barty Crouch, Senior, *Harry Potter and the Goblet of Fire*

FINISHED MEASUREMENTS
Height: 3.4 in. / 8.6 cm
Width when closed: 2.5 in. / 6.4 cm
Width when open: 3.5-4 in. / 8.9-10 cm

YARN
Worsted weight (#4 medium) yarn, shown in *Caron Simply Soft*, (100% acrylic, 315 yd. / 288 m per 6 oz. / 170 g hank).
Color A: #9701 White, 1 hank
Color B: #0008 Autumn Maize, 1 hank

Lace weight (#0 lace) yarn, shown in Hobbii *Go Handmade Glitter Deluxe*, (100% polyester, 1950 yd. / 1800 m per 1.1 oz. / 30 g cone).
Color C: #18121 Gold, 1 cone

HOOK
• US E 4 / 3.5mm crochet

NOTIONS
• Stitch markers
• Polyester stuffing
• Tapestry needle

GAUGE
Gauge is not critical for this project. Ensure your stitches are tight so the stuffing won't show through.

NOTE
• **Invisible finish:** Cut the yarn leaving around a 5-inch tail. Pull the hook up all the way to unravel the loop on your hook. Skip the next sc and with a tapestry needle, insert the yarn under the top (both loops) of the following sc. Pull the yarn through to the back. Then, insert the yarn under the back loop only of the last single crochet made in this round. Weave in the ends.

EGG

With **A**, make a magic ring.
Rnd 1: 6 sc in the ring—6 sc.
Rnd 2: 6 inc—12 sc.
Rnd 3: (1 sc, 1 inc) x 6—18 sc.
Rnd 4: 1 sc in each stitch—18 sc.
Rnd 5: (2 sc, 1 inc) x 6—24 sc.
Rnd 6: 1 sc in each stitch—24 sc.
Rnd 7: (3 sc, 1 inc) x 6—30 sc.
Rnds 8—16: 1 sc in each stitch—30 sc.
Rnd 17: (3 sc, 1 dec) x 6—24 sc.
Rnd 18: 1 sc in each stitch—24 sc.
Start to stuff the egg and continue as you go.
Rnd 19: (2 sc, 1 dec) x 6—18 sc.
Rnd 20: (1 sc, 1 dec) x 6—12 sc.
Rnd 21: 6 dec—6 sc.
Leave a 5 in. tail of yarn, then cut it. Pass the yarn through the loop to tie a knot.
With a tapestry needle, pass the yarn through the previous 6 stitches to close the circle. Hide the yarn with the needle and trim.

GOLDEN SHELL PARTS (MAKE 3)

With **B** and **C** held together and worked as one.
Row 1: 11 chs.
Skip the first ch and start crocheting in the 2nd ch from the hook.
Row 2: 1 sc in each of the next 9 chs, 3 sc in the 10th ch. Place a st marker in the 2nd of these last 3 sts. 1 sc back in each of the 8 chs on the other side of the chain, 3 sc in the 9th ch. Place a st marker in the 3rd of these 3 sts.
If the chains are gappy, you can darn them with the loose end from the chain base and a tapestry needle.
Rows 3—7: 1 sc in each stitch and 3 sc in the 2 marked sts. Place a st marker in the 2nd of these 3 sts (both times).
Invisible finish.

GOLDEN TOP PART

With **B** and **C** held together and worked as one, make a magic ring.
Rnd 1: 6 sc in ring.
Rnd 2: (1 sl st, 3 ch, skip the first ch and start crocheting in the 2nd ch from the hook, 2 sc along the ch and 1 sc in the next stitch) x 3.
Invisible finish.

ASSEMBLY

Sew the Golden Top Part to the top of the Egg (the most pointed part).
Sew the three Golden Shell Parts under the Egg, making sure they open and close without overlapping.

BEHIND THE MAGIC

The Golden Egg was completely waterproof as it would need to be submerged during the many takes for the scene. It also weighed over ten pounds, and would sink to the bottom of the prefects' bathtub if let go.

ELDER WAND

Designed by Krissy Linderman
Skill Level: ⚡⚡

The Elder Wand, considered to be the most powerful wand that has ever existed, is one of the three Deathly Hallows. It is no surprise Voldemort actively seeks out the wand, which has belonged to Albus Dumbledore for years. "Voldemort is under the belief that whoever possesses the Elder Wand would have supremacy," says actor Ralph Fiennes (Voldemort), "but it's more complicated than that, much to his frustration."

When the prop makers created Dumbledore's wand for *Harry Potter and the Sorcerer's Stone*, they had no idea of its importance. The team was always on the lookout for interesting woods to use for wands, choosing noteworthy textures or woods with burrs or knots in them. The Elder Wand was made from a sturdy piece of English oak with outcroppings of nodules every two or three inches. Being a long, thin wand also helped it stand out from the rest.

This Elder Wand amigurumi symbolizes the quest for mastery and captures the enchantment of handmade artistry. Worked in the round, this amigurumi wand showcases a blend of stitches, lending texture and detail that resembles the wand's intricate design. Each stitch is a nod to the wand's historical significance. The wand is constructed starting with the handle, and a small wooden dowel can be incorporated to lend structural integrity and ensure it retains its form.

"Just saying. That's the Elder Wand. The most powerful wand in the world."

Ron Weasley, *Harry Potter and the Deathly Hallows — Part 2*

FINISHED MEASUREMENT
Length: 15 in. / 38.1 cm

YARN
Worsted weight (#4 medium) yarn, shown in WeCrochet *Brava*, (100% premium acrylic, 218 yd. / 200 m per 3½ oz. / 100 g skein).
Color A: 29491 Carob, 1 skein
Color B: 29489 Espresso, 1 skein
Color C: 28410 Almond, 1 skein

HOOK
US E-5 / 3.5mm crochet hook

NOTIONS
• Stitch marker
• Polyester stuffing
• ⅛ in. / 3 mm diameter wooden dowel 12 in. / 30 cm long
• Stuffing tool
• Tapestry needle

GAUGE
22 sts and 24 rows = 4 in. / 10 cm in sc
Gauge is not critical for this project. Ensure your stitches are tight so the stuffing won't show through.

SPECIAL ABBREVIATIONS
2 Single Crochet Popcorn Stitch (2scpc): With B, make 2 sc in next st. Pull up a loop with the last st and remove hook. Insert hook into the first sc of the popcorn, yo with A, then pull the loop from the last st through the first st to complete the 2scpc. Pull B to tighten st.

Front Post Single Crochet (fpsc): Insert hook around the front of the post (from front to back to front), yo and draw up a loop, yo and draw through both loops to complete the st.

Back Loop Only (blo): Work through back loop only

Front Loop Only (flo): Work through front loop only

NOTES

- Wand is worked in continuous rounds unless noted. Place a stitch marker in the first stitch of each round.
- Stuff the handle using a stuffing tool through Rnd 24. The wooden dowel will be inserted once Rnd 96 has been completed. Rnds 25 to 96 will remain unstuffed.
- Do not cut yarn when changing colors unless otherwise noted. Drop yarn and pick up new color.

BEHIND THE MAGIC

The Elder Wand was crafted with a bone inlay on the handle, inscribed with rune-like symbols.

WAND

With **A**, make a magic ring.

Rnd 1: 6 sc in ring; do not join—6 sc.

Rnd 2: Inc in each sc around—12 sc.

Rnd 3: [Sc in next sc, inc in next sc] 6 times—18 sc.

Note: To create a jogless join for the next round, pull up a loop in the last st of Rnd 3. Insert hook from back to front in the first st of Rnd 4. Draw up a loop and pull through the st, pull tight. Ch 1 and tighten ch. Sc in blo for Rnd 4. Join and ch 1 do not count as a st.

Rnd 4: Sc in blo around—18 sc.

Rnd 5: [Sc in next 2 sc, fpsc in next sc] 6 times—18 sc.

Rnd 6: [Dec over next 2 sc, fpsc in next sc] 6 times—12 sc.

Rnd 7: [Sc in next sc, fpsc in next sc] 6 times—12 sc.

Begin stuffing the Wand.

Rnd 8: Dec around—6 sc.

Rnd 9: Inc around—12 sc.

Rnd 10: [With **A**, sc in next sc; with **B**, 2scpc in next sc; with **A**, sc in next sc, inc in next sc] 3 times—15 sc.

Rnd 11: [Dec over next 2 sc, sc in next 3 sc] 3 times—12 sc.

Rnd 12: [With **A**, sc in next 3 sc; with **B**, 2scpc in next sc] 3 times—12 sc.

Rnd 13: [With **A**, dec over next 2 sc, sc in next 2 sc] 3 times—9 sc.

Rnd 14: Sc around.

Rnd 15: With **A**, sc in next sc. [With **B**, 2scpc in next sc; with **A**, sc in next 2 sc] twice; with **B**, 2scpc in next sc; with **A**, sc in next sc—9 sc.

Rnds 16−17: Sc around.

Rnd 18: [With **A**, sc in next 3 sc; with **B**, 2scpc in next sc] twice; with **A**, sc in next sc.—9 sc.

Rnd 19: Sc around.

Stuff through Rnd 19.

Rnd 20: [Sc in next 2 sc, inc in next sc] 3 times—12 sc.

Rnd 21: [With **A**, sc in next sc, inc in next sc; with **B**, 2scpc in next sc; with **A**, inc in next sc] 3 times—18 sc.

Rnds 22−23: Sc around.

Rnd 24: [With **B**, 2scpc in next sc; with **A**, dec over next 2 sc, sc in next sc, dec over next 2 sc] 3 times—12 sc.

Lightly stuff through Rnd 24. The remaining rounds will be left unstuffed.

Rnd 25: [With **A**, sc in next sc, dec over next 2 sc] 4 times—8 sc.

Rnd 26: Sc around.

Rnd 27: [With **A**, sc in next 2 sc; with **B**, 2scpc in next sc] twice; with **A**, sc in next 2 sc—8 sc.

Rnds 28−29: Sc around.

Rnds 30−35: With **C**, sc around. Cut **C**.

Rnd 36: [With **A**, sc in next sc, inc in next sc] 4 times—12 sc.

Rnd 37: With **A**, sc in next sc; with **B**, 2scpc in next sc [with **A**, sc in next 3 sc; with **B**, 2scpc in next sc] twice; with **A**, sc in next 2 sc—12 sc.

Rnd 38: [Sc in next sc, inc in next sc] 6 times—18 sc.

Rnd 39: [Dec over next 2 sc, sc in next sc] 6 times—12 sc.

Rnd 40: Sc in next 4 sc [with **B**, 2scpc in next sc; with **A**, sc in next 3 sc] twice—12 sc.

Rnd 41: [With **A**, sc in next sc, dec over next 2 sc] 4 times—8 sc.

Rnds 42–53: Sc around.

Rnd 54: [Sc in next sc, inc in next sc] 4 times—12 sc.

Rnd 55: [With **A**, sc in next 3 sc; with **B**, 2scpc in next sc] 3 times—12 sc.

Rnd 56: [With **A**, sc in next 3 sc, inc in next sc] 3 times—15 sc.

Rnd 57: [Dec over next 2 sc, sc in next 3 sc] 3 times—12 sc.

Rnd 58: With **A**, sc in next sc; with **B**, 2scpc in next sc [with **A**, sc in next 3 sc; with **B**, 2scpc in next sc] twice; with **A**, sc in next 2 sc—12 sc.

Rnd 59: [Sc in next sc, dec over next 2 sc] 4 times—8 sc.

Rnds 60–70: Sc around.

Rnd 71: [Sc in next 2 sc, inc in next sc] twice, sc in next 2 sc—10 sc.

Rnd 72: [Inc in next sc, sc in next 2 sc] 3 times, sc in next sc—13 sc.

Rnd 73: [With **A**, sc in next 3 sc; with **B**, 2scpc in next sc] 3 times; with **A**, sc in next sc—13 sc.

Rnd 74: [Sc in next 2 sc, dec over next 2 sc] 3 times, sc in next sc—10 sc.

Rnd 75: [Sc in next sc, dec over next 2 sc] 3 times, sc in next sc—7 sc.

Rnds 76–84: Sc around.

Rnd 85: [Sc in next sc, inc in next sc] 3 times, sc in next sc—10 sc.

Rnd 86: [Sc in next 2 sc, inc in next sc] 3 times, sc in next sc—13 sc.

Rnd 87: [With **A**, sc in next 3 sc; with **B**, 2scpc in next sc] 3 times; with **A**, sc in next sc—13 sc.
Cut **B**.

Rnd 88: [Sc in next 2 sc, dec over next 2 sc] 3 times, sc in next sc—10 sc.

Rnd 89: [Sc in next sc, dec over next 2 sc] 3 times, sc in next sc—7 sc.

Rnds 90–96: Sc around.
Fasten off.

FINISHING

Insert the wooden dowel. Weave tail through each blo st of Rnd 96 and pull to close. Weave in ends.

Wrap a 30 in. piece of **A** yarn three 3 times around Rnd 30. Weave yarn though to Rnd 35 and wrap yarn three times around. Weave in ends.

ABBREVIATIONS

ch: chain

ch-sp: chain-space

dc: double crochet

dec: decrease

FO: fasten off

hdc: half double crochet

inc: increase

lp: loop

pm: place marker

rnds: rounds

RS: right side

sc: single crochet

sc2tog: single crochet two stitches together

sc3tog: single crochet three stiches together

sk: skip one stitch

sl st: slip stitch

sp: space

st: stitch

Str: strand

tr: triple crochet

WS: wrong side

yo: yarn over

YARN RESOURCE GUIDE

Yarnspirations

Yarnspirations.com

WeCrochet

Crochet.com

Scheepjes

Scheepjes.com

Premier Yarns

Premieryarns.com

Lion Brand Yarn

Lionbrand.com

Hobbii Yarn

Hobbii.com

YarnArt

Yarnart.com

Hobium

Hobiumyarns.com

Universal Yarn

Universalyarn.com

Rowan

Knitrowan.com

Sirdar

Sirdar.com

ACKNOWLEDGMENTS

I want to extend my heartfelt thanks to all who have been essential to this creative journey.

First, sending lots of love to my mom in heaven. Thank you for your patience and endless encouragement. You've opened the door to a world of making I never thought was possible. Wish you could see me now, Mom!

To my husband, thank you for your tolerance of my yarn-filled chaos. You are my biggest supporter. And thank you to my children who have always been the inspiration for my creations. I love you all to the moon and back!

A heartfelt thank you to the talented designers who poured your talent and creativity into this book. Your contributions have made this book a collaborative masterpiece that showcases the diversity and beauty of the crochet world.

Special thanks to the incredible team at Insight Editions for taking a chance on me and working tirelessly behind the scenes.

As this book finds its way into the hands of crochet artists of all skill levels, may the patterns within these pages bring joy, creativity, and a little magic to your crochet adventures.

With stitches and appreciation,
Juli Anne

I would like to express my gratitude and thanks to the talented people at Insight Editions, including Raoul Goff, Chrissy Kwasnik, and Vanessa Lopez, whose guidance and creativity are unparalleled. I would also like to thank Warner Bros. and The Blair Partnership, whose knowledge and expertise of the wizarding world is key to elevating the magic in our endeavors.

Much appreciation to Anna Wostenberg, who always earns an "Outstanding" as editor. Anna is amazingly deft at unraveling knots, and ensured no holes or dropped stitches happened in the execution of this book. Without her leadership and support, there would be a large tangle of yarn wrapped around us like Devil's Snare—Anna always brings the sunlight that counteracts unexpected Dark dangers.

Thank you to Judy Wiatrek Trum for her masterful design, and to the production team at Insight for their dedication, skill, and enthusiasm. Many thanks also to Insight's editorial team of project, associate, and assistant editors, copy editors, and proofreaders.

I am in awe of the crafty and creative pattern designers, whose executed concepts were inspirational to my work, in addition to being magical, and evocative of the Hogwarts aesthetic.

Thanks, finally, to my grandma, Sally, for showing me how to crochet, but also furnishing me head to toe (literally) with everything from hats to slippers made with a love similar to Molly Weasley's. And thanks to my family and friends, who sustain me with their patience, humor, and encouragement. For them and all mentioned above I am profoundly grateful.

—Jody Revenson

INSIGHT EDITIONS

PO Box 3088
San Rafael, CA 94912
www.insighteditions.com

Find us on Facebook: www.facebook.com/InsightEditions
Follow us on Instagram: @insighteditions

ISBN: 979-8-88663-394-8

Publisher: Raoul Goff
SVP, Group Publisher: Vanessa Lopez
VP, Creative: Chrissy Kwasnik
VP, Manufacturing: Alix Nicholaeff
Art Director: Stuart Smith
Senior Designer: Judy Wiatrek Trum
Senior Editor: Anna Wostenberg
Editorial Assistant: Alecsander Zapata
VP, Senior Executive Project Editor: Vicki Jaeger
Production Manager: Deena Hashem
Senior Production Manager, Subsidiary Rights: Lina s Palma-Temena

Patterns and Project Management: Juli Anne (Once Upon a Cheerio)
Additional Patterns: Aaron Hayden (The Crochet Carpenter), Abby Sy (Ollie + Holly), Amanda Molloy
(Loops and Love Crochet), Amy Ting (curiouspapaya), Camery Jacobsen (Cam's Crochet Creations),
Chanel Beauchamp-Snyder (CBFiberworks), Chloe Yuen (EMI Creations by Chloe), Christina Marie
(Whimsical Yarn Creations), Donna Beavers (3amgracedesigns), Heather C Gibbs (Keep Calm and
Crochet On UK), Irene Strange, Jacki Donhou (JackiStitchery), Joy Pham Sontakke (Anvi's Granny
Handicrafts), Julia Chiang (Little World of Whimsy), Krissy Linderman (Loopsy Daisy Crafts + Designs),
Larissa Soares (Pink Wip), Laura Rook (Kagooli Handmade), Lizette Lee Coreano (Chrisette Designs),
Mathilde Claiborne (CrochetPinkPumpkin), Nicole Rogowski (Woven Tales Designs), Pham Hien Hahn
(Beary Bearnita Design), Sam Savalle (Studio Savalle Crochet), Tera Kulling (Trifles N Treasures),
Tsui-Sie Baker-Wong (@tsuisie.wong), Valérie Prieur-Côté (Cozy Little Mess)

Technical Editor: BJ Berti

Photographer: Ted Thomas
Prop Stylist: Elena P. Craig